MW01036933

RACIAL ECOLOGIES

Racial Ecologies

EDITED BY
*Leilani Nishime and
Kim D. Hester Williams*

UNIVERSITY OF WASHINGTON PRESS

Seattle

Copyright © 2018 by the University of Washington Press
Printed and bound in the United States of America
Composed in Warnock Pro, typeface designed by Robert Slimbach

22   21   20   19   5   4   3   2

All rights reserved. No part of this publication may be reproduced or transmitted
in any form or by any means, electronic or mechanical, including photocopy,
recording, or any information storage or retrieval system, without permission in
writing from the publisher.

UNIVERSITY OF WASHINGTON PRESS
www.washington.edu/uwpress

LIBRARY OF CONGRESS CATALOGING-IN-PUBLICATION DATA ON FILE

ISBN (hardcover): 978-0-295-74371-4
ISBN (paperback): 978-0-295-74373-8
ISBN (ebook): 978-0-295-74372-1

Cover illustration by Christi Belcourt

Lucille Clifton, excerpt from "mulberry fields," from *The Collected Poems of
Lucille Clifton*, ed. Kevin Young and Michael S. Glaser. Copyright © 2000 by
Lucille Clifton. Reprinted with permission of The Permissions Company Inc.
on behalf of BOA Editions Ltd., www.boaeditions.org.

Nathaniel Mackey, excerpts from "Song of the Andoumboulou: 33," from
Whatsaid Serif. Copyright © 2000 by Nathaniel Mackey. Reprinted with
permission of The Permissions Company Inc. on behalf of City Lights,
www.citylights.com.

giovanni singleton, "Day 49," from the collection *Ascension* (Denver: Counterpath,
2012), reprinted by permission of the author.

CONTENTS

PART FIVE. SPECULATIVE FUTURES

RACIAL ECOLOGIES

A View from Ethnic Studies

CURTIS MAREZ

During the historic dot-com bubble, that period of explosive growth and enormous profits in the technology industry that began around 1995 and burst in 2001, I taught at the University of California, Santa Cruz, situated between the strawberry fields of Watsonville and Silicon Valley. At a time of shrinking state investments in public education and as part of his aspiration to globalize the humanities, our dean advised faculty to seek patrons by researching and writing hagiographies of the new high-tech elite. By contrast, the working-class students of color in my large undergraduate lecture course on US popular culture pressed me to research the Homies.

The last few decades have witnessed an explosion of collectible plastic figurines for sale, and leading the way have been the Homies, a popular line of small, plastic figurines representing the largely Chicanx inhabitants of an imaginary barrio somewhere near Silicon Valley. These finely detailed and painted figures of various barrio types, with names like Smiley, Shy Girl, and Spooky, were widely sold in gumball machines, at swap meets, on eBay, and on the Homies official website. Each of the almost two hundred figures has a name and a brief biography, and over one hundred million of them have been sold. Their creator, David Gonzales, developed the Homies merchandising empire in his office in Oakland, California, and he has based many of the figures on people from his hometown of San Jose, the diverse metropolis next to Silicon Valley.

The small brown dolls represent suggestive, iconic responses to the Silicon Valley financial bubble and the euphoric fantasies of technological and environmental progress that have accompanied it. The Homies invite us to reconsider the ways in which ideas and fantasies about high tech have emerged from material conditions of production that depend on poisoning people and their environments. Collectively, the figurines make up a particular neighborhood. The Homies' universe is a world-building project that indirectly references the toxic forms of segregation and uneven development that have accompanied high-tech industries. Silicon Valley, for example, is characterized by the contrast between the exclusive neighborhoods of the wealthy and the working-class barrios, many situated near Superfund sites created by the high-tech industry's dumping of toxic waste. The Homies thus represent the seeming intractability of spatial segregation, inequality, and environmental racism in Silicon Valley, an interpretation supported by Gonzales's new line of zombie Homies, which suggest the conditions of living death experienced by so many in the area.[1]

As representations of the low-wage workers of color in and around Silicon Valley, the Homies draw attention to the historic toxicities of labor segregation. The dot-com bubble depended on an expansion of low-wage jobs and the employment mainly of migrant women in Silicon Valley, the US-Mexico border region, and other parts of the world, particularly China. Many low-wage jobs in semiconductor factories and other high-tech manufacturing facilities place workers at risk of exposure to highly toxic chemicals. Since the Cold War, high-tech companies in Silicon Valley have been aggressively opposed to organized labor, becoming what David Bacon has called "laboratories for developing personnel-management techniques for maintaining a union-free environment." As a result, tech companies in the Valley remain largely nonunionized, and low-paid workers have few options but to accept the risks of illness, disability, and premature death from toxic chemical exposure. As David Naguib Pellow and Lisa Sun-Hee Park argue in *The Silicon Valley of Dreams*, these risks extend to the even more precariously situated workers in the "periphery jobs in printed circuit board, printer, and cable assembly, including home-based piecework and prison labor," disposable workers performing dangerous tasks.[2]

In response to some of the inequalities in Silicon Valley, low-wage immigrant workers have begun to organize unions and environmental organizations. Examples include the successful organization of janitorial workers at Apple and other companies. Environmental justice organizations, such as the Santa Clara Center for Occupational Safety and Health and the Silicon Valley Toxics Coalition, have fought to protect workers from exposure to industrial toxins.[3]

In this regard, the high-tech industry in Silicon Valley echoes the agricultural industry it partly succeeded. For those who profit, and for consumers who buy into it, the growth of the Silicon Valley high-tech economy has sustained an optimistic ideology of progress through technology. The promoters of the dot-com bubble projected that the high-tech economy would transcend many of the limitations of the industrial age. Silicon Valley companies claimed that theirs was a "clean, postindustrial, post-smokestack" enterprise representing progress over not only heavy industry but also the region's agricultural and canning industries.[4] As Pellow and Park point out, however, both farm workers and high-tech workers are vulnerable to toxic chemical exposures. Thus struggles over environmental racism in Silicon Valley share common ground with movements to organize farm workers, particularly the efforts by Cesar Chavez and the United Farm Workers, who were also active in support of Silicon Valley janitors.

The Homies would be at home in the pages that follow. Drawing on themes and methods familiar from critical ethnic studies, the contributors to *Racial Ecologies* persuasively demonstrate that environmental concerns are intertwined with differences of race, indigeneity, class, gender, and nation.

In the preface to a special issue of *American Quarterly* edited by Clyde Woods on the aftermath of Hurricane Katrina, I asked, "What is a disaster? To what extent is disaster 'exceptional,' and to what extent is it the norm? Does the term refer only to the moment when the levees broke, or does it also signify the political economic context that preceded the hurricane and the government response?"[5] As the contributors to this volume suggest, and as recent indigenous opposition to the Dakota Access Pipeline reminds us, ecological disasters are historic and ongoing features of colonialism, capitalist resource extraction, and racialized and gendered labor exploitation, from Puerto Rico to New Zealand and beyond.

Racial Ecologies also suggests that, assumptions of environmental progress notwithstanding, some of the most rapacious forms of resource extraction are occurring in the present. Revising Marx's concept of "primitive accumulation," which frames resource plundering as part of the prehistory of capitalism, David Harvey instead uses the term "accumulation through dispossession" to describe the ways in which environmental theft and degradation are persistent features of capitalism across time and space.[6] The contributors to this volume foreground ongoing antiracist, anticolonial struggles over the extraction of resources such as coal, natural gas, and oil. Indeed, this book suggests that different energy industries have historically mediated between settler colonialism and what Cedric Robinson famously theorized as racial capitalism.[7]

Racial Ecologies further reminds us that labor exploitation is an environmental issue. Historically, all sorts of racialized and gendered workers—slaves, indentured servants, farm workers, prisoners, and factory workers—have been exposed to toxins and subjected to environmental degradations. In the eighteenth and nineteenth centuries, for example, Spanish, Mexican, and Anglo-American settlers in what is now the US Southwest appropriated and despoiled Native land while attacking indigenous ecological epistemologies and practices and substituting settler modes of property and land use. Or, to revise George Lipsitz's famous concept, settlers developed a sort of possessive investment in white ecology.[8] Settler-colonial land appropriations made Indian labor vulnerable to exploitation. From about 1850 to 1870, during the formative period of the modern oil industry that Southern California settlers built on indigenous land and resources, the downtown Los Angeles plaza was the site of Indian slave auctions, where displaced indigenous peoples who had been arrested as vagrants were auctioned to the highest bidder as indentured servants. (Indian slavery occurred within the lifetimes of many of the early twentieth-century oil barons, not to mention the first producers and viewers of Hollywood Westerns.)[9]

Settler colonialism, environmental destruction, and racialized labor exploitation also come together in the Israeli occupation of Gaza, which displaces Palestinians from their land, poisons Palestinian water, destroys Palestinian agriculture, and situates Palestinians as migrant farm workers.[10] Most of the farm workers, including many children, in the occupied territories are undocumented Palestinians.[11] It is estimated that ten thousand Palestinians work the fields in the Jordan Valley year-round, and an additional twenty thousand work there during the date and grape harvests. Palestinian farm workers labor without union representation or protection from occupational hazards, including exposure to pesticides banned in Europe. And about 11 percent of Palestinian farm workers work on settlement land that originally belonged to their families.[12]

Different chapters in *Racial Ecologies* analyze related intersections of environmental violence and labor exploitation in agricultural fields, factories, and computer assembly plants. At the same time, this volume brings into relief indigenous, racialized, and gendered ecological ideas and practices that are often at odds with—and rendered invisible within—mainstream environmental movements and perspectives. African slaves, for example, emerge as fugitives in colonialist representations of the landscape, modeling relationships between the natural and the social that are opaque to European Enlightenment thinking. Moving from the philosophical to the practical, other authors examine gardening among Africans and the African diaspora, from Johannesburg to Detroit, as a means of antiracist, anticolonial survival, while still others examine creative environmental coalitions and strategies developed by working-class people of color.

An important theme in *Racial Ecologies* is the everydayness of ecological destruction and its consequences for food, water, and air. This is particularly true with regard to climate change, whose effects can sometimes be difficult to perceive and appreciate in the flow of everyday experience. Min Hyoung Song's chapter examines how climate change "alters experiences of the everyday," tapping into a pervasive but ill-defined "feeling of unease and a creeping sense that the relationship between humans and things is changing."

The everydayness of racial ecologies recalls a foundational concept in cultural studies: Raymond Williams's definition of culture as a whole way of life, including the vernacular cultural work of surviving and resisting ecological destruction, through gardening, singing, drumming, protests, and art. Many of the chapters here further suggest the significance of cultural studies as a critical optic that makes imaginative connections among peoples, places, and struggles.

The volume concludes with a group of chapters that discover critical insights for understanding racial ecologies in examples of speculative culture. Elsewhere, Julie Sze has written that "environmental activists, writers, critics and artists engage pollution across space and time using imagination and cultural ideas. . . . Imagination is a key resource in responding to environmental problems."[13] The provocative readings of speculative literature and film in this volume support and extend Sze's view that speculative fictions provide vital resources for understanding the scale of environmental problems.

NOTES

1   Curtis Marez, *Farmworker Futurism: Speculative Technologies of Resistance* (Minneapolis: University of Minnesota Press, 2016), 172–77.

2   David Naguib Pellow and Lisa Sun-Hee Park, *The Silicon Valley of Dreams: Environmental Injustice, Immigrant Workers, and the High-Tech Global Economy* (New York: New York University Press, 2002), 85.

3   David Bacon, "The New Face of Union Busting," *Stories and Photographs by David Bacon*, 1999, http://dbacon.igc.org/Unions/02ubusto.htm; Pellow and Park, *The Silicon Valley of Dreams*.

4   Pellow and Park, *The Silicon Valley of Dreams*, 18.

5   Curtis Marez, "What Is a Disaster?," in "In The Wake of Hurricaine Katrina," special issue of *American Quarterly* 61:3 (September 2009), x.

6   David Harvey, *A Brief History of Neoliberalism* (New York: Oxford University Press, 2007).

7   Cedric J. Robinson, *Black Marxism: The Making of the Black Radical Tradition* (Chapel Hill: University of North Carolina Press, 2005).

8   For Lipsitz's theorization of "the possessive investment in whiteness," see George Lipsitz, *The Possessive Investment in Whiteness: How White People Profit from Identity Politics* (Philadelphia: Temple University Press, 1998).

9   Curtis Marez, "Looking beyond Property: Native Americans and Photography," *Rikkyo American Studies* 29 (March 2007): 9–28.

10   Saree Makdisi, "Outsides," *Palestine Inside Out: An Everyday Occupation* (New York: W. W. Norton, 2008), 15–93.

11   "Ripe for Abuse: Palestinian Child Labor in Israeli Agricultural Settlements in the West Bank," Human Rights Watch, April 13, 2015, www.hrw.org/report /2015/04/13/ripe-abuse/palestinian-child-labor-israeli-agricultural -settlements-west-bank.

12   Ouessale El Assimi, "Palestinian and Migrant Agricultural Workers in Isreal and the Settlements, February 2011, www.agricultures-migrations.org/wp -content/uploads/2014/03/20140226_PalestinianMigrantAgriculturalWorker sInIsraelSettlementsOuessale.pdf.

13   Julie Sze, "Scale," in *Keywords for Environmental Studies*, ed. Joni Adamson, William A. Gleason, and David N. Pellow (New York: New York University Press, 2016), 179.

ACKNOWLEDGMENTS

The editors thank the Center for Communication, Difference, and Equity; the Department of Communication; the Center for Creative Conservation; the Department of the Comparative History of Ideas; and the Department of French and Italian Studies at the University of Washington for their support for the Racial Ecologies conference held in June 2017 at the University of Washington campus. We also thank Larin McLaughlin for her guidance as an editor and for her consistent advocacy for this project.

Leilani Nishime thanks Kim Hester Williams, who first proposed the idea for this book and who brings both the heart and intellectual rigor that animate it. She also thanks the Whiteley Center and the Women Investigating Race, Ethnicity, and Difference group for providing a space for contemplation and writing. Leah Ceccarelli, Christine Harold, Ralina Joseph, and Habiba Ibrahim gave their intellectual support to this book from the beginning. Most important, Leilani thanks her very patient family: Mark, her first backpacking partner; Kenzo, her most recent backpacking partner; and Takeo, who might someday learn to like backpacking. They help her remember why she does this work.

Kim Hester Williams first thanks Leilani Nishime for her friendship, generous spirit of collaboration, and commitment to intellectualism and beloved community. Her tireless efforts have most assuredly enriched this work. Kim also thanks the arts and humanities dean, Thaine Stearns, at Sonoma State University for research support; her colleagues in the English and American multicultural studies departments, especially Anne Goldman, for encouragement and for providing a public forum in which to develop ideas; Greta Vollmer for the wetlands trail-run "dates"; Ayana Jamieson, Shelley Streeby, the Octavia Butler Network community, the Huntington Library in San Marino, California, and its reader services coordinator, Emmy Zhang.

Heartfelt thanks, always, to her family: Henry Williams for his patience and care; her insatiably curious and conscious daughters, Mattea and Alanna; and her mom, Mary Hester, who provided the first and most enduring example of womanist ethics.

RACIAL ECOLOGIES

INTRODUCTION

Why Racial Ecologies?

LEILANI NISHIME AND KIM D. HESTER WILLIAMS

By centering attention on those most vulnerable to the fatal couplings of power and difference signified by *racism*, we will develop richer analyses of how it is that radical activism might most productively exploit crisis for liberatory ends.

RUTH WILSON GILMORE, "FATAL COUPLINGS OF POWER AND
DIFFERENCE: NOTES ON RACISM AND GEOGRAPHY"

THE essays gathered here concern ecological relations as they are troubled and frustrated by racialization and propelled by extract capitalism, colonialism, and hegemonic structures. *Racial Ecologies* offers a chorus of responses to environmental degradation fueled by what Ruth Wilson Gilmore calls the "fatal couplings of power and difference."[1] It details the devastations of environmental crisis and offers frameworks for analysis and action that are generative and continuously productive. *Racial Ecologies* resonates with the dying request of Toni Morrison's mystic Pilate to her nephew, Milkman, in *Song of Solomon*, to "sing a little something for me."[2] Put simply, we need song.

Racial Ecologies illuminates and underscores the interrelation of race and environmentalism through the interdisciplinary and activist traditions of ethnic studies. Environmentalism is often understood as universal and postracial, whereas environmental justice is seen as primarily, if not exclusively, concerned with racial equity. By contrast, we argue that race is

3

inextricable from our understandings of ecology, and vice versa. In fact, ideologies that define terms such as *nature* and *landscape* also subtend categories such as *self/other, Asian*, and *white*. This perspective allows for a broad definition of *ecology*, one that includes urban environments and agricultural systems. We consider nature and environment as relational sites for navigating both embodied racial identities and ecological space and place. Our use of the term *racial ecologies* instead of the more static term *environment* references these systems that shift and change over time but are always intertwined.

The contributors attend to the different racializations and positions within capitalist structures and analyze how these differences manifest themselves as distinct experiences of embodied ecologies and relations. We also recognize the particular place of Indigeneity, which often defies pressure to conform to US racial categories in order to stake a unique claim to land and nation. Rather than advance a singular vision of a prototypical racial ecology or even a binary ecology embodying Western and Other, the editors argue for a varied understanding of multiple ecologies. This enables us to consider the different ways in which racial groups and indigenous nations live in relation to landscapes and nonhuman beings. At the same time that *Racial Ecologies* recognizes the unique histories, stories, and approaches of racialized communities, it also expresses our interrelations by highlighting points of intersection and overlap as well as opportunities for political alliance.

Although the need for this intervention has long been with us, it has recently intensified. The water pollution crisis in Flint, Michigan, which emerged in 2014, stands as a glaring example of contemporary environmental and racial injustice. In an effort to save money, city officials in Flint, a city with a large African American population, made a catastrophic decision to switch the city water supply to Flint River water. The change led to corrosion of the system's aging water pipes, which leached toxic levels of lead into the city's water. Despite the revelation of links between the contaminated water and cases of illness and disease suffered by Flint residents, Flint officials offered only insufficient solutions and hollow apologies.[3] Victims of the Flint tragedy recognized and exposed the racism inherent in the state's neglect. Likewise, the independent task force that investigated the Flint crisis explicitly linked it to race and poverty, stating in their report that "race and economic status played an outsized role in explaining government neglect."[4] The Black Lives Matter movement rallied to call for the cleanup of Flint's water supply, demanding recognition of its disproportionate effect on African Americans.[5] These groups helped to shape a public commentary that highlighted the racially differential effects of ecological crisis.

Another stark and recent example of these disparate effects is the proposed construction of the Dakota Access Pipeline (DAPL) and the attendant standoff at Standing Rock in North Dakota. The proposal involves the construction of a 1,170-mile oil pipeline from western North Dakota to southern Illinois, passing underneath the Missouri River. The original route chosen for the pipeline passed close to the mainly white state capital of Bismarck, but a revised routing brought it near a primary drinking-water source for the Standing Rock Sioux Tribe. Although it received little attention, a tribal resolution against future pipelines was passed in 2012. Four years later, the Standing Rock Sioux, self-described as water protectors, formed and led a grassroots movement supported by over three hundred Indigenous nations as well non-Native allies from around the United States and the world. Local and North Dakota state police responded to the protesters' occupation of the pipeline site in a manner reminiscent of police brutality against civil rights protests in 1960s Alabama and Mississippi. They subjected the protesters to constant surveillance, assaulted them with pepper spray and high-pressure water hoses, and arrested them en masse. Meanwhile the builder of the pipeline, the Texas-based company Energy Transfer Partners, acted with impunity, using private security contractors to harass protesters and nonsanctioned maneuvers to occupy the land and build the pipeline.

Indigenous scholars such as Kyle Whyte and Dian Million remind us that the Lakota and Dakota have been fighting for over 150 years against the environmental ravages of settler colonialism. Whyte further explains that "in the 19th century, U.S. settlers sought to move to the places in which Dakota and Lakota peoples already had complex cultural, economic, and political relationships. . . . U.S. settler colonialism viciously imposed harms and risks on the ancestors of the Standing Rock Sioux Tribe that continue on through the DAPL ordeal."[6] Whyte insists that we recognize what LaDonna Brave Bull Allard of the Standing Rock Sioux calls "the larger story": namely that indigenous nations have a history and ethos of environmental stewardship, reciprocity, and responsibility that long predates the mainstream concept of environmentalism.[7]

Racial Ecologies attends to multiple ways in which the neglect of certain kinds of communities reproduces racial categories and how the systematic dispossession of targeted groups is reduced to a *naturalized difference*. In Flint, the callous disregard shown by public officials has marked the primarily

African American population as a group excluded from state recognition and protection. This group is defined through a constellation of factors, including neglected infrastructure, a polluted water supply, and historically segregated neighborhoods. At Standing Rock, colonized indigenous nations have been similarly designated as ineligible for state protection and subject to dispossession and genocide.

Both the Flint water and Dakota Access Pipeline crises reinforce a racial divide whereby communities are shaped by the uneven distribution of resources, discrimination, and structural racism. In law, custom, and practice, racially marginalized communities have historically been treated as inherently inferior and thus undeserving of quality housing, healthcare, or a healthy environment. Communities of color in the United States suffer disproportionately from high infant mortality rates, diabetes, and high blood pressure, conditions largely associated with lack of access to healthy food and the proliferation of food deserts. They also have high rates of asthma as a result of living in close proximity to oil refineries and freeways, and they are exposed to toxic pesticides as agricultural field workers. These are a few among many forms of environmental racism.

Rob Nixon refers to the gradual and visually mundane effects of environmental crisis on the poor as a "slow violence."[8] This is a form of what Michel Foucault refers to as biopower, a form that neglects targeted segments of the population and essentially allows them to die.[9] Despite assertions that environmental disaster is a universal threat, its effects are felt most profoundly by poor people and people of color. The dominant, racialized views of these groups as docile, unsophisticated, uncivilized, and unappreciative of the natural world serve to justify their continued endangerment by validating the idea that marginalized communities have created, or at least are complicit in, the degradation of their environment. On the contrary, dispossessed communities preserve memories, share knowledges, and enact ways of being that reflect an awareness of and resistance to the detrimental consequences of enduring structures of colonialism, imperialism, and neoliberal capital accumulation.

OVERVIEW

Racial Ecologies undertakes an interdisciplinary ethnic studies approach to environmental studies that is decidedly forward looking, even when we revisit the past. Our collection builds on the groundwork laid by earlier, discipline-specific collections while following the lead of newer single-authored or coauthored books that point to new directions in the study of race and ecology.[10] However, the collections that set the standard for our interdisciplinary approach feature scholars across a range of disciplines.[11] Like those collections, we draw attention to the ways in which similar questions and concerns cross disciplinary boundaries and the ways in which different kinds of methodologies and disciplinary orientations can give us distinctive responses to similar quandaries.

Racial Ecologies sets ethnic studies in conversation with ecological studies to trace a dialectics of race, environmentalism, and settler colonialism. Dorceta Taylor, Carolyn Finney, and Robert Gioielli have argued for a more expansive definition of environmental activism. While acknowledging important work in environmental justice, Finney expresses a concern about "how quickly anything related to African Americans and the environment" gets categorized as environmental justice.[12] Gioielli similarly argues that "all questions of power, privilege, class, and race get pushed to the field of environmental justice, removing them from consideration in the study of environmentalism."[13] As Taylor and Million remind us, people of color and Indigenous communities have been necessarily engaged in environmentalism, broadly and consistently, for centuries. While environmental justice scholars have noted that the issue of race is often marginalized in their field, they have yet to take seriously the theoretical contributions that ethnic studies might make to environmental studies. Questions that have long occupied researchers in ethnic studies, such as whether racial categories are biological or cultural, where the dividing line between animal and human lies, and the implications of the division between civilization and nature, all have ethical implications for environmental studies.

Conversely, ethnic studies has yet to develop a robust tradition of ecological analysis; yet ecological issues are inseparable from the articulation and perpetuation of difference. A growing number of critical ethnic studies scholars, including Claire Jean Kim, David Pellow, Lisa Sun-Hee Park, and Laura Pulido, are responding to this challenge.[14] Notably, Indigenous studies diverges from the field of ethnic studies in its steady focus on ecological concerns. This volume follows the lead of Indigenous studies in highlighting the emergence of settler colonialism as a fundamental concept for understanding both race and ecology.

Our collection grounds theory in case study, interviews, and accessible cultural analysis. It looks to the future of the field with attention to intersectional approaches, analyses, and imaginative narratives of subject formation and culture. The contributions are grouped into five broad categories that represent some of the most vibrant research areas in the study of race and ecology.

Part 1: Rethinking Race and Ecology

Rather than ask how we might incorporate ecological thinking into traditional fields of study, we combine interdisciplinary methods and an ethical commitment to racial justice as a way to think outside those standard intellectual boundaries. Our contributors foreground the "insubordinate spaces" of ecological struggle and likewise document how race, ethnicity, gender, and national identities are imbricated within empire and a neoliberal economic hegemony.[15] Min Hyoung Song's chapter conceives of ethnic studies as an epistemological tool that disrupts our familiar argumentative frames, jolting us out of our complacency in the face of ecological crisis. His approach brings to mind the civil-rights roots of the field of ethnic studies, with the belief in the centrality of culture and cultural change to revolutionary movements. Environmental exploitation is ideological, and our ability to address environmental degradation depends on our ability to name and resist those ideologies.

Chapters 2 and 3 similarly outline the larger arguments of the volume. These chapters on Indigenous "embodied ecologies" (Million) and African American "slave ecologies" (Haymes) constitute a deliberate move toward a paradoxical recognition of shared ecological concerns and, at the same time, of the crucial distinctions within and between racialized populations. All modes of racialization shape a group's relation to ecology while simultaneously reminding us that racialization necessitates that each group's response be unique. As Ikyo Day argues, "Putting colonial land and enslaved labor at the center of a dialectical analysis, we can see that blackness is neither reducible to Indigenous land nor Indigeneity to enslaved labor."[16] Instead, she argues, we must take into account the differing effects of settler colonialism and racial capitalism to understand the divergent trajectories of Indigeneity and Blackness in relation to land and labor. Haymes observes that the universalizing impulse of the founding fathers of environmental studies fails to account for the experiences of formerly enslaved African Americans. He does not go on to replace the earlier vision with an alternative, but equally universalizing, African American ecological epistemology: instead he posits the notion of "small ecologies," which allows for multiple ways of being and multiple scales for conceptualizing the ecological.

We draw from the work of Third World feminisms whose approach to racial politics has recognized the distinct histories and oppressions of racial groups rather than a liberal, multicultural vision of racial equivalence. The coalitional politics of those foundational feminist intellectuals, in the words of Grace Hong, "both mark the uniqueness of anti-Black violence as well as insist that it is possible to connect this violence to those experienced by other racialized, gendered, devalued people."[17] We don't attempt to smooth over contradictions or offer a totalizing solution: instead we leave arguments for alliance in the fight for government recognition of Indigenous treaty rights (Grossman) alongside studies of groups who reject state systems (Quizar). Million's chapter uses multiple scales to acknowledge the shared effects of neoliberal state violence while also attending to the different experiences and responses of separate Indigenous groups. In the chapters and sections that follow, the contributors take up these themes and others to show us the complexity as well as the convergence of race and ecology.

Part 2: Landscapes of Racialization

Chapters 4–6 focus on improvised forms of resistance and survival by racialized subjects against the regulation, financialization, and subjugation of life. As Wendy Brown argues, "Neoliberalism transmogrifies every human [animal, plant, species] domain and endeavor . . . according to a specific image of the economic."[18] The chapters in this section ask what happens when subjects (especially human and nonhuman subjects designated as Other) resist instrumentalization under conditions of settler colonialism, enslavement, apartheid, economic hegemony, dispossession, and environmental distress. They show how our very perceptions of land and place are shaped by liberal economic rationality, a rationality imbricated in persistent systems of slavery and its afterlife, domination, subjection, colonialism, and empire.

Our framework of race and landscape expands on Keeanga-Yamahtta Taylor's affirmation of the tenacious link between racism, capitalism, and the spatial distribution of people and resources, as exemplified by climate apartheid, urban blight, the proliferation of oil refineries, toxic chemical exposures, and the subprime mortgage lending crisis. There is overwhelming evidence of the disproportionate effect of capitalist extractive industries on communities already living in conditions of scarcity and the resulting environmental violence. Taylor argues that understanding this process requires "locating the dynamic relationship between class exploitation and racial oppression in the functioning of American capitalism."[19] We must be attentive, as well, to the interlocking dynamics of racial capitalism and colonial structures, which produce intersectional processes of racialization that historically have been met with related yet distinct methods of resistance from dispossessed communities.

While many chapters in this book address issues of capitalism (Million, Rosas, Grossman, de Onís, and McNeil), we include in this section contributions that directly address capital accumulation and make visible the aesthetics, fungibility, and fugitive nature of Blackness in New World colonial contexts (King). When we complicate the Marxian frame of worker-as-commodity to include "Blackness as experienced," we can then challenge some other fundamental divides between categories such as nature and culture. Likewise, a discussion of urban farming in Detroit helps us to understand the racialized politics of defining livable environments, producing food, and negotiating labor markets.

Contributors discuss the hegemony of structural political geographies and colonial spatial control and highlight the ways that racialized subjects seek to recover their ecological relations, especially their relation to land. In chapter 6, Dominique Bourg Hacker identifies other possibilities and forms of consciousness in the work of writers such as the South African author Bessie Head, whose iconic novel *A Question of Power* offers metaphors for healing and reenvisioned social relations through imaginative responses to racial formation and apartheid.

Part 3: Vulnerable Embodiments

There can be no planetary and multispecies justice without direct attention to the interdependence in neoliberalism of what Grace Hong identifies as disavowal and modes of erasure. The contributions in this section offer new insights into the study of race and environment, engaging theories of trans-corporeality and the politics of avowal and disavowal and expanding the scope of intersectionality. In "staying with the trouble," as Donna Haraway suggests, we continue to oppose the "inversion of freedom" and the death machinery of capital by exploring different ways of conceptualizing life and ecosystems.[20]

This section highlights intersectionality through the examination of bodies that are especially subject to disruptive ecological relations and domestic alienation. Julie Sze and Ana Elizabeth Rosas draw from interviews and archival sources to demonstrate the disproportionate effect of large-scale ecological change on the most vulnerable bodies, from farmworkers exposed to toxic chemicals in California's Central Valley to the limited options for women left behind in the wake of mass male emigration from Mexico in search of work on US farms. For the Latinas discussed in these articles, the demands of capital exacerbate patriarchal norms.

Perspectives from the field of animal studies can broaden the scope of critical race studies and intersectional approaches. Erica Tom draws attention to the complicated implications of equine prison programs by analyzing the ideological underpinnings of attitudes about human animals and nonhuman animals.

Part 4: Organizing Racial and Environmental Justice

As the Flint water crisis reveals, environmental degradation disproportionately affects people of color. However, the crisis in Flint is unusual in this respect because it has often been represented in the popular media and elsewhere as a racialized issue. This shift is due, in part, to waves of research documenting the high incidence of environmental threat and crisis in communities of color and the rise of racial-justice groups such as Black Lives Matter.[21] Chapters 10–12 explore ways in which the fight for racial justice can work in tandem with environmental movements.

All the examples in these chapters illustrate the significance of culturally specific organizing. Histories of colonialism and transnational migration shape both the environmental threat and community responses to those threats. While debates over the correct response of environmental groups to immigration seem endless, the authors of these chapters all recognize the extent to which the global flows of people have already shaped the ecologies of settler-colonial nations like the United States, and they refuse to scapegoat recent immigrants.[22] All three chapters discuss the histories of imperialism and labor migration that force marginalized groups into antagonistic relationships with the state in order to address environmental destruction. The struggles of many environmental groups to organize across racial lines are complicated by the alignment of race with and against national identifications. Organizing across national boundaries, or organizing within a nation that does not recognize all citizens equally, requires a rethinking of the terms of environmental justice organizing itself. Ultimately, successful organizing efforts must recognize the links between environmental justice and issues of racial equity, sovereignty, and power.

Part 5: Speculative Futures

Speculative literature can offer ways of thinking about race and ecology that move beyond anthropocentric subjectivities. How do we imagine a posthuman future that is not scripted by a European-centered liberalism and by economic logics that privilege freedoms and rights for the ideal liberal subject, "man," as Lisa Lowe states, "while relegating others to geographical and temporal spaces that are constituted as backward, uncivilized, and unfree"?[23] How do we engender, make, and preserve kin and kinship, as Donna Haraway proposes?[24] How might we see our way past the Anthropocene to Octavia Butler's radical re-visioning of hybrid categories of subjectivity? How do we envision culture and "race" beyond human hegemony?

A growing body of work on people of color and speculative fiction highlights the crucial role of a racial imaginary in creating possible futures.[25] Less attention has been paid to how these visions of the fantastic have also addressed issues of scarcity and sustainable ecologies. Chapters 13–15 discuss a range of texts, including Karen Tei Yamashita's *Arc of the Rainforest*, to analyze how the novel asks us to extend our conception of the subject beyond the human, destabilizing an anthropocentric worldview. Yu-Fang Cho's examination of the Godzilla movie franchise and its Japanese, American, and transpacific contexts demonstrates how popular culture actively mediates "the ongoing struggles with (neo)colonial nuclearism in Asia and the Pacific that have remained largely absent from Western public discourses." Finally, with her exploration of the dialogic landscapes of race, gender, and ecology in the film *The Book of Eli*, and the novels *Wildseed* and *Parable of the Sower* by Octavia Butler, Kim Hester Williams highlights Butler's focus on a womanist ethics of care and communalism as an intervention against environmental degradation. These chapters ask what futures might be possible—or inescapable—if we recognize the crucial place of race in shaping our ecological consciousness.

In *Dangerous Crossings*, Claire Jean Kim challenges readers to develop "a reorientation toward an *ethics of mutual avowal*, or open and active acknowledgement of connection with other struggles."[26] *Racial Ecologies* seeks to offer a clarifying perspective on the contemporary moment of ecological degradation and to address the possibilities of a more just future. In its wide-ranging articulations of race and ecology, racial subjects continue to renegotiate the relationship between embodied identities and the "natural" environment. Ultimately, *Racial Ecologies* participates in and promotes the long tradition of forging a path toward freedom from ecological subjugation and oppression—for all beings.

1   Ruth Wilson Gilmore, "Fatal Couplings of Power and Difference: Notes on Racism and Geography," *Professional Geographer* 54 (2002): 1.

2   Toni Morrison, *Song of Solomon* (New York: Penguin, 1977), 336.

3   Mona Hanna-Attisha, Jenny LaChance, Richard Casey Sadler, and Allison Champney Schnepp, "Elevated Blood Lead Levels in Children Associated with the Flint Drinking Water Crisis: A Spatial Analysis of Risk and Public Health Response," *American Journal of Public Health* 106, no. 2 (February 2016): 283–90. See also see Lawrence O. Gostin, "Lead in the Water: A Tale of Social and Environmental Injustice," *JAMA* 315, no. 19 (May 2016): 2053–54.

4   Gostin, "Lead in the Water," 2053–54.

5   Susan Douglas, "Without Black Lives Matter, Would Flint's Water Crisis Have Made Headlines?," *In These Times*, February 10, 2016.

6   Kyle Powys Whyte, "The Dakota Access Pipeline, Environmental Injustice, and U.S. Colonialism," *Red Ink* 19, no. 1 (Spring 2017): 160. Whyte defines settler colonialism as "social processes in which at least one society seeks to move permanently onto the terrestrial, aquatic, and aerial places lived in by one or more other societies who already derive economic vitality, cultural flourishing, and political self-determination from the relationships they have established with the plants, animals, physical entities, and ecosystems of those places" (158).

7   LaDonna Brave Bull Allard, "Why the Founder of Standing Rock Sioux Camp Can't Forget the White-stone Massacre," Yesmagazine.org, 3 September 2016.

8   Rob Nixon, *Slow Violence and the Environmentalism of the Poor* (Cambridge, MA: Harvard University Press, 2013), 1.

9   Michel Foucault, *The History of Sexuality, Volume 1: An Introduction*, trans. Robert Hurley (New York: Vintage, 1990), 140–45.

10 Two exemplary collections of essays on environmental justice are David E. Camacho, ed., *Environmental Injustices, Political Struggles* (Durham, NC: Duke University Press, 1998), and Elizabeth DeLoughrey and George B. Hadley, eds., *Postcolonial Ecologies: Literatures of the Environment* (New York: Oxford University Press, 2011).

11 These collections include Joni Adamson and Kimberly N. Ruffin, eds., *American Studies, Ecocriticism, and Citizenship: Thinking and Acting in the Global Commons* (London: Routledge, 2012); Donald S. Moore, Jake Kosek, and Anand Pandian, eds., *Race, Nature and the Politics of Difference* (Durham, NC: Duke University Press, 2003); Catriona Mortimer-Sandilands and Bruce Erickson, eds., *Queer Ecologies* (Bloomington: Indiana University Press, 2010).

12 Carolyn Finney, *Black Faces, White Spaces: Reimagining the Relationship of African Americans to the Great Outdoors* (Chapel Hill: University of North Carolina Press, 2014), 68–69.

13 Robert Gioielli, *Environmental Activism and the Urban Crisis* (Philadelphia: Temple University Press, 2014), 6.

14 Claire Jean Kim, *Dangerous Crossings: Race, Species, and Nature in a Multicultural Age* (Cambridge: Cambridge University Press, 2015); David N. Pellow and Lisa Sun-Hee Park, *The Silicon Valley of Dreams: Environmental Injustice, Immigrant Workers, and the High-Tech Global Economy* (New York: New York University Press, 2002); Lisa Sun-Hee Park and David N. Pellow, *The Slums of Aspen: Immigrants vs. the Environment in America's Eden* (New York: New York University Press, 2011); Laura Pulido, *Environmentalism and Economic Justice: Two Chicano Struggles in the Southwest* (Phoenix: University of Arizona Press, 1996).

15 George Lipsitz and Barbara Tomlinson, "Insubordinate Spaces for Intemperate Times: Countering the Pedagogies of Neoliberalism," *Review of Education, Pedagogy and Cultural Studies* 35, no. 1 (2013): 3–26.

16 Iyko Day, "Being or Nothingness: Indigeneity, Antiblackness, and Settler Colonial Critique," *Critical Ethnic Studies* 1, no. 2 (2015): 13.

17 Grace Kyungwon Hong, *Death Beyond Disavowal: The Impossible Politics of Difference* (Minneapolis: University of Minnesota Press, 2015), 13.

18 See Wendy Brown, *Undoing the Demos: Neoliberalism's Stealth Revolution* (Cambridge, MA: MIT Press, 2015), 10.

19 Keeanga-Yamahtta Taylor, *From #BlackLivesMatter to Black Liberation* (Chicago: Haymarket Books, 2016), 206.

20 Donna Haraway, *Staying with the Trouble: Making Kin in the Chthulucene* (Durham, NC: Duke University Press, 2016), 50–51.

21 Robert Doyle Bullard, *Dumping in Dixie: Race, Class, and Environmental Quality*, vol. 3 (Boulder, CO: Westview Press, 2000); Melissa Checker, *Polluted Promises: Environmental Racism and the Search for Justice in a Southern Town* (New York: New York University Press, 2005); Luke W. Cole and Sheila R. Foster, *From the Ground Up: Environmental Racism and the Rise of the Environmental Justice Movement* (New York: New York University Press, 2001); David Naguib Pellow, *Resisting Global Toxics: Transnational Movements for Environmental Justice* (Cambridge, MA: MIT Press, 2007); Pellow and Park, *The Silicon Valley of Dreams*; Gioielli, *Environmental Activism*; Dorceta Taylor, *Toxic Communities: Environmental Racism, Industrial Pollution, and Residential Mobility* (New York: New York University Press, 2014), and *The Environment and the People in American Cities, 1600s–1900s: Disorder, Inequality and Social Change* (Durham, NC: Duke University Press, 2009).

22 Priscilla Huang, "Anchor Babies, Over-breeders, and the Population Bomb: The Reemergence of Nativism and Population Control in Anti-immigration

Policies," *Harvard Law and Policy Review* 2 (2008): 385; Park and Pellow, *The Slums of Aspen.*

23 Lisa Lowe, *The Intimacies of Four Continents* (Durham, NC: Duke University Press, 2015), 3.

24 Haraway, *Staying with the Trouble.* In her introduction, Haraway proposes making "odkin; that is, we require each other in unexpected collaborations and combinations. . . . We become with each other or not at all" (4).

25 See David S. Roh, Betsy Huang, and Greta A. Niu, *Techno-orientalism* (New Brunswick, NJ: Rutgers University Press, 2015); Sandra Jackson and Julie Moody-Freeman, eds., *The Black Imagination: Science Fiction and the Speculative* (New York: Routledge, 2010); Jane Chi Hyun Park, *Yellow Future: Tracing the Significance of Oriental Style in Contemporary Hollywood Cinema* (Minneapolis: University of Minnesota Press, 2010); Adilifu Nama, *Black Space: Imagining Race in Science Fiction Film* (Austin: University of Texas Press, 2008); Walidah Imarisha and Adrienne M. Brown, eds., *Octavia's Brood: Science Fiction Studies from Social Studies Movements* (Chico, CA: AK Press, 2015).

26 Kim, *Dangerous Crossings,* 20.

PART ONE

RETHINKING RACE AND ECOLOGY

CHAPTER ONE

"WE ARE THE LAND, AND THE LAND IS US"

Indigenous Land, Lives, and Embodied Ecologies in the Twenty-First Century

DIAN MILLION

On April 1st, 2016, tribal citizens of the Standing Rock Lakota Nation and ally Lakota, Nakota, & Dakota citizens, under the group name "Chante tin'sa kinanzi Po," founded a Spirit Camp along the proposed route of the bakken oil pipeline, Dakota Access. The Dakota Access Pipeline (DAPL), owned by Energy Transfer Partners, L.P., is proposed to transport 450,000 barrels per day of bakken crude oil (which is fracked and highly volatile) from the lands of North Dakota to Patoka, Illinois.

STATEMENT, CAMP OF THE SACRED STONES, 2016

The death of a traditional food system is the death of a nation . . . physically and culturally. We can and must protect and restore practices that can make us healthy and well as indigenous people.

SECOND GLOBAL CONSULTATION ON THE RIGHT TO
FOOD AND FOOD SECURITY FOR INDIGENOUS PEOPLES,
NICARAGUA, SEPTEMBER 7–9, 2006

i loved the fish
and now the fish are scarce here
i think i must believe it will better further north
at home whatever place you cannot bear to see stripped not
always somewhere else
what is left is sacred   no reason is enough
no one can tell me   this will not be about the water my

frantic love
laughs out loud
tells them not to spray paint their lawns green

DIAN MILLION

T HE Standing Rock Lakota's 2016 effort to protect the Mni Sose, the
Missouri River, from the Dakota Access Pipeline rallied Indigenous
peoples and myriad ecological warriors of different stripes worldwide.
In many ways, Standing Rock presents us with a heretofore unimagined
assemblage in solidarity to protect water, the source of life on this planet.
The Lakota people led with a powerful prayer of hope. As the winter of 2016
set in with unprecedented blizzard conditions, Donald Trump, a New York
real estate baron, was elected president of the United States, and Energy
Transfer Partners, the Dakota Access pipeline's corporate sponsors, pre-
vailed. The subsequent drilling beneath the Missouri River (at Lake Oahe)
was an act of rape, a violence that ignored Standing Rock's long-embodied
sovereignty in that Lakota place. The amount of militarized police mobilized
against the allied Lakota Water Protectors to "finish the job" testifies loudly
to the ongoing matrix of uneven power relations between the United States
and the Lakota. These are relations that Standing Rock has negotiated and
struggled with for over a century.[1]

Now, in late December 2017, the United States is again poised to invade
an Indigenous place, Iizhik Gwats'an Gwandaii Goodlit (the sacred place
where life begins), as it is known in Gwich'in Athabascan, and in English as
the Arctic National Wildlife Refuge (ANWR). The porcupine caribou calving grounds that have sustained a way of life for millennia are about to go
under the knife, casually sacrificed as an add-on to a tax bill that few have
read. Again, this move is about oil, and need, and places that are not imaginable to most of the citizens of the United States (and Canada).

Any appeal in this moment to liberal "human" rights for the Indigenous
can never bring the entirety of the Gwich'in or Standing Rock people's full
relations to entities like rivers, air, land, and other beings into its logic. A
just inclusion of the nonhuman in this place already exists under Lakota law
that far exceeds any "rights"-based appeal for states to be better actors. Thus,
at Standing Rock, the Lakota, Nakota, and Dakota obeyed their own sacred
law, their ages-old responsibilities that they do not shirk. These Indigenous

laws are often in direct opposition to national and international laws, whose primary responsibility is to protect the "property" of global enterprise and a settler imperative of emptying sacred places of Indigenous relations. This is settler colonialism as it is lived in our Indigenous places now, in this moment. The stepped-up intensity of our Indigenous-led resistance movements— Standing Rock, Idle No More in Canada, and the Gwich'in's defense of Iizhik Gwats'an Gwandaii Goodlit—should be understood as decision points, moments when we, as inhabitants, victims, and recipients of benefits wrought by the destruction of our own conditions for life on this planet, might do something different. It is critical that we imagine a future for more than "just us."

In this chapter, I join in conversation with others who foreground our lives lived, in different locations, ones that come from our racialized, gendered, and class experiences of ecological life and death in the presence of globalized capital. I seek first to acknowledge our relations as we come together, in this collection, rather than to just identify differences. At the same time, I believe that there is great worth in learning from the interstices, rivulets, and streams that represent meetings and differences that our peoples' histories and different economic, political, and cultural positions give us. The Indigenous peoples of this continent hold up a difference that is not fully captured by the matrix of race and "ecology." I enter the conversation titled "Racial Ecologies" by problematizing its terms. This chapter seeks to present Indigenous experience in its ability to complicate what we imagine as "justice" if we cannot imagine our relations. I first examine the myth of our Indigenous absence but racialized presence in the heart of capitalism. I then turn to the land, to argue for what Indigenism means where it can be read, not through any pristine or primordial lens, but in its worth as a different matrix of values. I do so that we might ask harder questions about what "ecology" is to any equitable, safe, or healthy lives we might desire. I end with a discussion of the relations of Indigenous survivance and presence in an Arctic "last frontier." Imagined as a great empty space, the Arctic is actually the site of one of the oldest ongoing struggles in North America.

HUBS

One increasingly antithetical split created in our minds is that there is an "urban" and a "rural." What exactly do these terms mean? In the 2016 US presidential election, that split was imagined by one political party as a racial and class divide, between "multicultural" and "educated" white urban dwellers and poor rural uneducated "whites." We should be suspicious of this oversimplification.

In the configurations of race, class, and gender that map the megacities that now cover huge swaths of the United States, Indigenous peoples are disappeared. In the statistics that account for the racial and economic fabric of the United States, the racialization of American Indian and Alaska Native peoples disappears them. These cities rose in the ashes of Indigenous places and gained their prosperity from capitalizing on the same abundance that nourished our economies for thousands of years. These megacities, the "urban," now serve as hubs for a capitalism that operates transnationally and globally. These are places that are served up as imaginary nodes of progress, cited as epitomes of "freedom" for a mobile "creative" class.

In 2002, Richard Florida, the economist author of *The Rise of the Creative Class*, graphically illustrated five major cities, with their "creative" classes surrounded by poorer, suburban "service" classes, and with small pockets of "working class" residents in their peripheries. These "class" geographies reflect the intensity of financial centers, surrounded by those there to service them while being pushed to the periphery, unable to live in the intensified gentrification created by housing-market values and shifting racial codes.[2] This core embedded in these inner cities represent "creative class" jobs and housing that are 73.8 percent white.[3] The racial and multicultural are mostly accounted for in "service class" jobs, which they are often pushed into once white suburbs are transformed by immigration, while any "working class" thins.

In the United States and Canada, capitalist interests have sought to represent their labor policies as benign among peoples pushed into diaspora. Capitalism in North America presents in the establishment of *multicultural* democracies that have promised equity, progress, and opportunity for all. This benign reading of capitalism has become eclipsed in the twenty-first century as the facts of capital's voracious needs and the violence of resource wars have now pushed myriad peoples into the realities of established settler-colonial xenophobia.

The Indigenous peoples of the North American continent are not represented in these megacities (even when they are greatly present) because they are associated with another narrative, that of "frontiers" and of a past rather than a future. Indigenous peoples, characterized as the primitive past, anchor the narratives of progress that built these megacities on their lands, cities that disappear their difference within the hierarchies that keep our capitalist relations in place. Indigenous peoples are very present in these cities and the environments that they are also a part of. A US Census report states that "in 2010, the majority of the American Indian and Alaska Native alone-or-in-combination population (78 percent) lived outside of American Indian and Alaska Native areas." In this same report much is made of race: "Nearly half of the American Indian and Alaska Native population reported multiple races."[4] The US Census produces a "rationalized" statement of the nation-state's biopolitical interest in the management of its "populations." In the above assessment, the United States declares that the population deemed "American Indian and Alaskan Native" statistically exceeds a state expectation of its place and composition. It is a "population" that exceeds the boundaries of its colonization and its racialization. When the myriad peoples of Turtle Island were colonized, they were rationalized, singularly reduced to *a* race, "Indian," putting a numerical quantity on their bountiful multiplicity.

The implication of this constant numerical assessment of the assimilation of Indigenous peoples reveals an ardent hope. The nation-state (the United States, in this case) dutifully accounts for the moment when such people are no longer numerically significant; until the moment when no "pure" population defined by the original "contracts" of their status exists. At that time, "Indians" pass into the general population with "other" mixed, minoritized, and racialized populations without claims to treaties and sovereignties. In the face of this rational epistemology, those who attempt to live on as Indigenous often report the affective weight of being an ontological and moral challenge to the dominant order. In this setting, the relations that inform the fight for the Mni Sose at Standing Rock and for the Arctic seem absent, or unrecognizable. In urban settings Indigenous peoples suffer from the same kinds of "environmental" disasters that have become familiar to many. We suffer from the failure of systems that serve capital but not people who are insignificant to it, from the fate of those whose labor is not needed, or who are no longer legible—the homeless, the addicted, and the old. These great hubs of capitalist life have relations and a "lifestyle" that is now so ascendant that we might mistake it as a natural force. Yet, these lives we live, however nourished or abandoned by capitalist infrastructure, are actually lives with profound relations.

What are these relations? How do they make us? Glen Sean Coulthard (Yellow Knives Dine) reminds of these relations in his *Red Skin, White Masks: Rejecting the Colonial Politics of Recognition* in his Indigenous reading of Marx: "[A] mode of production must not be considered simply as being the production of the physical existence of the individuals. Rather it is a definite form of activity of these individuals, a definite form of expressing their life, a definite mode of life on their part. As individuals express their life, so they are. What they are, therefore, coincides with their production, both with what they produce and with how they produce [it]."[5]

The modes of life that capitalism produces are profoundly anchored by hierarchies of race, class, and gender. They present as places of great excitement, great extremes of income and consumption, and the capitalist *vie joyeuse* for some. Yet, these are increasingly "urban," cities within cities that are themselves only nodes in great streams of capitalist activity that stretch across our worlds. As sociologist and geographer Deborah Cowen points out, our cities are now shaped by their roles in the three great flows of capital: production, consumption, and distribution.[6] The wars that nations like the United States now fight are primarily those in protection of these flows, those of data, of goods or energy. The outsized presence of a state and corporatized (and militarized) police force in protection of the Black Snake at Mni Sose, the Missouri River, makes more sense when you understand the needs of global capital to protect these infrastructures, these flows, capitalism's bloodstreams.

These homes and hubs of capital are always undergoing renovation, reorganized for the goods and labors that are capitalism's business. Aaron Bady reminds us that "bourgeois reformers never *solve* the problems created by capitalism, because they cannot address the root causes; since you can't just kill the poor, the next best thing is to move 'blighted' populations elsewhere, out of sight and out of mind. To 'revitalize' a city center, therefore, is to make room for capital development by moving unwanted and unproductive (and uncapitalized) people elsewhere."[7] In Richard Florida's initial argument, the active players are a creative class of biotech, dot.com, and financial innovators seemingly detached from the land/resource production of an earlier, more voracious era. I would argue that these "creative" financiers and entrepreneurs are more dependent on the resources being extracted from the land now than in the past, and increasingly detached from any knowledge of their dependency. I believe that most of us cannot name the relations that we are profoundly a part of when we live in these hives of capitalist relations that we denote as urban. I want to just bring to the fore that capitalisms do indeed produce "ways of life." But I would not differentiate these by geography from something called the "land." Any divide between these "geographies" is now oversimplified in an assessment of the United States as the pinnacle of neoliberal globalism as urban and rural: the rich urban elites versus the primarily poor rural white family forgotten by capital.

These great city-state nodes of capitalist urbanism are juxtaposed to places that continue to provide the United States with an imaginary that retains status as "the Real America." These are places with frontier values, whose people's hard work and moral standards are what is needed to be "made great again." Rural areas are not barren; nor are they frontiers, although the nostalgia for a "virgin frontier" lives on deeply in the white desire to be armed and landed. Moreover, they have never been solely "white," not in history and not in the present, in regions that have known global settler immigration for two to three centuries.

The actual relations of land need to be clarified, and I begin this discussion with Standing Rock, itself, a place of long relations. The Lakota, a society that preceded the United States and the state of North Dakota by millennia, are presences that forever confound and question the imaginaries of the formation and legitimacy of the United States. For the United States, the Lakota always exist in "the barrens," where rural white America demands a replaying of "the Indian Wars" every time the nation moves to take resources from Indian lands. These barrens are places where a pipeline route can be moved so as not to endanger settler capitalist water sources. Indigenous places are often imagined as isolated empty places, disposable, or usable places subordinate to national need. Indigenous peoples are not isolated, in a past, outside of capital, or without capitalist relations: we are central to them. We get past some kinds of "geographical" differences when we foreground other relations: the relations revealed, for instance, between the necessity and desire for life and clean water in African American communities in Flint, Michigan, juxtaposed with these needs in Standing Rock.[8]

THE "LAND"

When we enter the imaginary of the "pristine" or the "ecological" sans a human hand, we enter a dangerous illusion about "land." Scott Lauria Morgensen mused on this feature of settler colonialism: "'Empty land' reminds us that the ontology of settler colonialism has been premised on its own boundlessness: always capable of projecting another horizon over which it might establish and incorporate a newest frontier."[9] The ideology of unbridled Western progress resides in the worship of development. "Development," even when debunked, underpins numerous assumptions about what non-Western epistemologies, ways of knowing, have to inform the present. We lose any sight of another set of relations, other values, when we discuss Indigenous peoples in multicultural discourses as minority populations in hierarchies of race. We lose the point of justice when we reduce the Indigenous to an appeal to liberal justice systems based on an additive formula for rights. I posit that environmental racism and environmental justice may have important overlapping interests with Indigenous interests, but we cannot go forward without acknowledging their profound difference. There is a shift in relations between working from the perspective of Indigenism to working against environmental racism and for environmental justice. Here I want to take these differences, differences in epistemologies (ways of knowing) and ontologies (ways of being) into account.

The premise of a different knowledge organizing human life undergirds Indigenous relations in place. As Peter Morin (Tahltan) writes in "This Is What Happens When We Perform the Memory of the Land," *the land is us, it is in us*, in memory and resonance with living generations lived in close relation with places.[10] The difference between Western epistemological "land" as an environment and ecology and Indigenous place as relations with responsibility is a critical philosophical difference. Indigenous peoples' lifeways as ancient nations are different ontological and material interpretations of life that question and offer alternative imaginaries outside capitalism. The myriad Indigenous peoples who continue today practicing their heritage knowledge as daily, lived action, performed in ongoing relation with place, have ways of governing that perform what "ecology" implies. While none of these peoples are "outside" capitalism after hundreds of years of entanglement, they continue to act on principles and values that hold up different ideas about what might be lived. Their "modes of production," as Coulthard observes above, produce a different way of life, even when they have been severely disrupted.

Settler colonialism is evoked here when we position land as the primary desire of colonizing Western nation-states, a desire that forever seeks the death and disappearance of the Indigenous peoples who hold and who remain in deep relations with places.[11] Indigenous feminist theories illuminate statements and acts grounded in epistemologies representing more than "environmentally friendly" ways of being. These theories represent counterknowledge to capitalism itself. The Indigenous do not uniformly seek equality with nation-states, nor their recognition. Indigenism in practice often seeks to challenge capitalist ways of life for a futurity. As Sami feminist theorist Rauna Kuokkanen notes, "Indigenous peoples' struggle for self-determination, therefore, is also a struggle to exist as a collective in the future, which implies being able to decide about and have control over that future as a people."[12] This quest for autonomy rather than "equality" within capitalism's democracies marks an important difference. The ways of life that Indigenism practices are not inherent in Indigenous peoples' DNA but the result of myriad centuries of relations with places. Altered and sometimes compromised, these ways of life, "cultures," continue to serve up values that need to be understood as alternative imaginaries that once existed all over the world.

Indigenous women are often foregrounded in these struggles for our values. Capitalism is a gendered hierarchy and violence against Indigenous women; this dominating characteristic of our lives in capitalism is not a just a by-product of settler colonialism, but one of its operating logics. In Indigenous societies, Kuokkanen reminds us, "Indigenous women play a crucial role in envisioning models of autonomy that do not merely replicate patriarchal, hierarchical structures that often reproduce the marginalization and subjugation of sections of society . . . [they] play a crucial role in maintaining and cultivating practices, systems, and bodies of knowledge, values, languages, modes of learning."[13] The outsize presence in this generation and past generations of women leaders in Indigenous resistance is not by chance. In each case, the leadership of LaDonna Brave Bull Allard and Faith Spotted Eagle among the Lakotas, and so many others, ground these movements. In the remainder of this chapter I ground myself to speak as one of myriad Northern peoples. As Natives, Alaskan Natives, or First Nations, we are reduced into the Western colonial imagination of an "Arctic" or "subarctic." As homelands, our names are many and varied. Dena, Inuit, Inupiaq, Unungan, and more are experiences of beauty in a scale of life and being that arrests the human mind from imagining itself as omnipresent. When confronted by what Standing Rock really means to me in this moment of personal, social, and political readjustment and recalibration, I want to go home in this chapter, because that is where my care is visceral.

The "Arctic" is a place where the capitalist nations imagine a world most alien from their own idea of a good life. These are places that the United States and Canada did not originally see as permanent homes for their citizens but only as places of extraction, of animals for fur, and of ores and oil. These places are now closely centered in the US and Canadian militarized need for security aroused by two twentieth-century wars and the rapidly melting ice that separates North America from Russia and Asia. We become the poster children for "climate change," more recently darkly characterized by Katherine McKittrick in a Twitter post as "ecocides of racial capitalism" (@demonicground, December 1, 2016). Our homes in circumpolar lands across the top of the globe have continuously been reimagined as a perpetual "last frontier." What is meant by this perpetual "last frontier" status of our Indigenous homelands in the North? In the crosshairs of Jodi Byrd's "transits of empire" for three centuries, Indigenous lives in the Arctic have not been lived in isolation but in a frenzy of global capitalism.[14]

HUNGER

I believe your nation might wish to see us, not as a relic from the
past, but as a way of life, a system of values by which you may
survive in the future. This we are willing to share.

PHILIP BLAKE (DENE FORT MCPHERSON)

Sandra Gologergen and Wilfred Miklahook, residents of Savoonga, stand
together with Wilfred's arm encircling Sandra's small shoulders. Resolutely
looking into the photographer's camera, they smile, capturing this moment
in their lives. Behind them, their Yupik community goes about its business.
Savoonga is one of two communities on St. Lawrence Island in the Bering
Sea, 2,100 miles from Seattle and 37 miles from the Chukchi Peninsula of
Russia. Interviewed for the National Public Radio (NPR) program *The Salt*
by Clare Leschin-Hoar about Alaska's food insecurity, Sandra Gologergen
speaks about the changes that have altered her relations to her people's food.
In NPR's story, Savoonga residents do not speak only for their own experience; they become a proxy for a food crisis across the Arctic. NPR's story is
related to hundreds of news stories now popping up in US and Canadian
media outlets highlighting the warming of the Arctic. These St. Lawrence
Island Yupik stand as a symbol for a multitude of changes in the Arctic, sur-
facing in the consciousness of the mainland United States, Canada, and the
rest of the world as climate change. The interdependent relations between
the land, the sky, and the animals that Savoonga once knew are changing
faster than anyone anticipated.

Leschin-Hoar reported that Alaska's food insecurity rate averages around
14.4 percent, only a sliver above the US national average. The difference is
how directly Alaskan Native peoples rely on their traditional foods, 295-plus
pounds per person a year. At the same time, both distance from commercial grocery outlets and the price of shipping and fuel make replacing this
diet in their home communities difficult, a serious problem with no easy
answers. Food flown in from urban centers costs well above what these families can afford and is of notoriously poor nutritional quality. This "hunger"
is deeper than it looks.[15]

Leschin-Hoar points to Savoonga's precarious relations with the capitalist food infrastructure, the chain of supply that feeds other places and
peoples—or doesn't. Yet, Leschin-Hoar's NPR story ignores the full complexity of what the failure of the ice means in another set of relations. In
Savoonga, a failure of old Yupik relations with ice and animals hastens the
necessity of contemplating how to adapt to a rapidly melting homeland. The

Yupik's direct relations with the land, sea, and other life-forms, so at the level of obscurity in the capitalist imagination, have always meant more to them than a job that pays money that buys food. Food, in the sense that Sandra Gologergen speaks of it here, means something more that NPR doesn't fully articulate.

"Food," in an Indigenous sense, always evokes something larger than the direct consumption relations that the Indigenous have with animals, waters, and beings that give us life. "Food" necessarily evokes and produces cultures, economies, languages, kinships, reciprocal relations, and responsibilities that form a way of acting toward something larger than our individual human bodies and lives. For instance, there is no way to speak to a "Yupik culture" that does not evoke larger Yupik relations with and to the places that present generations inherited from the many hundreds of generations before them. These generations and their deep knowledge represent more than ten thousand years of experience with places and the changes that occur in those relations. Marie Battiste (Mi'kmaq) and James Sakej Henderson (Choctaw) have written that "place" is an "expression of the vibrant relationships between people, their ecosystems, and other living beings and spirits that share their lands. . . . All aspects of knowledge are interrelated and cannot be separated from the traditional territories of the people concerned."[16] Indigenous place is infinitely more than geographical location. It is in every sense holistic, where all entities are bound in relations that interactively form societies, human and nonhuman. St. Lawrence Island is, in every Indigenous sense of the word, an Indigenous "place."

The 2002 study by Carol Jolles and Yupik elder and resident Elinor Mikaghaq Oozeva, *Faith, Food and Family in a Yupik Whaling Community*, chronicled life in Savoonga and Gambell (sister communities on St. Lawrence Island) as late as the early 1990s. Savoonga and Gambell were already experiencing rapid change then, but food wasn't the dire issue that it has now become. "Food" had a prominent place: "Food was obviously important. . . . The kinds of food consumed by a Gambell family and the manner in which food is served are considered to be the heart of being Yupik." While both communities had adapted Christianity to their needs in the same way that they had adapted technology, it was clear that an older order they practice was at the heart of their identity. In Gambell, the entire year and the community's social structure emerged from their relations with whales. As Jolles, who knew the community from 1987 on, observed, "Nowhere is that sense of identity, purpose, and distinctive order so evident as in the experience and tradition of sea mammal hunting, especially the hunt for *aghveq*, the great bowhead whale." The community's life was ordered by the hunt. The account given by Jolles and Yupik elder advisor Elinor Oozeva is compelling: "Children's games, courting activity, menstruation, pregnancy, maintenance of the land, and entry onto the land were regulated either partially or entirely by their relationship to hunting. Family celebrations, healing the sick, exchange [in marriage]—all were articulated with the hunt."[17] These are relations with place and "environment" that are hardly imaginable in Westernized lives. In every sense of the word *environment*, then, the lands, waters (and ice) where these intimate interactions between people and marine life occurred over countless generations formed society, governance, and responsible relations among all present.

Glen Coulthard quotes a famous Dakota scholar, Vine Deloria Jr.: "[A] fundamental difference is one of great philosophical importance. American Indians hold their lands—places—as having the highest possible meaning, and all their statements are made with this reference point in mind."[18] Thus, Savoonga is not endangered by a food shortage, where "food" is an interchangeable substance without relations, an abstract. The St. Lawrence Island peoples face an epistemological minefield in the years ahead as an order of life changes, with the changes to all their relations in their place. There is a rapidly changing environment that will alter many basic tenets of Northern life forever, and subsistence hunting in particular. The hunger families are reporting is real.

Yet, St. Lawrence Island, even as Elinor Oozeva gave her account of her people's close-knit relations, had already lived in the midst of profound change for centuries. The lives of its people do not anchor any narrative about the inevitable march of progress and their transformations from some imagined pristine life. These Yupik, along with other Alaskan Natives, have already lived through several iterations of capitalist infrastructural invasions—enslavement, numerous "resource" extraction activities, and then as the center of a military logistics buildup that made them the first line of defense against a Soviet missile strike and turned one island into a nuclear testing site.[19] Along with numerous places in Alaska, St. Lawrence Island was a military site during and after World War II. After the war, the military abandoned many of these places, leaving dangerous chemicals in Inuit, Yupik, and Alaskan Native hunting and gathering places. It was Annie Alowa, a Savoonga elder and midwife, who sought attention to and research of the problem after she noticed high numbers of miscarriages and birth defects occurring in her community. Her findings sparked a United Nations Permanent Forum on Indigenous Issues report in 2012 reporting the acute levels of toxic chemicals found on St. Lawrence and beyond.[20]

The Arctic is not and never has been Terra Nullis or the West's "last frontier": it is a crossroads and heart of Indigenous nations and their lifeways. What Westerners may mean by "last frontier" is that as a place, a frontier, it is imagined as "empty": it becomes an empty signifier, a place perpetually reimagined for different Western interests. In part, this is Patrick Wolfe's settler colonialism: a "land," while not wholly imagined as a permanent home for settlers (as yet), is imagined as a process, a frontier of perpetual settler extraction. In the American Southwest these Indigenous places have been imagined as "national sacrifice areas." The metamorphoses of different capitalist energy interests that have been undertaken in our Indigenous midst are the ecology of change in the North. Radical changes to our old relations are not recent. Indigenous lifeways must be examined as enduring rather than just precarious.

If the Arctic has long been touted as the last frontier in North America, our histories bear the marks of what this frontier means as "structure," as an ongoing process rather than as an "event." As a structure, "frontier" means the ongoing opening, abandonment, and reopening of extraction and transient exploitation of our lives and our places without Native consent. Settler colonialism's interests in such "rural" or imagined "open" spaces are never naive or disinterested. To ignore so-called flyover places in the geo-imaginary of our present politics is to ignore the significant control of lands and resources basic to the capitalist economic need to consolidate its powers. To represent these places as "underdeveloped," or merely as a disgruntled domain of right and alt-right white settlers who assert their "God-given" rights to land, guns, and employment, is to make an egregious misreading of what land and capital interests actually are in North America. The interests in these places, both in the United States and Canada, increasingly demand local white settler control (or conservative multicultural cooperation) to exploit resources at the same time they would like to disappear Native ways of life. The rural United States and interior Canadian provinces are home both to nation-states' energy preserves and the Indigenous peoples that often bar access. The cities are interdependent with, never separate from, these places.

The stakes seem different when we do not understand Indigenism within its own relations. Our environmental and racial justice demands are made depending on our ability to reform capitalisms whose relations serve a deep axiom: the "survival of the fittest." This axiom is often attributed to "nature." These are not the only relations possible with "environments." The "survival of the fittest" never existed except in Darwin's mistaken humancentric,

Eurocentric nineteenth-century theory of life's relations as a mirror of nineteenth-century capitalism—a mistake that could be rendered only by a capitalist mind. Indigenism writ large knows that there are other readings of what our relations might be, other values that could be held, that must come into the conversations that inform all our struggles, that we must include—not to admonish, but to suggest.

In a scene from the 2004 film *Oil on Ice*, then-senator Frank Murkowski (R-Alaska) holds up a large, blank piece of white paper in a 2002 Senate hearing on the fate of the Arctic National Wildlife Refuge. "This is what it looks like about nine months of the year," he said.[21] Murkowski's depiction erases Iizhik Gwats'an Gwandaii Goodlit's relations to the planet, to the Gwich'in, to us all. This is a blindness that is far beyond the blank piece of paper the senator imagines. It is a world in which he cannot recognize any relations, where there are no relations that exist for him in a place he cannot imagine. It always comes back to the matter of relations. Now, in 2017, it is Frank Murkowski's daughter, Senator Lisa Murkowski (R-Alaska), who engineers the inclusion of oil-drilling incursions in ANWR into the Republicans' grand tax scheme, now being celebrated in Washington, DC. Gwich'in elder Sarah James, a forty-year veteran of the fight for the caribou calving grounds central to her people's way of life, articulates the stakes of what the opening of ANWR means to her people: "We are the ones who have everything to lose."[22] Our loss is most certainly not the Gwich'in's alone. Who and what are your relations?

NOTES

1   See Audra Simpson and collective's outstanding online syllabus and activist open forum site "#StandingRockSyllabus," https://nycstandswithstandingrock .wordpress.com/standingrocksyllabus, accessed August 9, 2017.

2   Richard Florida, *The Rise of the Creative Class* (New York: Basic Books, 2012).

3   Richard Florida, "The Racial Divide in the Creative Economy," *City Lab*, 2016.

4   Norris, Vines, and Hoeffel. "American Indian and Alaska Native Population," 1.

5   Glen Coulthard, *Red Skin, White Masks: Rejecting the Colonial Politics of Recognition* (Minneapolis: University of Minnesota Press), 2014, 65.

6   Deborah Cowen, *The Deadly Life of Logistics: Mapping Violence in Global Trade* (Minneapolis: University of Minnesota Press), 2014.

7   Aaron Bady, "None of You," Zunguzungu: The New Inquiry, November 28, 2016, https://thenewinquiry.com/blog/none-of-you.

8   Stephanie Latty, Megan Scribe, Alena Peters, and Anthony Morgan, "Not Enough Human: At the Scenes of Indigenous and Black Dispossession," *Critical Ethnic Studies* 2 (2016): 143.

9   Scott Lauria Morgensen, "Theorising Gender, Sexuality and Settler Colonialism: An Introduction," *Settler Colonial Studies* 2, no. 2 (2012): 2.

10 Peter Morin, "This Is What Happens When We Perform the Memory of the Land," in *Arts of Engagement: Taking Aesthetic Action in and beyond the Truth and Reconciliation Commission of Canada*, ed. Dylan Robinson and Keavy Martin (Waterloo, ON: Wilfred Laurier University Press, 2016).

11 Patrick Wolfe, "Settler Colonialism and the Elimination of the Native," *Journal of Genocide Research* 8, no. 4 (2006).

12 Rauna Kuokkanen, "The Politics of Form and Alternative Autonomies: Indigenous Women, Subsistence Economies, and the Gift Paradigm," Globalization Working Papers, McMasters University (2007), 1.

13 Ibid., 2.

14 Jodi A. Byrd, *The Transit of Empire: Indigenous Critiques of Colonialism* (Minneapolis: University of Minnesota Press, 2011).

15 Clare Leschin-Hoar, "In Alaska's Remote Towns, Climate Change Is Already Leaving Many Hungry," *The Salt*, National Public Radio, July 27, 2016.

16 Maria Battiste and James Sakej Henderson, *Protecting Indigenous Knowledge and Heritage* (Saskatoon: Purie, 2000), 20.

17 Carol Zane Jolles and Elinor Mikaghaq Oozeva, *Faith, Food, and Family in a Yupik Whaling Community* (Seattle: University of Washington Press, 2002), 41, 289, 292.

18 Quoted in Glen Coulthard, "Place against Empire: Understanding Indigenous Anti-colonialism," *Affinities: A Journal of Radical Theory, Culture and Action* 4, no. 2 (Fall 2010): 79.

19 See Jennifer Sepez, Christina Package, Patricia Malcolm, and Amanda Poole, "Unalaska, Alaska: Memory and Denial in the Globalization of the Aleutian Landscape," *Polar Geography* 30, nos. 3–4 (September 2007): 195. Also see Dorothy Miriam Jones, *A Century of Servitude: Pribilof Aleuts under U.S. Rule* (Lanham, MD: University Press of America, 1980). Also see Dean Kohlhoff, *Amchitka and the Bomb: Nuclear Testing in Alaska* (Seattle: University of Washington Press, 2002).

20 Andrea Carmen and Viola Waghiyi, "Indigenous Women and Environmental Violence: A Rights-Based Approach Addressing Impacts of Environmental Contamination on Indigenous Women, Girls and Future Generations," paper presented at the United Nations Permanent Forum on Indigenous Issues Expert Group Meeting, "Combatting Violence against Indigenous Women and Girls," United Nations Headquarters, New York, January 2012.

21 *Oil on Ice*, directed by Dale Djerassi and Bo Boudart (Oley, PA: Bullfrog Films, 2004).

22 Sarah James, "We Are the Ones Who Have Everything to Lose," in *Arctic Voices: Resistance at the Tipping Point*, ed. Subhankar Banerjee (New York: Seven Stories Press, 2012).

CHAPTER TWO

AN AFRICANA STUDIES CRITIQUE OF ENVIRONMENTAL ETHICS

STEPHEN NATHAN HAYMES

T HIS chapter addresses some of the serious limitations of environmental ethics regarding what is recognized as an ecological perspective or point of view. The Eurocentric epistemic logic of environmental ethics, a logic supported by the knowledge systems of the (post)settler-plantation societies that authorize colonizing ecologies, negates the phenomenological origins and epistemic practices that emerged from the way black people of African descent in the Americas experienced the "natural environment." Their lived experiences of the natural world have been constituted in and through a distinct structure shaped by European colonial expansion into the Western Hemisphere, in particular the establishment of slavery and the violent insertion of enslaved Africans into the New World settler-plantation complex. From this lived experience, or what the Africana existential philosopher Lewis R. Gordon calls "lived context or meaning of concern," they forged moral and ethical identities with a distinctive, value-laden perspective on and orientation to the natural world.[1] How did their ecological experiences and cares during and after the period of slavery contribute to the establishment of the moral and ethical identities of African-descended black communities?

Eurocentrist environmental ethics ignores these kinds of questions and sees them as irrelevant to environmentalism, a term which, broadly defined, is a liberal rights-based philosophy and social movement concerned with protecting and bettering the environment. However, this ideology is fundamentally a European and Euro-American historical phenomenon. It implicitly expects that questions about the environment, nature, and ecology be framed in the moral, ethical, and epistemological traditions of Europeans and Euro-Americans without considering the lived context or meaning of concern in which the ideology itself emerges. For this reason it has also been referred to as "green imperialism," suggesting that the origins of environmentalism are linked with colonial expansion.[2] The concept of racial ecologies is integral to Africana studies' because of its critique of antiblack racial ecologies and its consideration of the significance of enslavement for shaping African-descended peoples' historical experiences of and orientation to the natural world. Emerging from this experience are what I call "slave ecologies," or Africana ecologies of liberation.

While there are differences between and within Africana ecologies and epistemologies with respect to such criteria as gender, sexuality, class, and geography, this project examines the distinct set of relations between the natural world and "lived" body consciousness that shaped the desire of enslaved Africans in the New World to persevere—that is, the desire for joyful living even in the midst of the calamitous and catastrophic.

GLOBAL ENVIRONMENTAL ETHICS AND
THE CONTEMPORARY ECOLOGICAL CRISIS

The contemporary concern for the ecological well-being of the planet, particularly with the ecological crisis expected to result from global climate change, has made Aldo Leopold's "earth ethics" a principal reference for formulating a "global" environmental ethics. The axiological preferences of Western "holism" regarding what is valued or worthy of moral consideration exclude the ecological experiences and cares of colonized non-Europeans, particularly black communities of African descent.

This view, dismissing as basically nonexistent the cares, experiences, knowledge systems, and modes of existence that enable particular kinds of "life projects," arises because the current Eurocentric environmental ethics perceives itself as a universal moral point of view. In reality, though, environmental ethics is linked to particular, Eurocentered epistemological assumptions about the environment. The following example illustrates the point of view that there is just one big environment, the biosphere:

> Moral progress has consisted in widening the moral constitu-
> ency, with the gradual recognition of the rights of foreigners,
> women, people of different races, and so on. Such progress is
> stunted, however, if it remains anthropocentric. Indeed, it
> cannot rest until the moral status not only of flora and fauna, but
> of whole ecosystems, is recognized. A "new" ethics is therefore,

an extension of justice. Such an ethic will promote attitudes of reverence, awe, and respect towards living things and systems, the whole environment in fact. For these have their own sanctity and *intrinsic value*. Underlying these attitudes will be the appreciation that our world is a *seamless whole*, an ecosphere, *Gaia*, in which every being, including man, has its integral place. The ethic will be a naturalistic one, since it is gleaned from the observation—no longer distorted by anthropocentric science and philosophy—of natural systems. Only such an ethic will have the force to reverse the process of environmental destruction.[3]

This passage promotes a Western notion of holism in which everything in nature, humans included, is seen as an integral element in a seamless whole. This perspective does not take account of particular ecological systems but is preoccupied with sweeping claims about universal unity and connection. The moral imperative here is that we should feel reverence or veneration for the whole natural order, of which we ourselves are integral parts. All of our environmental concerns are supposed to extend to everything.

Slave ecologies, by contrast, are relational ecologies: they do not accord final moral value to nature, the ecosystem, or the environment. Such a view is analogous to kin relationships, in which each individual part—humans, soil, plants, lands, waters—is cared for and nurtured by the community or family. The ecologies of enslaved Africans were ethically grounded in a precolonial, indigenous sub-Saharan African religious view of the natural world. The African environmental ethicist Kevin Behrens describes this worldview as different from Western holism because of its emphasis on *relationality*.[4] This emphasis, he argues, is captured in the southern African term *ubuntu*, expressive of African communitarianism, in which full moral personhood is ethically attainable only in and through communal relationship with other living beings.[5] Humans, as well as the physical landscape, plants and animals, are embraced as sharing in relationship.[6] Communal or shared existence, viz. moral personhood, is achieved by engaging in moral actions that commit to what Behrens describes as "harmonious relationships" expressive of wholesome kin relations.[7] These relationships "begin with affective bonds that in turn lead to developing a sense of moral responsibilities to others," namely solidarity, friendship, care and seeking the common good.[8] Commitment to these moral virtues entails a commitment to the security and material and emotional well-being of living others in the

STEPHEN NATHAN HAYMES

family, even at one's own expense.⁹ According to Behrens, being part of a family "implies not just acknowledging an interdependence, illustrative of Western holism, but also obligation to communal relations" representative of "African relational environmentalism." But this is an obligation that "refuses to firmly prioritize either the interests of individuals or the interest of the communities."¹⁰ For communities are social relations that enhance each member's understanding of every other member's value and uniqueness. Thus, a person's identity is constituted with other people but also with other living beings. This relationality is respectful of both the individual and community, whereas Western holism subjugates the individual to the community or greater whole.

Environmental ethics promotes itself as a moral response to the modernist—and also Eurocentric—paradigm of nature: the subjugation and control of nature through technology. But what is interesting is that this notion of environmentalism produces a more objectified, totalizing, and unifying vision of the world than the modernist paradigm does. At stake in the environmentalist effort to save nature is not modernist culture but power, meaning the ability of a certain group to define the meaning of the world for everyone, yet again. The epistemic logic and moralism that govern this ethics are the cultural logic of the Same, inherited from modernity, in which there is one paradigm or vision for being human. In comparison, slave ecologies are governed by a cultural logic of difference that ethically entails respect for individuality within the community.

The so-called global environmental ethics has resulted in a Eurocentric view of the contemporary ecological crisis, entangling and grounding it in what the decolonial theorist Walter Mignolo refers to as the "Western Code": it is "sustained by and anchored in the rhetoric of modernity and the logic of coloniality." It thus implicitly subscribes to the idea that there is one sustainable system of knowledge, and, by extension, of landscape and land ethics. "Such a system of knowledge," Mignolo argues, "serves not all humanity, but only a small portion of it that benefits from the belief that in terms of epistemology there is only one game in town." To believe in such a system of knowledge, he states, is "pernicious to the well-being of the human species and the life of the planet."¹¹

By producing and regulating the concept of ecological crisis, environmental ethics normalizes that crisis from a Eurocentric perspective and thus prescribes a moralistic response from the same perspective. Its cultural logic emphasizes ecological crisis rather than a wider social crisis that includes both the destruction of human life-worlds and the environment in which they are situated.

One of the epistemic features of environmental ethics, indeed, is its denial of the existence of the social world. To disassociate ecological crisis from social crisis is to ignore the distinctive ways in which local environments assemble soils, plants, animals, waters, and land into ecosystems.

ENVIRONMENTAL ETHIC AND COLONIZING ECOLOGIES

Today, across the Americas, black communities of African descent continue to live in death-bounded ecological spaces—not those of the plantation now, but of cities. These spaces are born of systemic forced removal, displacement, dispossession, and the diminution of these communities into "surplus humanity." Colonializing racial ecologies perpetuate the idea that African-descended communities are historically incapable of having ecological experiences and concerns. Euro-American environmentalists who are complicit in this assumption have based their views on the genetic evolutionary theory of the sociobiologist, conservationist, theorist, Harvard University professor, and two-time Pulitzer Prize winner Edward O. Wilson.[12] Epistemologically, Wilson is committed to a positivist scientific perspective that regards nature as an ontological domain distinct from the knowing subject's construction or representation of nature. Wilson turns to human genetics, or to a "gene-centric" argument, to suggest that human beings have a natural disposition not only to exploit but also to protect their environment. Thus Wilson coined the term *conservation ethic*, which is a type of broad environmental ethics concerned with protecting biodiversity (another term coined by Wilson) as a whole.[13]

Wilson's theory of human evolution owes much of its popularity to his influential notion of *biophilia*, defined as "an innate tendency to focus on life and lifelike processes, [an] innate emotional affiliation of human beings to other living organisms," or an "inborn affinity human beings have for other forms of life, an affiliation evoked, according to circumstances, by pleasure, or a sense of security, or awe or even fascination blended with revulsion."[14] Two aspects of this definition are especially relevant. First, "biophilia is innate and is therefore part of [humanity's] genetic heritage and [its] evolved human nature. Second, biophilia is an emotional response akin to feeling a sense of pleasure and well-being, or it can stimulate emotions that motivate exploration."[15]

Wilson presents a connection between the genetic basis of biophilia— "the human bond with other species"—and the kind of "livable" habitats preferred by human beings. These preferences are learned aesthetically through a cognitive, rule-based process of biocultural evolution. According to Wilson, the ecosystem of the savanna—small forest, scattered trees, and grassland, as opposed to rainforest or desert—was the milieu desired by prehistoric human beings. In contrast, other primates (including monkeys, apes, and baboons) flourished in both the rainforest and the deserts, but the "prehistoric species of the *Homo*, the ancestor of modern human beings," had a preference for an "intermediate topography—the tropical savanna." According to Wilson, this is because "the bipedal locomotion and free-swinging arms fitted these ancestral forms very well to the open land, where they were able to exploit an abundance of fruits, tubers, and game." In Wilson's view, this innate human preference for a savanna ecosystem persists even today: "People work hard to create a savanna-like environment in such improbable sites as formal gardens, cemeteries, and suburban shopping malls, hungering for open spaces but not a barren landscape, some amount of order in the surrounding vegetation but less than geometric perfection. . . . When people are confined to crowded cities or featureless land, they go to considerable lengths to recreate an intermediate terrain, something that can tentatively be called the savanna gestalt."[16]

Wilson presents this assumed genetic proclivity to colonize and shape all lands into savanna-like landscapes as a universal phenomenon. His concept of biophilia naturalizes this Eurocentrism by representing it as a form of the global holism and antiblack ecologies of Western environmental ethics. So, for example, the colonial epistemic logic of Western environmental ethics accepts "green capitalism" as an approach to protecting the tropical rainforests of Asia, Africa, and Latin America. This has forcibly disassembled and reassembled the lands of African-descended and indigenous communities into savanna-like landscapes and in many cases has displaced and disposed these communities. Environmental ethics accepts "green gentrification" (or ecogentrification) to the same effect in the cityscapes of African Americans (and Latinos) in the United States. For example, in some major US cities, like Chicago, Detroit, Los Angles, and Oakland, urban agriculture has been initiated by local residents as a grassroots food-justice movement. These movements have transformed abandoned vacant lots or brownfields into greenfields through the practices permaculture. What began as a grassroots people's movement for food justice has now been commandeered by upscale gentrifiers, alternative food markets, and city planners promoting ecofriendly urban growth. This has increased property values and led to the displacement of local residents from their neighborhoods.[17]

EUROCENTRIST CONSERVATIONISM AND AFRICAN-DESCENDED PLACE-MAKING ECOLOGIES

In *The Value of Life: Biological Diversity and Human Society*, the social ecologist and urban designer Stephen Kellert, a Wilson protégé, embraces Wilson's biophilia and conservation ethics. He adopts the concept of biophilia to account for differences in the ways specific "ethnic groups . . . value living diversity." Kellert's conclusions are based on the data he collected for his 1978 US Fish and Wildlife Service national survey and sociopsychological analysis. This national study questioned the American public on wildlife-related values, interests, and activities and analyzed the responses by age, gender, education, occupation, location (urban or rural), and ethnic group. Kellert developed a taxonomy that included nine basic values: aesthetic, dominionistic, ecologistic and scientific, humanistic, moralistic, naturalistic, symbolic, utilitarian, and negativistic.[18]

These basic values, Kellert argues, accord with Wilson's definition of biophilia, which posits that people innately tend to focus on life and lifelike processes. Thus each of the values represents "a range of physical, emotional, and intellectual expressions of the biophilic tendency to associate with nature." And, like Wilson, he emphasizes that "these are weak biological tendencies, [and unlike] the 'hard-wired' instincts of breathing or feeding, which occur almost automatically, the biophilic values must be cultivated to achieve their full expression. They depend on repeated exposure and social reinforcement before emerging as meaningful dimensions of human emotional and intellectual life."[19] Kellert suggests a positive trend away from dominionistic values (the mastery, physical control, and dominance of nature) and negativistic values (the fear of, aversion to, and alienation from nature) and toward the other seven values that, to different degrees, encourage attitudes and interests that value biological diversity.

Most of the demographic groups in the study expressed a positive inclination toward a conservationist ethic. However, Kellert observes that "most Americans remained fixed on a narrow segment of the biotic community—largely vertebrate animals, particularly creatures of special historical, cultural, and aesthetic significance." He concludes that concern "for biodiversity and natural process continues to be limited and superficial."[20] Among the positive values identified, the weakest according to the criterion of valuing living diversity, is the utilitarian perspective—the view that nature may be exploited for the material benefits it offers (such as food, medicine, clothing, fuel, tools, and other products). The strongest of the values is the ecologistic and scientific, an approach to the natural world that emphasizes, first, "interdependence among species and natural habitat, and second the structures and processes below the level of whole organisms and ecosystems such as morphology, physiology, and cellular and molecular biology." Nonetheless, for Kellert the general positive trend toward valuing "living diversity" and a conservation ethic among most Americans indicates "environmental progress."[21]

Kellert identifies African Americans as the only group that does not value "living diversity." According to Kellert, members of this group "reveal less appreciation, less recreational interest, and less willingness to support the protection of nature and wildlife. They express a greater inclination to endorse the practical exploitation and control of the natural world."[22] His comments seem to suggest that this demographic group represents a hindrance to "environmental progress."

Kellert explains this finding by asserting that slavery arrested the development of biocultural maturity and biophilia among African Americans: "The experience of slavery was so traumatizing that African Americans ever since have tended to view progress in terms of distance from land and its resources." He adds that "the historical persecution of blacks in association with rural areas may also elucidate why relatively few visit national parks and other protected natural areas, perhaps largely viewed as pleasure grounds for European Americans."[23]

In contrast, in my book *Race, Culture, and the City*, I suggest that many African Americans migrating from the rural South to southern and northern cities engaged in forms of place-making ecologies that often reinvented rural traditions in their city neighborhoods.[24] In other words, the meanings and uses assigned to their surroundings were defined around a popular memory of black rural southern culture, which was rebuilt through shared folk traditions related to gardening, by exchanging medicinal plants and delicacies, and by fishing and feasting. Additionally, visits and exchanges with rural relatives who brought their harvest to the city contributed to the making of black solidarity economies, which are described as black collectively owned and operated cooperative enterprises (e.g., credit unions, restaurants, grocery and retail stores, and utilities) and mutual aid societies.

Thus the ecological knowledge of African Americans has historically been embedded in their place-making practices and in their practices of emplacement. These practices, borrowing a term from bell hooks, were about the making of "homeplace"—about assembling plants, animals, water, land, and human beings into spaces of care and nurturance.[25] These spaces are sites, says hooks, "where one could confront the issue of humanization, where one could resist, . . . where all black people could be subjects, not objects, where we could be affirmed in our minds and hearts despite poverty, hardship, and deprivation, where we could restore to ourselves dignity denied us on the outside in the public world."[26] The biophilic conservationist ethics of Kellert and Wilson, and Kellert's assumptions about the biophilic immaturity and past history of African Americans, are blind to these orientations and practices. Furthermore, their perspectives reflect a Eurocentric environmental ethic that narrows the definition of ecological knowledge, cares, and concerns.

FROM DEATH-BOUNDED ECOLOGIES TO HOMEPLACE ECOLOGIES OF CARE AND LIBERATION

Wilson's biophilic perspective not only underpins Kellert's views but also provides an epistemological footing for the "ecocentric holism" of environmental ethics. Ecocentrism is an axiological environmental ethics that extends moral consideration, and therefore value or worth, to all living and nonliving entities within an ecosystem. Thus, unlike biocentrism, ecocentrism focuses on extending value or worth to nonhuman individuals not because they are sentient beings that are aware of their own suffering and go through their own life process, viz. subjects of a life, but rather because the individual entities of local ecosystems are interdependent and cooperatively contribute to the integrity of the whole ecosystem of the earth. Thus value, or moral standing, is conferred on whole ecosystems, not discrete entities. In slave ecologies, by contrast, ecosystems are assembled locally, through the daily reproduction of community life. Thus, the moral standing of humans, plants, animals, land, and water is relational and is achieved through the quotidian activities of assembling local "black environments," "black worlds," or, better yet, "homeplaces," intimate spaces where black people can be themselves.

The "ecocentrism" of environmental ethics has rendered this relational ecology nonexistent. The epistemic legacy of ecocentrism, which is Western holism, has been supported by ecological discourses that are grounded in Western modernity's colonial-hierarchical knowledge systems and modes of existence. (Post)settler-plantation ecologies are a creation of the Americas; they were born out of the European conquest of the planet and genocide of indigenous peoples and the enslavement of Africans.

Usually, settler societies in the Americas have been viewed separately from the plantation complex. The European settler is not seen as a slave master. To preserve this distinction is to disconnect the disassembling of indigenous lands from the enslavement of black bodies—bodies that were forced

STEPHEN NATHAN HAYMES

to clear indigenous lands, transform their ecology, and reassemble them into Euroscapes. The constitution of the black body into a slave body and unit of perpetual property satisfied the slave master's need for bodies to clear and cultivate the land, and the appropriation of indigenous lands satisfied the slave master–settler's need for space. So, in other words, the place-making practices integral to the spatial construction of the settlement as a Euroscape, the clearing and genocide of indigenous peoples, and the construction of the European as the quintessential human are intimately linked to the rendering of the black body into perpetual bondage. Black bodies, then, were fundamental to the construction of the plantation as a white space where the white settler-master could dwell and self-actualize as the archetypical human. The slave's racialized body is used to construct this space as the space of civil society, as the space of the living.

In (post)settler-plantation societies, black existence is "below-Otherness," to use a phrase from Lewis R. Gordon, and it is the zone of nonbeing, that is, the zone of the nonhuman or nonliving. As Frantz Fanon reminds us in *Black Skin, White Masks*, the Hegelian master-slave dialectic of recognition, in which the master's self-actualization depends on the slave's recognition of the master through the alienation and exploitation of the slave's labor, is not applicable to the black slave.[27] Because black presence is incapable of appearing as human presence, it is incapable of recognizing or being recognized by the Other. The implication is that the black body is purged from all ethical relations. And in an antiblack racist world, this means that the self-realization of the settler-master as human is achieved through the gratuitous violence inflicted on the slave's black body. It means that "whiteness" is therefore synonymous with *human*. The emotional constitution of whiteness, and therefore the pleasure of being white, is psychically invested in unwarranted violence towards the black body, so as to render it a perpetual slave body.

Similarly, Gordon says, "The absence "of a Self-Other dialectic in racist situations means the eradication of ethical relations. . . . [It] means living with [a] 'death-bound subjectivity.' It means living with the possibility of one's arbitrary death as a legitimate feature of a system. It also means witnessing concrete instances of arbitrary death and social practices that demonstrate that one group of people's lives are less valuable than others' to the point of their not being considered to be really people at all."[28]

(Post)settler-plantation ecologies are therefore "death-bounded ecologies" that conspire with the "colonial matrix of power" to diminish the social vitality or life force of African-descended black communities in the New World.[29] Subsequently, to speak of the death of the black body as a complex ecological system is not only to speak of physical death but also of what Orlando Patterson refers to as "social death." This is distinct from the alienation experienced by workers in the labor process described by Marxist theories of capitalist exploitation. The peculiar alienation experienced through the capture of the black body is rooted in an enslavement process that is unique to the Americas. That process renders black people nonpersons through its practices of "natal alienation," in which the black body is a "genealogical isolate." This is the constitutive feature of black slaves and of their descendants. Natal alienation produces "the loss of ties of birth in both ascending and descending generations, the loss of native status, of deracination."[30] Alienation from familial lineage results in the slave's having no socially recognized existence separate from his or her master—becoming a social nonperson.

Ontologically speaking, (post)settler-plantation ecologies are premised on the antiblack worldview that black people are incapable of enacting their own worlds or of realizing sociality on their own terms. This is because the black body is constituted as property and as the object of unwarranted violence. The black body's eradication from Georg Hegel's Self-Other dialectic also means that the black body has no capacity for labor. According to this dialectic, human value is constituted through mutual human recognition, which is a function of the product of human labor. In other words, human activity, in contrast to nonhuman activity, is illustrative of labor because it transforms nature into something of human value. Labor, then, confers human status on individuals and groups, even if their labor is exploited and alienated.

In the antiblack world of (post)settler-plantation societies, *black labor* is an oxymoron because the black is nonhuman. This means that the slave's activity cannot be subjugated or estranged like white-human labor. So the nonhuman black body is incapable of being exploited and alienated: it is simply a tool in the perpetual service and extension of white desire and its will to power, meaning the determination (or will) of whites, as settler-masters, to order the world.

From this perspective, the impossibility of black sociality is simultaneously linked to the view that African-descended black people are incapable of territoriality and place making, meaning that they are incapable of having an ecological perspective with regard to the environments they inhabit or of assembling the ecosystems of their local environments. The basic assumption of (post)settler-plantation ecologies is that blacks do not have the capacity—that is, labor—that enables them to inhabit environments. Given this incapacity for labor, and given that labor is constituted

STEPHEN NATHAN HAYMES

within the Self-Other dialectic and that even black mutual recognition is inconceivable, blacks are not naturally predisposed to inhabiting environments and making a homeplace. Their rendition as tools and extensions of the white will to power place them outside the contingencies and therefore outside the human possibilities of space and time, in which human labor is necessary to the assembling of environments.

Another pioneer of ecocentric ethics was Aldo Leopold, an American wildlife ecologist. Leopold's ecocentrism was defined in relation to his theory of land ethics, which, he writes, simply enlarges the boundaries of the community to include soils, waters, plants, and animals—or, collectively, the land. For Leopold, land is a community of all the living things, terrestrial and marine, that shape an ecosystem, or what he refers to as a biotic community. A land ethics changes the role of *Homo sapiens* from conqueror of the land-community to plain member and citizen of it. It implies respect for fellow members, and also respect for the community as such. In this ecological order, the individual is irrelevant: biotic communities are a closely organized cooperative commonwealth of plants and animals. For the [Western] holism defining Leopold's land ethics constructs ecosystems as individuals, namely biotic communities, and not as the sum of their member entities. According to Leopold, "A thing is right when it tends to preserve the integrity, stability, and beauty of the biotic community. It is wrong when it tends otherwise."[31] As J. Callicott, a Leopold protégé and renowned environmental ethicist, comments: "The land ethic, thus, not only has a holistic aspect; it is holistic with a vengeance."[32]

Leopold anticipated that because his original land ethics describes biotic communities, namely local or regional ecosystems, it was not globally scaled to the whole of the planet Earth to account for biospheric changes, such as changes to the climate, soils, or oceans. In "Some Fundamentals of Conservation in the Southwest," a previously unpublished manuscript written in the 1920s, and posthumously published in 1979 in the journal *Environmental Ethics*, Leopold offered a new land ethic. The term Leopold coined for this new land ethic was *earth ethic*, anticipating the Gaia principle expounded by J. E. Lovelock in 1972. The Gaia principle proposed that organisms interact with their inorganic surroundings to form a self-regulating, complex system that contributes to maintaining the conditions of life on the planet. Leopold refers to the Earth as a living organism:

> It is at least not impossible to regard the earth's parts—soil, mountains, rivers, atmosphere, etc.—as organs, or parts of organs, of a coordinated whole, each part with a definite

function. And, if we could see this whole, as a whole, through a great period of time, we might perceive not only organs with coordinated functions, but also possibly also that process of consumption and replacement, which in biology we call the metabolism, or growth. In such a case we would have all the visible attributes of a living thing, which we do not now realize to be such because it is too big, and its life processes too slow. And there would also follow that invisible attribute—a soul, or consciousness—which many philosophers of all ages, ascribe to all living things and aggregations thereof, including the dead earth.[33]

In support of this passage, Callicott declares: "Fortunately, Leopold left us at least a point of departure for constructing an environmental ethic that is globally scaled spatially and millennially scaled temporally—an Earth ethic—to complement the land ethic."[34] However, in her critique of Leopold's holistic foundation, the ecofeminist Marti Kheel states that Leopold collapses individual beings into these larger, abstract constructs.[35] This means that the existence of individual biotic communities is relevant only to the extent that they are folded into and contribute to the earth as a living organism. It is on this basis that contemporary African relational environmentalism challenges Leopold's environmental holism.

As a diasporic antecedent to African relational environmentalism in the New World, slave ecologies challenge the holistic foundation and universalistic declarations of Leopold's earth ethics. They contest the Eurocentric globalism and colonizing ethos that proclaim that there is only one earth ethics, and it is white. Slave ecologies assemble, care for, and nurture local ecosystems through quotidian efforts to reproduce community life in all its dimensions—ecological, emotional, intellectual, spiritual, and physical. Here, community encompasses all living beings as kin or family. This means, in the words of Sara Ahmed, that orientation is a matter of how we reside in space, a matter of residence; of how we inhabit spaces as well as "who" or "what" we inhabit spaces with.[36]

In this regard, slave ecologies forged ecological homeplaces of care, in which the desires of enslaved Africans to persevere were entwined with their care of other living entities. Desire, in this instance, is to exist and be active in pursuit of one's desires. Slave ecologies, as embodied in enslaved Africans striving to assemble a human or social world in and with the natural world, allowed for a joyful existence, even in the midst of the calamitous and the catastrophic. As ecologies of liberation, slave ecologies enabled

STEPHEN NATHAN HAYMES

forms of belonging that allowed for experiences of black joy through social communion. Cornel West says that joy tries to get at those values—love, care, kindness, service, solidarity and the struggle for justice—values that provide the possibility of bringing people together. We might add that joy is a collective's alternative way of knowing itself. Through their ecologies of liberation, or ecologies of joyful living, or ecological homeplaces, enslaved Africans sought to address epistemological and ethical concerns: how do we come to know what we know, and how must we act? Although Cornel West does not address slave ecologies per se, he summarizes the ethical and epistemological motivations and concerns of these ecologies when he writes:

> The genius of our black foremothers and forefathers was to create powerful buffers to ward off the nihilistic threat, to equip black folk with cultural armor to beat back the demons of hopelessness, meaninglessness, and lovelessness. These buffers consisted of cultural structures of meaning and feeling that created and sustained communities; this armor constituted ways of life and . . . values. . . . [T]raditions of black surviving and thriving under usually adverse New World conditions were major barriers against the nihilistic threat. . . . If cultures are, in part, what human beings create in order to convince themselves not to commit suicide, then black foremothers and forefathers are to be applauded.[37]

West adds that these traditions consist primarily of black religious and civic institutions that sustained familial and communal networks of support.[38] I would add that the genius of Africana or black ecological traditions, inspired by enslaved ancestors throughout the Americas, equipped black folk with more cultural armor to beat back these demons. As bell hooks also reminds us, "Recalling the legacy of our [slave] ancestors, who knew that the way we regard land and nature will determine the level of our self-regard, black people must reclaim a spiritual legacy where we connect our well-being to the well-being of the earth."[39]

NOTES

1   Lewis R. Gordon, "Existential Dynamics of Theorizing Black Invisibility," *Existence in Black: An Anthology of Black Existential Philosophy*, ed. Lewis R. Gordon (New York: Routledge, 1997), 3.

2   Richard H. Grove, *Green Imperialism: Colonial Expansion, Tropical Island Edens and the Origins of Environmentalism, 1600–1860* (New York: Cambridge University Press, 1995), 9, 224.

3   David E. C. Cooper and Joy A. Palmer, *Environment in Question: Ethics and Global* (New York: Routledge, 2005), 164.

4   Kevin Behrens, "Exploring African Holism with Respect to the Environment," *Environmental Ethics* 19, no. 4 (2010): 466.

5   Ibid., 468.

6   Ibid., 477–78.

7   Ibid., 471–76.

8   Ibid., 477.

9   Ibid., 475.

10   Ibid., 477.

11   Walter D. Mignolo, *The Darker Side of Western Modernity: Global Futures, Decolonial Options* (Durham, NC: Duke University Press, 2011), xvii, xii.

12   Edward O. Wilson. *Biophilia: The Human Bond with Other Species* (Cambridge, MA: Harvard University Press, 1984), 128–40; Edward O. Wilson, "Biophilia and the Conservation Ethic," in *The Biophilia Hypothesis*, ed. Stephen R. Kellert and Edward O. Wilson (Washington, DC: Shearwater Books, 1993), 31–41.

13   Wilson, *Biophilia*, 128–40; Wilson, "Biophilia and the Conservation Ethic," 31–41.

14   Edward O. Wilson, *Naturalist* (Washington, DC: Shearwater Books, 1994), 360.

15   Judith Heerwagen, "Biophilia," in *Encyclopedia of Environmental Ethics and Philosophy*, ed. J. Baird Callicott and Robert Frodeman (New York: Macmillan USA Reference, 2008), 109.

16   Wilson, *Biophilia*, 109, 110–11.

17   Julie Guthman, "If They Only Knew": The Unbearable Whiteness of Alternative Food," in *Cultivating Food Justice: Race, Class and Sustainability*, ed. Alison Hope Alkon and Julian Agyeman (Cambridge, MA: MIT Press, 2011), 263–78.

18   Stephen R. Kellert, *The Value of Life: Biological Diversity and Human Society* (Washington, DC: Island Press, 1997), 60–62, 3, 7, 34.

19   Ibid., 26, 7.

20   Ibid., 26, 62.

21   Ibid., 13, 62.

22   Ibid., 60, 62.

23   Ibid., 61.

24   Stephen Nathan Haymes, *Race, Culture, and the City: A Pedagogy for Black Urban Struggle.* (Albany: State University of New York Press, 1995).

25   Ibid., 71, 112, 113, 129).

26   bell hooks, *Yearning: Race, Gender, and Cultural Politics* (Boston: South End Press, 1990), 42.

27 Frantz Fanon, *Black Skin, White Masks* (New York: Grove Press, 2008), 219–20.

28 Lewis R. Gordon, "Essentialist Anti-essentialism, with Considerations from Other Sides of Modernity," *Quaderna: A Multilingual and Transdisciplinary Journal* 1 (2012): 11.

29 Anibal Quijano, "Coloniality and Modernity/Rationality," *Cultural Studies* 21, nos. 2–3 (March–May 2007): 169.

30 Orlando Patterson, *Slavery and Social Death: A Comparative Study* (Cambridge, MA: Harvard University Press, 1985), 6.

31 Aldo Leopold, *A Sand County Almanac* (New York: Oxford University Press, 1968), 213.

32 J. Baird Callicott, *Thinking Like a Planet: The Land Ethic and the Earth Ethic* (New York: Oxford University Press, 2013), 150.

33 Aldo Leopold, "Some Fundamentals of Conservation in the Southwest," *Environmental Ethics* vol. 1 (1979), 139–40.

34 Callicott, *Thinking Like a Planet*, 150.

35 Marti Kheel, *Nature Ethics: An Ecofeminist Perspective* (Lanham, MD: Rowman & Littlefield, 2008), 118.

36 Sara Ahmed, *Queer Phenomenology: Orientations, Objects, Others* (Durham, NC: Duke University Press, 2006), 2.

37 Cornel West, 1992, "Nihilism in Black America," in *Black Popular Culture*, ed. Gina Dent (Seattle: Bay Press, 1992) 40.

38 Ibid.

39 bell hooks, *Sister of the Yam: Black Women and Self-Recovery* (Boston, MA: South End Press, 2005), 175.

CHAPTER THREE

THE ARTFUL THINGS OF CLIMATE CHANGE

MIN HYOUNG SONG

O NE of the most memorable recent contributions to the environmental humanities is Rob Nixon's idea of slow violence, which focuses attention on actions that can harm individuals, their children, and whole communities over long periods. This kind of violence is often ignored in favor of the "highly visible act that is newsworthy because it is event focused, time bound, and body bound." We are all familiar with the latter, but how do we make sense of the former? As Nixon puts this question, "How can we convert into image and narrative the disasters that are slow moving and long in the making, disasters that are anonymous and that star nobody, disasters that are attritional and of indifferent interest to the sensation-driven technologies of our image world?"[1] One ready-made answer offered by literary critics is the practice of close reading: the scrupulous attention to the text by which each word and sentence and passage is carefully analyzed and thought through, so that we force ourselves to slow down and make sense of effects that are often registered as something that happens in the background, as noise, as the unmarked massing of phenomena.

Close reading is one practice that the humanities can contribute to a discussion about climate change. It can lead us to question habits of thought and in their place offer creative ways of imagining how humans relate to each other, their environments, and their feelings. Through their sensitivity to issues of power and disenfranchisement (though of course not all, and not exclusively), and the myriad ways in which some lives simply matter less than others, writers and scholars who focus on the poor and people of color, and on a history of colonial expansion in particular, can help readers understand how disparate concerns are related to the problem of tracking the effects of slow violence as it relates to the climate. Even when they are not explicitly talking about race, what they have to say may nevertheless be informed by racial concerns. As Stephen Sohn asks with respect to literature by Asian Americans that does not foreground Asian American characters, "If a strategic essentialist approach persists as one of the primary modes for defining Asian American literature, what then of thinking about the strategic antiessentialism of fictional worlds?"[2]

This idea of a "strategic antiessentialism" feels important to me. It reverberates in discussions about nonhuman agency and the Anthropocene, where the "human" often remains racially unmarked.[3] Given the global nature of the phenomenon, climate change offers a powerful frame for understanding how seemingly unrelated struggles for justice are in fact connected. At the same time, it is too big a frame: it needs intervening levels of descriptive and narrative devices to become more a part of everyday reality.

There are, however, some questions that linger around such efforts. Can humanities scholars and creative artists, who excel at exploring uncertainty, contribute to a task that calls for exacting clarity of purpose? Or can they offer only a greater tolerance of uncertainty and a willingness to sit with feelings of unease? Are these latter qualities necessary for the important work of linking climate change to everyday experiences, especially the kind butting up against racial differences, so that action does not depend on a perfection of knowledge?

Here I look for instances where the everyday is reinterpreted in the light of what is now widely known about climate change and what must be done in response. Humanities scholars have already explored the ways in which climate change challenges ideas about history, geography, the human, and time.[4] I want to examine how it alters experiences of the everyday. I ask how phenomena that lie beyond human perceptual limits can manifest themselves in ways that can be, or at least should be, immediately apparent. So far, this has happened primarily through a growing feeling of unease and a creeping sense that the relationship between humans and things is changing. Literature, television, journalism, and film can highlight and prolong such emotional states. They can also, however, act as barriers to connecting such feelings to a wider context, as emphasized in my discussion of Teju Cole's 2011 novel *Open City*.

In thinking climate change and race together, this chapter tests the possibility that an effective way of talking about either subject is to do it indirectly, focusing on their attendant affects and observable material consequences. Indeed, talking about climate change might be a powerful way to talk indirectly about race, and vice versa. Each can act as a frame that helps us to imagine the everyday as other than what it may serenely appear.

Yet there are limits to this strategy that require us to be bold about the arguments we want to make.

"SOMETHING MORE TROUBLING WAS AT WORK"

Open City features an impressively erudite, cosmopolitan, and sensitive narrator. A psychiatry fellow at a hospital, Julius spends his evenings and days off walking around the city of New York. When he accrues enough vacation time, he travels to Brussels, where he befriends a Moroccan clerk, Farouq, working at the Internet cafe where he catches up on his e-mails. Farouq is friendly and well versed in Western continental philosophy. The two have heated conversations about colonialism, literature, racism, and Zionism. Throughout his travels, the narrator notes not only the physical landscape but also the history of that landscape. He sees a church in Harlem and recalls the building's history as a theater, "America's third largest when it was built, seating over three thousand. . . . Al Johnson had played there, as had Lucille Ball, and back then it had been surrounded by expensive restaurants and luxury goods shops."[5] Visiting the former site of the World Trade Center, he finds himself musing about what was there before the towers went up and then fell down: "There had been communities here before Columbus ever set sail, before Verrazano anchored his ships in the narrows, or the black Portuguese slave trader Esteban Gómez sailed up the Hudson; human beings had lived here, built homes, and quarreled with their neighbors" (59).

Julius thinks about his own privileged childhood in his family's home in Nigeria and the poverty he encountered, as when getting a suit made by a tailor in a poor neighborhood to wear to his father's funeral: "These children stared when my aunt and I emerged from her car because, from their point of view, we would have represented unimaginable wealth and privilege" (223). Race and the role it has played in a history of colonial exploitation saturate these ruminations. As Sohn writes about the work of a different author, because these ideas "exhibit a kind of geographical and historical expansiveness that could be mislabeled as a postracial aesthetic, these works demand that readers attend to the relational power structures arising in colonial and postcolonial contexts."[6]

Race is something that readers have to notice deliberately in *Open City*, because nothing seems to escape Julius's perceptiveness, and his observations can blend into each other. He is keenly aware of how racism and colonial exploitation have shaped the very buildings and places he walks through. He is comfortable with people of every background, class, gender, and sexuality, even as he is quietly scornful of the hypocrisies of others. Just as important, his interests include bird watching, classical music, literature, philosophy, independent film, history, poetry, photography, and architecture. Everything about his character suggests that he is someone who notices race because he notices everything.

And yet, for all his sensitivity, weaknesses in his perception slowly appear.[7] He visits a detention center for undocumented immigrants in Queens and hears the testimony of a Liberian man whose family was slaughtered during the civil war there and who himself narrowly escaped being conscripted as a child soldier. Julius responds, "I wondered, naturally, as Saidu told his story, whether I believed him or not, whether it wasn't more likely that he had been a soldier" (67). Later he has a chance encounter with Moji, the sister of a childhood friend, and he flatters himself that she must have had a crush on him. She invites him to a party hosted by her boyfriend. At the end of the party, she confronts him with an accusation of rape: "Things don't go away just because you choose to forget them. You forced yourself on me eighteen years ago because you could get away with it, and I suppose you did get away with it. But not in my heart, you didn't" (245).

It is possible that Julius's skepticism about Saidu's story is well founded, and even that Moji is somehow misremembering what happened between her and Julius when they were much younger. Still, both moments suggest troubling gaps in Julius's thinking. His use of the word "naturally" in questioning Saidu's story suggests that any attentive listener would also harbor doubts. Julius never refutes Moji's claim. Rather, he withdraws from it, and the next chapter moves on to tell of something else that happens to him. Such moments shock the reader precisely because Julius is so aware of his surroundings and so careful to place what he sees in historical contexts stripped of self-serving narratives and erasures of atrocity.

What does he fail to see despite his perceptiveness? What does he allow himself to forget? What do such gaps reveal about the extent to which an individual can make meaning of what he or she sees? In an important moment early in the novel, Julius observes, "But I was no longer the global-warming skeptic I had been some years before, even if I still couldn't tolerate the tendency some had of jumping to conclusions based on anecdotal evidence: global warming was a fact, but that did not mean it was the explanation for why a given day was warm. It was careless thinking to draw the link too easily, an invasion of fashionable politics into what should be the ironclad precincts of science" (28).

At this point in the novel, readers have encountered Julius's rich thought processes but not any of the doubts about his character that are introduced later. This makes it easy to interpret these sentences as another sign of his sharp reasoning. It *is* naive to think that a single day of heat—or of cold—reveals anything about a phenomenon that requires years of meticulously collected data to verify. Indeed, the tendency to conflate weather and climate has been highlighted by James Hansen, one of the scientists most responsible for helping to make climate change an important public concern. As he and his coauthors write: "The greatest barrier to public recognition of human-made climate change is probably the natural variability of local climate. How can a person discern long-term climate change, given the notorious variability of local weather and climate from day to day and year to year?"[8]

At the start of *Open City*, Julius acknowledges what Hansen's article goes on to demonstrate: that the increasing volatility of the weather is due to something other than normal variability. Julius observes, "The absence of this order, the absence of cold when it ought to be cold, was something I now sensed as a sudden discomfort" (28). Hansen and his coauthors would likely respond, "The climate dice are now loaded to a degree that a perceptive person old enough to remember the climate of 1951–1980 should recognize the existence of climate change."[9] Julius, however, shakes off what his senses tell him by expressing fears of confirmation bias. He worries that he is reading into signs the meaning that he already expects: "Still, the way my thoughts returned to the fact that it was the middle of November and I hadn't yet had occasion to wear my coat made me wonder if, already, I was one of those people, the overinterpreters. This was part of my suspicion that there was a mood in the society that pushed peopled more toward snap judgments and unexamined opinions, an antiscientific mood" (28).

Julius insists that inferences of anthropogenic climate change are wild leaps of logic, "a more general inability to assess evidence" that fuels a political climate in which "partisanship was all" (28). His skepticism is heightened, so much so that it seems an affectation, a way to communicate to the reader that despite the Nigerian heritage bequeathed to him by his father (his mother is German), he considers himself someone who can rise above ethnic-seeming superstitions and quaint ways of thinking. His skepticism is a proud badge of his high educational attainment, intellectual sophistication, social status, and knowledge of the world around him.

Julius's reasoning, and the cultural associations it might conjure, is what Wendy Hui Kyong Chun questions when she observes that the public respect for science has ironically created expectations of an impossible standard of scientific certainty: "The debate continues . . . because of the reification of science as absolute and certain; a significant number of those who have reservations regarding the existence of global climate change are not dupes, ideologues, or postmodern theorists but rather vocal supporters of science."[10] The views of these doubters rest on the assumption that science can arrive at irrefutable truths and provide perfect understandings of how phenomena occur. Julius echoes the plea for better science that many deniers make, one that is founded rhetorically on a concern that political causes can cloud scientific reason. As a result, the public continues to be misled by interpretations of data that can be stretched to mean many different, and often contradictory, things. For someone to insist that an unusually warm winter is a sure sign of climate change is just as irresponsible as James Inhofe, the Republican chair of the Senate's Environment and Public Works committee, throwing a snowball during a committee session to show that climate change is not real.[11] The only apparently logical position to take in the face of such extremes is the one Julius takes: to treat both sides of the argument with skepticism and refuse to commit to either one.

In the rest of the novel, Cole works to unravel this simple stance. He does so first by revealing that Julius is an unreliable narrator. Despite his sensitivity, his thinking fails him at key moments, most notably in his relationship to Moji. What he initially mistakes as reawakened sexual interest is actually revulsion. Moji, meanwhile, speaks with an earnest passion that calls into question Julius's habitually skeptical stance: "On our way into the park, Moji had said to me that she was more worried than ever about the environment. Her tone was serious. When I responded that I supposed we all were, she corrected me, shaking her head. What I mean is that I actively worry about it, she said, I don't think that's generally true of other people" (198). Moji becomes in this moment an example of someone who ruins the mood of a social gathering by bringing up something too serious. By doing so, she challenges Julius's glib remark. While everyone may pay lip service to environmental concerns, she takes them seriously in a way that Julius simply does not. Perhaps she is being parochial, and even ethnic (in a way that Julius seems to associate with being unscientific), in being so earnest, but such concerns do not seem to matter to her. Her stance is a notable contrast to Julius's habit of distancing himself from ethnic particularity by embracing a cool and discerning cosmopolitanism.

The rightness of this kind of earnest concern about the environment is buttressed throughout the novel by observations Julius makes about the weather he has been experiencing. At the start of the second half of the book, alluding to Wallace Stevens's poem "The Snow Man," he undercuts the tone of the poem by noting what the weather has actually been like:

I made an effort to develop a mind of winter. Late last year, I
actually said to myself audibly, as I do when I swear these oaths,
that I would have to embrace winter as part of the natural cycles
of seasons. . . . But it was to be a year without a real winter. The
blizzards for which I braced never came. There were few days of
cold rain, and one or two cold snaps, but heavy snow stayed away.
We had a series of sunny days in the middle of December, and I
was unnerved by that mildness, and when the season's first snow
did eventually fall, it was while I was in Brussels, getting drenched
by the rain there. The snow was in any case short-lived, melted
away by the time I returned to New York in mid-January, and thus
did the impression of unseasonal, somewhat uncanny, warm
weather persist in my mind, keeping the world, as I experienced
it, on edge. (149–50)

An exceptionally mild winter can be explained as an anomaly. When
successive winters, however, are noticeably warmer than usual—or so
extremely cold and snowy that hundred-year-old records are broken—it
becomes harder to argue that nothing is happening. Words like *usual* or
natural lose their meaning, and a sense of unease begins to dominate, growing into an inchoate sense of dread, foiled expectations, and uncanniness.
The recognition of such emotions may not lead to an aesthetic practice that
can connect climate change to the everyday, but it does point to the gap
between the two. To say that anomalous weather is happening because of
climate change is at once true and maybe too sweeping and obvious a statement. Climate change may seem like such a large topic that others respond
with a shudder and a shrug. The unease is what lingers, and it needs compounding to prevent the weirdness of what is happening to the weather from
receding into the background.

Unease mounts throughout the rest of the novel, culminating in an anecdote about how the Statue of Liberty, until 1902, used to be a working light-
house. "The birds," Julius tells the reader, "many of which were clever enough
to dodge the cluster of skyscrapers in the city, somehow lost their bearings
when faced with a single monumental flame" (258). For years, Colonel Tassin, "who had military command of the island," kept a detailed record of the
birds who died in this way. Before his arrival on Liberty Island, other officials
had sold the carcasses to hat makers and other merchants in the city. After-
wards, the dead birds were donated to museums. The narrative concludes:
"The average, Colonel Tassin estimated, was about twenty birds per night,

although the weather and the direction of the wind had a great deal to do with the resulting harvest. Nevertheless, the sense persisted that something more troubling was at work. On the morning of October 13, for example, 173 wrens had been gathered in, all dead of impact, although the night just past hadn't been particularly windy or dark" (259). From the obvious allegorical nature of concluding the novel with a story about the Statue of Liberty, which inevitably connects this story to a larger national context and its guiding mythologies, to the use of a word like *harvest* to refer to the number of dead birds, this ending seeks to conjure for the reader a heightened mood of foreboding.

Several implicit and unanswered questions contribute to this unease. In the absence of obvious causes, what brought about the birds' death? Why couldn't the birds steer clear of a single spotlight after having successfully navigated past the much brighter lights of the city? Why does Tassin record so meticulously the gruesome facts of the number and species of the birds that died, and their time of death? The reader is left with haunting mysteries, an uncertainty that partially unravels the standard of scientific certainty that Julius conjures in his skepticism about global warming. The more diligently Colonel Tassin documents what has happened, the greater the reader's sense that something is evading such record keeping. There is a strange, perhaps occult force at work. Science itself becomes an imperfect instrument, less the search for certainty and more, as Chun argues, a start toward building "habits" that shape responses to the challenges ahead.[12] The unease generated by this final anecdote reminds the reader simultaneously of a history of colonial expansion and nation building, the crashing of planes into the Twin Towers and the wars that followed, and something else even more difficult to put into words.

In death, the birds are made into things—objects of trade and scientific curiosity. They might remind the reader of the way racism can make humans into things that occupy the space between the living and the dead. Slavery, for instance, was a form of social death, making slave bodies into objects that could be traded or studied. The birds might also remind the reader that humans, too, are subject to forces beyond their understanding that can lure them into danger and suddenly end their existence. The mystery of death conjured in the final pages of Cole's novel thwarts claims of human mastery, self-awareness, and exceptionalism. We are like the birds, a part of the world rather than some entity that can stand fully apart from it. Some of us more than others are also, because of history and group differences and greater vulnerability, more aware of these similarities.

What can span the apparent gap between the abstract phenomenon of climate change and the everyday? This is a question I continue to struggle with, alongside many other humanities scholars. One approach is to seek examples of artistic and literary creativity, like *Open City*, that enable discussion of how climate change can affect ordinary ideas about how the world operates. The following is a journalistic description of Staten Island after Hurricane Sandy in 2012: "Shrubs and saplings had been cut off at the roots—not cleanly, but as if scratched away by fingernails. Deep gouges in the banks undercut fences and asphalt biking trails, and the scrubby trees far above the usual high-tide line hunkered down as if some massive creature had slept on them. Shreds of plastic bags hung among the branches everywhere, while the ocean, distant and calm at low tide, offered its quiet wavelets and asked, 'Who, me?'"[13]

The verbs in this passage are words ordinarily reserved for human or animal agency: *scratched, hunkered down,* and *asked.* The metaphoric representation of the forces of wind and ocean as an organic being (an entity with "fingernails," a "creature") is somewhat heavy-handed, as if the journalist does not trust the reader to grasp his meaning. The words *gouges* and *shreds* are used as nouns, but they also connote human or animal action. The ocean is imagined to have not only the ability to enact great violence but also to coyly dissemble. Things not only speak in this passage: they can also lie.

In these kinds of rhetorical flourishes, inanimate things seem capable of action, and often, as in the case of Hurricane Sandy, they act with a force that humans can barely comprehend. As one illustration of this point, consider what may be the most memorable passage in Michael Pollan's book *The Omnivore's Dilemma* (2006), his description of the corn that is at the base of the United States' industrial food system (itself a significant contributor to climate change): "Basically, modern hybrids can tolerate the corn equivalent of city life, growing amid multitudes without succumbing to urban stress. You would think that competition among individuals would threaten the tranquility of such a crowded metropolis, yet the modern field of corn forms a most orderly mob. This is because every plant in it, being an F-1 hybrid, is genetically identical to every other. . . . There are no alpha corn plants to hog the light or fertilizer. The true socialist utopia turns out to be a field of F-1 hybrid plants." Later in this chapter, Pollan returns to his conceit of the anthropomorphized corn: "And then of course there's the corn itself, which if corn could form an opinion would surely marvel at the absurdity of it all—and at its great good fortune."[14]

Consider one final illustration, from the film *Beasts of the Southern Wild* (2012, directed by Benh Zeitlin). Intercutting the narrative of a poor black man and his daughter living in an impoverished tidal community, threatened both by floods and by dams meant to protect a more affluent nearby community, are scenes of icebergs breaking apart and falling into the ocean on the other side of the planet. As the icebergs break, they awaken giant, boar-like creatures that march across an abstracted landscape, until at the very end of the film they face the girl, who snarls angrily back at them. Rather than confrontation, however, the film suggests that a form of communication occurs, a moment of mutual acknowledgment. A movement that at first seems threatening turns out to be more profoundly contiguous, a metonymic line connecting melting ice, charging animals, and snarling human. As the African American girl comes face to face with the melting ice, as embodied by the animals, she acknowledges the animals as the manifestation of the ice's changing form and growing force.

Attempts like these to describe a phenomenon that clearly lies outside ordinary habits of perception (a lying ocean, a city of corn, the ice-animal-girl assemblage) can resemble what Seo-Young Chu calls the lyrical: "What makes a lyric poem 'lyrical' is a constellation of interrelated attributes that have characterized Anglophone poetry from the Renaissance (if not earlier) to the present. Lyric poetry is frequently soliloquy-like. Lyric voices speak from beyond ordinary time. Lyric poems are inhabited by situations and tableaux transcending ordinary temporality. Lyric descriptions are charged with depictive intensity. Lyric poetry is musically expressive. Lyric poems evoke heightened and eccentric states of consciousness."[15]

This original characterization of the lyrical is then extended to science fiction (SF) narratives: "SF is frequently soliloquy-like. SF voices speak beyond ordinary time. Works of SF are inhabited by situations and tableaux transcending ordinary temporality. SF descriptions are charged with depictive intensity. SF is musically expressive. And works of SF evoke heightened and eccentric states of consciousness." There is no analogy in this argument. SF is not *like* lyric poetry. Rather, Chu insists that SF is a form of the lyrical. Even when it is not in verse, it remains lyrical in that even its prose begins to take on attributes of free verse. So although there may be few examples of SF poetry, its prose narratives and movies and comics are necessarily lyrical, because lyric alone has enough power "to convert an elusive referent into an object available for representation."[16] By definition, SF is always interested in the "elusive referent," since it seeks to represent a world that does not yet exist or is said to exist in some alternative universe.

sharing borders, communicating, touching

the elusive referent

Perhaps, following Chu's lead, it might be possible to speak about a climate lyricism: a way of turning the use of anthropocentric habits of expression back on itself, so that the nonhuman is given human characteristics and, in the process, asserts powers similar to those assumed to be uniquely human. A world made knowable by climate lyricism could make people more aware of their own fragility and their dependence on processes that far exceed their powers of control. This is a world that many in the global South and in the growing sacrifice zones of industrialized countries already know too well, but which remains alien to much of the elite who dictate governmental and business policy. This is also, thus, a world marked by racial difference and racism, and by class and a history of capitalist exploitation.

When a novel like *Open City* taps into the power of this lyricism, it speaks to sheltered viewers and readers in the global North to convey something that those living in the global South may very well experience as the everyday. That is, a perception of a gap between climate change and the everyday is most likely a position of privilege, one enabled by socioeconomic status, geographical location, and racial expectations. This gap is as much constructed by race and a history of colonial and capitalist exploitation as by an innate human inability to perceive a slowly approaching calamity. An attunement to climate lyricism, then, might reveal that the birds in *Open City* are speaking, that they are artful things conveying the same message that many vulnerable humans have been conveying for some time. The challenge remains: how to amplify and make more immediately discernible this cry?

NOTES

1   Rob Nixon, *Slow Violence and the Environmentalism of the Poor* (Cambridge, MA: Harvard University Press, 2011), 3.

2   Stephen Sohn, *Racial Asymmetries: Asian American Fictional Worlds* (New York: New York University Press, 2014), 3–4.

3   See, for instance, Timothy Morton, *Hyperobjects: Philosophy and Ecology after the End of the World* (Minneapolis: University of Minnesota Press, 2013); Jane Bennet, *Vibrant Matter: A Political Ecology of Things* (Durham, NC: Duke University Press, 2010).

4   See, for example, Dipesh Chakrabarty, "The Climate of History: Four Theses," *Critical Inquiry* 35, no. 2 (Winter 2009): 197–222; Ursula Heise, *Sense of Place and Sense of Planet: The Environmental Imagination of the Global* (New York: Oxford, 2008); "Climate Change Criticism," ed. Karen Pinkus, special issue, *Diacritics* 41, no. 3 (November 2013); Nixon, *Slow Violence*.

5   Teju Cole, *Open City* (New York: Random House, 2011), 235. All subsequent citations to this work appear in parentheses in the text.

6   Sohn, *Racial Asymmetries*, 138.

7   Criticism of the novel centers primarily on its critique of cosmopolitanism. See, for instance, Pieter Vermeulen, "Flights of Memory: Teju Cole's *Open City* and the Limits of Aesthetic Cosmopolitanism," *Journal of Modern Literature* 37, no. 1 (Fall 2013): 40–57; Katherine Hallemeier, "Literary Cosmopolitanism in Teju Cole's *Every Day Is for the Thief* and *Open City*," *Ariel: A Review of International English Literature* 44, nos. 2–3 (2013): 239–50. See also James Wood, "The Arrival of Enigmas: Teju Cole's Prismatic Début Novel *Open City*," *New Yorker*, February 29, 2011. Cole describes Wood's review of his novel as crucial to its wide circulation and attention (personal communication). Notably, none of this criticism addresses the novel's references to climate change or its careful attention to the weather.

8   James Hansen, Makiko Sato, and Reto Reudy, "Perception of Climate Change," *Proceedings of the National Academy of Sciences* 109 (August 2012): 14726–27.

9   Ibid.

10 Wendy Hui Kyong Chun, "On Hypo-real Models or Global Climate Change: A Challenge for the Humanities," *Critical Inquiry* 41, no. 3 (Spring 2015): 681.

11 Jason Plautz, "Watch James Inhofe Throw a Snowball on the Senate Floor," *National Journal*, February 26, 2015, www.nationaljournal.com/energy/watch-jim-inhofe-throw-a-snowball-on-the-senate-floor-20150226.

12 Chun, "On Hypo-real Models," 679.

13 Ian Frazier, "The Toll: Sandy and the Future," *New Yorker*, February 11 and 18, 2013, 41.

14 Michael Pollan, *The Omnivore's Dilemma: A Natural History of Four Meals* (New York: Penguin, 2006), 37, 56.

15 Seo-Young Chu, *Do Metaphors Dream of Literal Sleep? A Science-Fictional Theory of Representation* (Cambridge, MA: Harvard University Press, 2010), 13–14.

16 Ibid., 14.

PART TWO

LANDSCAPES OF RACIALIZATION

CHAPTER FOUR

RACIAL ECOLOGIES

Black Landscapes in Flux

TIFFANY LETHABO KING

NEW analytic frames that emerge from a number of interdisciplinary traditions within Black diaspora studies trouble conventional practices for seeing, thinking, and conceptualizing Blackness within ecologies of the Americas. Fine arts, literature, history, gender and sexuality studies, and other interdisciplinary traditions within Black diaspora studies have shifted the focus from static Marxian and humanist narratives of Black labor and commodification to more agile and elastic ones. Marxian frames that focus on the worker as commodity also reify Cartesian and humanist distinctions between the discrete realms of the natural and the human and cultural. A much more salient method of describing Black life and ecosystems is through attention to the texture, sense, feel (Black aesthetics), fungibility (Afropessimism), and fugitivity (Black optimism) of Blackness, as experienced, performed, and represented as flux.[1]

As early as 1997, scholars like Saidiya Hartman were theorizing and elaborating the significance of Black fungibility—of Black bodies and the idea of Blackness as fungible—for thinking about how slavery and its afterlife imagines Black people. In *Scenes of Subjection*, Hartman applies the political-economic term *fungibility* to the elasticity and exchangeability of Black bodies.[2] She argues that the enslaved embody the abstract "interchangeability and replaceability" endemic to the definition of a commodity.[3] But unlike a strict political economic framework's emphasis on the one to one exchangeability of a commodity-form, Hartman's Black body has figurative and metaphorical value. Explaining this elasticity and fluidity, Hartman defines fungibility's relationship to Blackness by stating that "the fungibility of the commodity makes the captive body an abstract and empty vessel vulnerable to the projection of others' feelings, ideas, desires, and values."[4]

While the theorization of Black fungibility begins in the violence of slavery, Black scholars have transformed Black openness, elasticity, and fungibility into a resource. Following the tradition of the enslaved, Black scholars have been able to use Blackness's capacity for flux and change into an opportunity for flight.[5] This chapter experiments with reading an eighteenth-century map of the coast of South Carolina and Georgia that depicts Black people cultivating indigo through the lens of fungibility rather than labor. This experiment asks the reader to consider what new ways of seeing and thinking emerge if fungibility becomes the focus.

In the words of Mart Stewart, William de Brahm's 1757 *Map of South Carolina and Georgia* "has gained a reputation as the first 'scientific' or 'modern' map of southeastern North America." It became the standard source for geographic knowledge of the British colonies in North America.[6] Measuring approximately four feet by four feet, the map is an arresting and imposing work split diagonally by a rendition of the coastline of southern North Carolina, all of South Carolina, and Georgia. Land and sea appear to occupy approximately equal areas of the map.

The cartouche, placed in bottom right corner of the map (in the Atlantic Ocean), is a large-scale etching that effectively zooms in on daily activity on the shores of the Atlantic. The cartouche is elaborately detailed and animated by the motions of the enslaved, a coastline, the sea, ships in the distance, foliage, plant life, and a multistage depiction of indigo processing. To the left of the cartouche, anchoring the map, is a legend listing the owners of property (land and slaves). The map labels identify different kinds of territories, units of property, soil types, larger geographic units like the ocean, and colonial boundaries. Most important, this text supports the overall story told by the cartouche.

READING A MAP IN MOTION

I read de Brahm's map against the grain (yet within the context of colonial orders) in order to illuminate the ways that both nature (plant and nonhuman life) and Black bodies (and ideas of Blackness) needed to be rendered as open and moving processes before they could be represented as ontologically fixed. I draw on literature from environmental history as well as methods from postcolonial visual analysis to trace the conventions that transform the renderings and representations on the map from fixed and inert, already knowable objects into dynamic processes. Rather than view

TIFFANY LETHABO KING

the map as simply a representation of plants, ocean, shoreline, and Black laboring bodies on a plantation, I reimagine and re-present the map as a scene of motion, movement, and flux that have not yet been given fixed borders or placed in colonial categories.

Rereading de Brahm's map attends to a temporary epistemic break, or stop-gap, in which Black bodies, nonhuman plant life, and other natural matter function as symbols of transition and flux. The natural sciences that emerged during the European Enlightenment ordered people's perceptions—their ideas of what it was possible to see and think. Cartesianism distinguishes between human (culture) and nonhuman biomatter (nature). Further, human and nonhuman organisms are imagined as inert objects rather than interrelated, dynamic, ever-changing systems.

Recently, the environmental historian Mart Stewart has intervened in the fields of environmental history and critical cartography by reading the eighteenth-century plantation scene in the de Brahm map as a colonial landscape in process. This chapter extends on this important visual and spatial analysis but also contends with the forgotten landscape of Blackness. I extend upon Stewart's work in taking the depictions of Black bodies on the plantation as depictions of figures and bodies in process.

Commissioned in 1753 by British subjects and settlers and completed in 1757, de Brahm's map depicts a number of dynamic landscapes: the ocean, the flora and fauna, Black enslaved figures in motion, and the process of turning the indigofera plant into dye. In Stewart's words, this map, like many others of this century depicting British territories, "both described and hoped for an agenda of development."[7] My visual analysis maps the imagination and the epistemological systems that the conquistadores and settlers relied on to create spatial representations of empire. I also show how the Cartesian landscape in de Brahm's map and the figures within it had to be thrown into a state of flux (movement, process, and boundlessness) before they could be imaged as inert forms that could be captured and fixed in space.

Paradoxically, the need to render life forms as discrete, knowable, containable, and fixed simultaneously required them to be represented as unstable and changing. Cartesianism's fixed boundaries are a colonial ruse: boundaries continually needed to be made malleable and thrown into flux in order for them to be reorganized and reconstituted with new, humanist boundary markers.[8] Mart Stewart notes that de Brahm, "a student of alchemy and a natural philosopher," understood that every "landscape was always in a process of change and transformation, and each statement about it was conditional."[9]

I also use de Brahm's map as an ideal place to situate and interpret Blackness and Black bodies as processes or representations of states of change. Of particular importance to this analysis is the cultivation and processing of indigo dye that is represented in the map's cartouche. The kinetic energy and processes of indigo dye cultivation—in which enslaved Black and fungible bodies, the cells of plants, lye, and water are juxtaposed and thrown into motion.

Thinking about this map in this fashion enables a way of seeing and imagining Blackness as a set of ecotones, or transitional processes: water yielding to shore, shore to clearing, clearing to plantation, plantation to indigo processing site, indigo processing site to moving Black bodies, moving Black bodies to indigo dye. This visual sensibility and perspective undermine coloniality's visual imperative to categorize all living and nonliving matter as discrete, countable objects. If objects cannot be visualized and understood as discrete elements, the empiricist grounding of humanism and its distinctions is undermined. For example, I argue that de Brahm's map depicts Black forms not as human workers but as states of process. Reading Black fungibility as flux is to read it as opacity. If the Black figure on the plantation landscape is obscure and not yet known, it can elude certain forms of representation that attempt to fix it in space and time. Black forms on the landscape are yet to be understood rather than always already known.

A focus on process and states of change (things that can't be pinned down) also exposes the colonial ruse of empiricism—by exposing the "Black" phantasmic or imaginary—within hegemonic visual regimes. My scrutiny of the imaginative and speculative nature of eighteenth-century cartography, an emerging science, reveals the fiction of empiricism and its production of the idea of truth through an accounting of the "real." The imaginative landscapes of this eighteenth-century map reveal that there was not necessarily a discrete, inert, and visible catalogue of real bodies, nature, and land that could be truly captured and known. Therefore, Black bodies, nonhuman life forms, and the ways they were categorized through humanist forms of Cartesianism can be called into question. The categories of human and nonhuman laborer, plant, land, animal, and other forms of life, and the boundaries between them all become suspect political projects. Black bodies function outside these categories and simultaneously call into question the borders placed around them.

Like the coasts, waterways, and ocean, the prominent Black bodies in the cartouche work to link discrete and nonindigenous ecological features of the empire (palm trees from different regions, chemical processes) into a coherent whole. Within this fluid economy and system of exchange, Blackness comes to represent the fluidity of the British Empire's economy as well as the larger flows of the Atlantic world.

In a footnote, Stewart mentions that the palm trees represented as natural features of the coastal landscape would not actually have been present: they are coconut trees that grew only in the Caribbean at the time.[10] Is it plausible that the trees, like the Black enslaved bodies in the cartouche, are represented as easily uprooted and transported from their place of origin? Blackness, particularly Black fungibility, figures here as an important symbolic, conceptual economy and a universe of unending metaphoric possibility. Within the de Brahmian imaginary, Blackness becomes a metaphor for other liquescent forms, like water, transportable plants, varying soil types, chemical processes, and other states of change.

THE CARTOUCHE

The juxtaposition of rigid boundary lines on the map and the fluid, dynamic space depicted in the cartouche evinces the tensions in colonial depictions of conquest and territory. Both the position of the cartouche and the depictions it contains represent the flux and movement needed to establish the map's depiction of rigid spatial and property boundaries. Rendered in fine detail, the flora and fauna represent what the "natural eye" might perceive (someday). The cartouche also represents the abundance being achieved and hoped for on the individual plots of property delineated on the map.

Lush trees and vegetation in the foreground recede into a sandy, shore-like landscape in the background. Ships are docked just offshore. Even farther in the background of the territory pictured, the landscape recedes into a hilltop. In the left foreground, fruits, vegetables, and leaves symbolize an imminent harvest and also form a decorative border around the large stone stela that bears the map's title.[11] The arrangement of the flora and produce, reminiscent of a still-life painting, contrasts with the more languid and organic vegetation depicted in the background.

At least two competing landscapes coexist in the frame of the cartouche. A landscape representing "natural" transitions between the sea, shore, grassland, trees, and hills is held in tension with another, compelled into transition through man-made alterations, structures, activities, and uses. Depicting the sheer diversity of the landscape as well as its potential yield was essential for sustaining support for settlement in the Americas.[12] At a time when blue dyes were rare and prized, the representation of indigo cultivation was included to convince the British Empire of the future promise of the colonies. Stewart observes that "indigo production was already successful in the British

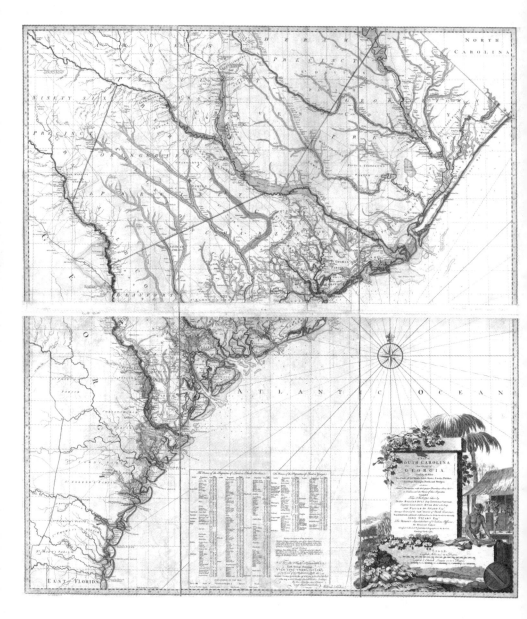

William de Brahm, *Map of South Carolina and a Part of Georgia, Containing the Whole Sea-Coast*, 1757. Printed in London by Thomas Jefferys, 1780. Library of Congress, www.loc.gov/item/74692514.

TIFFANY LETHABO KING

colonies in the Caribbean, and it was a crop that had begun to diversify the market chances for profitable success by South Carolina rice planters."[13]

The cultivation of indigo to supplement the rice industry was a sign of the progress and development of the region as well as a symbol of speculation and expansion. As Stewart argues, it represented "land claimed and land yet to be claimed." The viability of indigo also assured the planters (including de Brahm himself) that the soil had the potential for multiple or fungible uses. On the map, de Brahm's careful marking of soil types showed that "he was considering the relationship of soil with everything else, and indicating the potential for transformation as well."[14]

The theme of transformation and the potential for continual change is important. It was Black bodies that mediated the rotation and transition between the cultivation of rice and indigo, which occurred on the same plot of land. Growing rice, unlike growing indigo, requires flooding the soil. Black bodies are both facilitators and initiators of this temporal change from indigo time to rice time.[15] Even though dictated by the demands of early mercantile capitalism, this temporality depended on those enslaved bodies. Black bodies thus become the intercessors or intermediary figures between multiple agricultural processes, spaces, and temporalities.

Recently, scholars in the humanities have returned to the environmental sciences, and specifically the literature on ecotones as a metaphor for mapping power and systems of representation in postcolonial contexts.[16] The cartouche depicts a scene on the shore, where water meets the land and sand meets soil—a space of transition. Just as waterways represent connections between property plots, colonies, and regions, Black bodies can be read as points where things meet. The Atlantic Ocean, while abutting and partly constituting the shore, also flows into and feeds the aquatic ecosystem, made up of marshes, streams, rivers, and tributaries. Black bodies similarly linked the colonies to the larger British economy. Further, Black bodies effected smaller and even microscopic chemical connections and changes, like those that occurred during indigo processing.

The Black flesh depicted in this map conforms to its overall themes of transition, flux, and process. Spatially and ecologically, Black figures function as sites of transit or passageways. Like the coconut tree that links landscapes separated by miles of oceans, Black bodies function as symbols and sites of transit that enable diverse ecological forms and cycles to work together rhythmically. The Black bodies in this cartouche also represent the chemical changes, molecular breakdown, and phases of atomic change that occur as indigofera plants are transformed into the commodity of indigo dye. The moving bodies provide the kinetic energy for the processes of dissolution and fermentation required to derive the indigo compound from indican. Black muscles repeatedly extend and contract to prepare and ferment the solution in indigo vats.

In the cartouche, three Black male bodies represent various stages of indigo processing. Their poses also conform to Enlightenment notions of the linear progression of time. Two of the figures are framed by the large wooden vat immediately behind them. One is extending a paddle into the air; the

Cartouche from de Brahm, *Map of South Carolina and a Part of Georgia*, showing indigo processing

other, apparently stirring the vat with another paddle, represents the opposite phase of this task. Their motions represent the first stages of indigo fermentation, which includes oxidizing a solution of lye, water, and indigo plant material.

The slaves in the background are almost, but not quite, shown in profile. They are also drawn in a generic, ethnographic style. Their bodies and activities represent the process of breaking down the plants, with water and lye, into chemical elements—and perhaps the process of breaking down human bodies, by strain and fatigue, into the elementary forms of muscles, lactic acid, and sweat. In a sense, then the movements of Black musculature are not simply the labor needed to create the kinetic energy but constitute the very process of fermentation itself. Black bodies are actual chemical processes.

Moving forward and left, a direction that represents progress in linear time, we move into the later phases of the chemical process. In the foreground, the undifferentiated solution of chemical elements has been reduced to a solid mass. The dried indigo is being cut into dye blocks, a sophisticated and exacting process that requires attention to detail, precise and consistent measurement, and good timing if the indigo is to become a marketable commodity. Thus the movements and progressive placement of the three Black bodies in the cartouche represent the stages of a modern chemical process and mark linear progressions within Enlightenment notions of time.

The male figure cutting the blocks in the foreground is distinguished from the other two by posture and scale. He faces forward, and his facial features are distinct. His mouth appears to be moving, lips perhaps curving from a state of relaxation into a smile. He is cutting the dried indigo paste into the uniform-sized cubes in which the commercial dye is eventually shipped and sold.

This figure also wears a head wrap that contrasts with his dark skin. This could simply function to keep the sweat out of his eyes. According to Stewart, however, the quality of the dye could be compromised through contamination by insects, dirt, and even sweat: we might therefore surmise that the head wrap is intended to protect the dye blocks from the cutter's sweat. Thus the kinetic energy produced by Black bodies may represent a tacit threat to the practices and property regime that constituted slavery. Black fungibility, construed as a state of continual movement, change, and exchange in the service of accumulating property and persons, can also work against the aims of the slave regime. Rendered as fungible and perpetually changing, Black bodies also have the capacity for unexpected and unanticipated movements that could upend proprietors' or slave owners' claims to them as property. Black bodies on the move not only sweat but can also flee.

To date, Black studies continues to debate whether spending too much time in the hold of the slave ship or in the terror of plantation violence is productive. I would argue that tracing the lines of fugitive flight by Black bodies also entails mapping the sites and locations of violence and accumulation that seek to make Black people fungible. As fungible and fugitive figures, Black bodies in flux are dynamic and kinetic sites to which the slave owners and proprietors listed on de Brahm's 1757 map had only tenuous claims at best.

NOTES

Parts of this chapter have been revised from Tiffany L. King, "The Labor of (Re)reading Plantation Landscapes Fungible(ly)," *Antipode* 48, no. 4 (2016): 1022–39.

1   Fred Moten, *In the Break: The Aesthetics of the Black Radical Tradition* (Minneapolis: University of Minnesota Press, 2003), 71.

2   Saidiya Hartman, *Scenes of Subjection: Terror, Slavery, and Self-Making in Nineteenth-Century America* (New York: Oxford University Press, 1997), 21.

3   Ibid., 21.

4   Ibid.

5   See King, "The Labor of (Re)reading Plantation Landscapes,"; C. Riley Snorton, *Black on Both Sides: A Racial History of Trans Identity* (Minneapolis: University of Minnesota Press, 2017).

6   Ibid.

7   Mart Stewart, "William Gerard de Brahm's 1757 Map of South Carolina and Georgia," *Environmental History* 16 (July 2011): 524–35.

8   Here I follow Donna Haraway's argument that all boundary making that differentiates one object from another is a social and political project. See *Simians, Cyborgs, and Women: The Reinvention of Nature* (London: Routledge, 1991), 421.

9   Stewart, "William Gerard de Brahm's 1757 Map," 532.

10   Large coconut trees are also placed immediately behind the title. Stewart explains that these coconut trees could be found in the Caribbean but not in the Carolinas or Georgia (ibid., 53n11). See also Krista Thompson, *An Eye for the Tropics: Tourism, Photography, and Framing the Caribbean Picturesque* (Durham, NC: Duke University Press, 2006), 47. As Thompson argues, coconut trees were not indigenous to the Caribbean or the low country in North America even though they are depicted as parts of the natural landscape in eighteenth-century maps of the empire like de Brahm's.

11   The title of the map is inscribed on a stone stela within the cartouche. According to Stewart, the stela operated as a fixed marker of territorial possession. See Stewart, "William Gerard de Brahm's Map."

12   During the eighteenth and nineteenth centuries, the British were uncertain
     whether the material and economic costs of settlement in the Atlantic
     world made it a worthwhile endeavor. See Carole Pateman, "Settler Contract,"
     in Carole Pateman and Charles W. Mills, *Contract and Domination*
     (Cambridge: Polity, 2007).

13   Stewart, "William Gerard de Brahm's 1757 Map," 528.

14   Ibid, 528, 532.

15   Ibid, 529. Stewart explains that the indigo and rice cycle was created for
     efficiency.

16   While ecotone literature has been evolving since 1965, scholars in the
     humanities have more recently been appropriating this concept from the
     environmental sciences in order to think through and articulate relations of
     power in the social realm. See P. G. Risser, "The Status of the Science
     Examining Ecotones," *BioScience* 45, no. 5 (1995): 318–25, as well as presenta-
     tions from the 2015 conference "New Ecotones," Université Paul-Valéry
     Montpellier, France, available at www.coastal.edu/media/academics
     /collegeofhumanities/specialprojects/newecotonesjune2015/Programme%20
     New%20Ecotones%202015%20V4.pdf, accessed December 17, 2017. See also
     Eddy van der Maarel, "Ecotones and Ecoclines Are Different," *Journal of
     Vegetation Science* (1990): 135–38.

CHAPTER FIVE

WORKING TO LIVE

Black-Led Farming in Detroit's Racialized Economy

JESSI QUIZAR

F EEDOM Freedom, a small urban farm on Detroit's Far East Side, is a riot of color in midsummer—the deep purple shine of eggplants hanging heavily under fuzzy leaves; tomatoes striped in shades of yellow, burgundy, and red; and habanero peppers as electric orange as highway cones. The beets that Feedom Freedom grows are a variety that bears the name of the city and an early nickname of the iconic Black power leader Malcolm X: Detroit Red. And of course, like everywhere else in Michigan's sticky summer heat, the farm is saturated in bright, ecstatic green.

Feedom Freedom is a family farm started by lifelong Detroiters Myrtle Thompson-Curtis and Wayne Curtis. Wayne Curtis (anyone under forty who knows him calls him Baba Wayne) was a member of the Detroit Black Panther Party. He was inspired to begin the farm in part by the party's survival programs, especially the children's breakfast and free food distribution programs. Wayne and Myrtle's narrative about the garden—why it is necessary and its political possibilities—draws its genealogy from longer conversations in the city on Black survival and self-determination, as well as critiques of an economy that structurally works against the well-being of Black Detroiters.

In this chapter, I examine the work of Detroit's Feedom Freedom Growers and their analysis of the links between work, urban farming, and the freedom of Black and poor people. I conducted this research between 2011 and 2013 through interviews and participant observation (or, as I told Myrtle once, "deep hanging out"). Despite its small size, Feedom Freedom is one of the best-known farms in the city: it has appeared in documentaries and local, national, and international media.[1] Feedom Freedom uses urban agriculture in the city as a site of praxis from which to vigorously critique the conditions under which most Black people in the city labor, and to envision and experiment with alternative economic forms.

Feedom Freedom and other growers frame Black-led urban agriculture in the city in three ways: as a means of survival and security; as a route toward reframing what it means to live a fulfilling life; and as a tool for promoting self-determination for Black and poor people. These views are rooted in a long Black radical tradition of challenging racial capitalism. Feedom Freedom farmers, along with many other organizations in the city, argue for a politics and practice of collective Black self-reliance—for developing collective ways to supply basic necessities while reducing dependence on unreliable capitalist economic structures. Crucially, they promote a system of work that values workers' humanity, relationships, creativity, and intellect, as well as the cultivation of more secure working lives for Black and poor people in the city.

WORKING IN THE D

Detroit has long been a center from which Black people in the United States have opposed the operation of racial capitalism and imagined a liberatory future. The city was a site of struggle for militant Black labor, particularly in the 1960s and 70s, through organizations like the League of Revolutionary Black Workers, which married the labor struggles of Black workers in auto-manufacturing plants with the philosophy and militancy of Black power. Feedom Freedom's analysis of labor is distinct from that of these earlier movements and has developed in response to neoliberalism. Nevertheless, the intellectual work and practice of the growers is very much a legacy of the radical audacity with which these earlier movements envisioned and worked toward a world beyond capitalism, one that valued and nurtured Black life.

Following the success of neoliberalism in the past forty years, the questions that Black people in the city face now are about survival. Massive waves of white flight in the mid-twentieth century left the city in a state of constant economic crisis, as it had to maintain infrastructure built for many more people than actually lived and paid taxes there. This has led to increasingly severe waves of municipal austerity, including the closing of schools and social service offices, the privatization of city services, and cuts in public health and transportation. These surges of austerity culminated in a state "emergency" takeover of the city's finances in 2012–13, leaving locally elected officials with no power to set public policy.[2] The state-appointed emergency manager of Detroit declared the largest municipal bankruptcy in US history.

In the United States, families tend to hold wealth through homeownership, and this wealth appreciates through rising property values. However, in Detroit, as in many US cities, Black homeownership has been as likely to diminish family wealth as to increase it. In the 1960s and 70s, as Black residents were finally able to buy homes in neighborhoods that had been exclusively white, white residents left for the suburbs—often explicitly to avoid living in integrated neighborhoods. In their wake, property values plunged.[3] In other words, the very presence in a neighborhood of Black people caused a mass exodus of white people, which lowered property values. As a result, in Detroit, as in most cities in the United States, it has been virtually impossible for Black homeowners to accrue the same level of value buying homes as whites have done.[4]

Detroit's population continued to decrease, but by the 1990s most of those leaving the city were Black. Many middle-class Black families moved from the city to adjacent suburbs like Oak Park—a once-white suburb that was 54 percent Black by 2010.[5] And after 2000, much of the flight from the city could be better described as displacement, as hundreds of thousands of Black residents of the city lost their homes to either mortgage foreclosure or tax foreclosure.[6]

These waves of flight from the city have left a visual landscape that lays bare the ways in which capitalist cycles produce "organized abandonment." Almost every neighborhood has buildings or houses that have been burned or otherwise massively degraded, and in some areas these structures dominate the landscape. However, in contrast to many portrayals of Detroit as a city completely depopulated, all neighborhoods in the city are still occupied, albeit with much more open space than they had in the mid-twentieth century. Detroit currently has about seven hundred thousand residents, more than Washington, DC, or Boston.[7] However, the specter of poverty—both individual and municipal—is unavoidable. As Feedom Freedom Grower Kezia Curtis observes,

> Detroit is really no different than any other city. But in every
> other city there's this really nice backdrop of, like, oh, there are
> rich people here and they spend money, and you can walk around
> and feel safe. But, you know, that has nothing to do with really

building a sense of community. It just has to do with, like, we
need to get these poor people out of the way because we don't
want people to see them. . . . You come to Detroit and you see it.
You see it. It's just a lot more apparent here that there are poor
people.[8]

Residential flight was compounded by industrial flight, as the auto man-
ufacturers that had been at the heart of Detroit's astronomical growth in the
first half of the twentieth century left in the second half. Detroit's industries
had also been a center of labor organizing, some of it quite militant. Partially in response to the power of Detroit's exceptionally organized work-
force, industrial plants relocated to sites in the southern United States and
abroad, where labor laws were weaker and conditions were less favorable to
union organizing. There remain some well-paying jobs in the city, particularly in government and in the city's large medical district. However, white
suburbanites are much more likely to commute into the city to these higher-
wage jobs, while Black Detroiters tend to commute out of the city to low-
wage service-sector jobs in the suburbs. While Detroit was 83 percent Black
and only 11 percent white in 2012, 55 percent of those employed in the city
are white.[9]

Compounding the difficulties of many Black Detroiters who have jobs
that are quite far from home and pay relatively little, public transportation
in the city is infrequent, with many routes running only once every hour.
To make matters worse, 2008, 22 percent of Black households in the city had
no vehicle to buffer them against the dramatic cuts to public transportation
that took place in 2012.[10] Car insurance in Detroit in 2014 was the most
expensive of any city in the United States, costing an astonishing annual
average of $10,723 in a city where the average annual household income is
$26,955.[11] For many Detroit families, car insurance is simply unobtainable.
All of this makes it incredibly difficult, both logistically and financially, to
actually get to work. And service-industry employers are often extremely
unforgiving of lateness and the scheduling considerations of their low-wage
employees.

This spatial mismatch between jobs and housing contributes to the
city's high unemployment rate. In 2014 Detroit's unemployment rate was
the highest of the fifty largest cities in the United States, at 23 percent.[12]
This statistic does not include those who are no longer looking for
work. By the 1970s, the city was home to a generation that James Boggs
called "the outsiders"—young working-age people who did not see any

possibility of meaningful formal employment for themselves in a capitalist economy.[13]

MAKING A WAY OUT OF NO WAY

Even in Detroit's supposed heyday in the mid-twentieth century, Black workers never enjoyed the same prosperity as white workers. Consequently, Black Detroiters employed a wide variety of strategies to make do in an economy that was structured against them. Most new migrants came from rural areas and brought with them agricultural traditions, which many continued to practice in Detroit's backyards, supplementing their diet with home-grown fresh food.[14] As in other cities in the north to which migrants moved, there developed a rich network of Black self-help organizations.[15] In the 1960s and 70s, this tradition gave rise to Black organizations with much more explicitly radical politics. Perhaps most notably, the Black Panther Party in Detroit, as elsewhere, developed and sustained long-term "survival programs" for Black people in the city, which included a breakfast program for school children, massive food giveaways, and some basic medical services, including testing for sickle-cell anemia.

Feedom Freedom Growers was founded in the tradition of these radical programs of self-help with the ultimate goal of Black self-determination. Wayne Curtis was for a time the manager the of the Black Panthers' breakfast program. He had also gained experience with gardening while teaching art at the African-centered Nsoroma Institute, a charter school on the East Side of the city.

Feedom Freedom began informally. Wayne and Myrtle planted vegetables in the vacant lots adjacent to their home. Both of them had paying jobs, Wayne as an art teaching assistant and Myrtle as a short-order cook. Their adult children, particularly Kezia Curtis, Monique Little, and Tyrone Thompson, helped with the work of building a small urban farm. As the garden grew, they began to develop educational programs for children, teens, and adults in the neighborhood. The teen program was particularly representative of the Feedom Freedom approach of combining political discussion, writing and research, training in facilitation and leading group discussions, and building farming skills. Feedom Freedom youth participants led monthly roundtable discussions to which the local community was invited, discussing, among other topics, the ways that food was and is used as a tool of both oppression and liberation, links between food in schools and food in prisons, and transportation and food justice.

My father is from Guatemala, and I grew up part-time in the United States and part-time in Central America in the 1980s, as civil wars raged. I had certainly been around revolutionaries who were thinking practically and acting concretely to build independent economies, but I very rarely encountered them in the United States, where activists and poor people's movements seemed to involve an endless treadmill of fighting against neoliberal horror to defend dwindling social safety nets.

As I prepared to leave my first graduate program in 2006, I got peripherally involved in the struggle to save South Central Farm in Los Angeles. This was the largest urban farm in the United States, occupying fourteen acres in the middle of a warehouse district. Collectively operated, the farm provided food to about three hundred families, mostly immigrants from Central America. In 2005, the farmers were given an eviction notice. They fought it vigorously, first in the courts and then in a six-month occupation of the land. Many if not most of the South Central Farmers had experienced land struggles in Central America. The younger generation of farmers had grown up with the Zapatistas as their models of revolutionary organizing. They linked their struggle for the farm with the need to build alternatives to global capitalism. I embraced their politics and felt urgently for the first time that we need to place food and food production at the center of any vision of a "people's economy."

I first came to Feedom Freedom in 2007, on a tour organized through the Allied Media Conference, a national activist gathering that happens every year in Detroit. The garden was beautiful, I remember, but what was most striking to me was Wayne and Myrtle's goal of working to build an economy that could advance poor Detroiters' self-determination. When I came to work at Feedom Freedom a year later, I was intrigued by their analysis, but perhaps even more, I was struck by the fact that it came from people who had spent their whole lives in the United States. Indeed, the work and analysis of Feedom Freedom and other Black farmers in the city emerged from the specific context of US capitalism and its failures to meet even the very basic needs of Detroiters, from the experience of Detroit's economic crisis, and from specifically American forms of anti-Black racism.

I moved to Detroit in 2011. While conducting interviews, I was also working in the garden, particularly in their summer program for teenagers. I helped (and continue to help) with farming tasks like weeding, as well as with the organization of a monthly roundtable discussion. When Feedom Freedom incorporated as a nonprofit entity in 2015, I accepted a position on the board.

Given the context of economic crisis and the long tradition of Black theorization and movement building around issues of race and the economy in Detroit, it is perhaps unsurprising that much of the impetus for farming in Detroit and analysis by Detroit farmers is focused on labor—both through a critique of the kinds of work available to most Detroiters and in wrestling with the questions of how to create meaningful working lives and what systems of labor best facilitate those ends. Feedom Freedom growers often characterize farming, accessing food, and having control over one's own food supply as issues of survival—of day-to-day livelihood and also more broadly of Black and poor people's survival. Their visions also draw on the common experience of Black Detroiters for whom available jobs are generally difficult to get to, unfulfilling, poorly paid, and unreliable. Indeed, the question that arguably dominates most grassroots work in Detroit, and certainly most Black-led agricultural work, is how to shape an economy in which people can meet their basic needs while gaining greater control over their lives.

Myrtle Thompson-Curtis, the cofounder of Feedom Freedom, associates the development of urban agriculture in the city and the support it has received in her neighborhood with the fact that Detroiters often live precariously and are seeking better options. We sat on her porch one day in the muggy Detroit heat, saying hello to neighbors as they walked by the house on their way to the nearest gas station—the closest and most convenient source of food. She told me, "Lately, when we talk to people, people are ready to hear. They're ready to listen. They know we're at a very crucial, critical point. You know?" When I asked her why she thought that was, she said, "The lack of. It's harder to get simple things. Driving a car in the city is difficult because of the cost associated with it. It's difficult. And if you're on any kind of minimum-wage paying job or anything like that . . . Most folks out here are driving illegal [driving unregistered and/or uninsured cars]. Or they're sacrificing one bill to pay for the other—they're juggling. Or it's taking everybody to do half of the stuff that we used to do ten years ago, maybe."[16]

Feedom Freedom farmers often reiterated that growing food on abandoned urban land was a survival strategy, a hustle—one among many that poor people in Detroit employed in order to stay afloat in an economy that was failing to meet even their most basic needs. Accessing affordable and healthy food is one of their more difficult problems. There are few large grocery stores in the city, and many Detroiters rely on what in Detroit are called party stores—liquor stores—for food.[17]

Drawing from Black Detroiters' long-standing practice of kitchen gardening, farming is foremost a survival strategy—a way to ensure that even amid unstable employment, unreliable transportation, and low wages, Black people in the city can grow food to eat well. Feedom Freedom heavily emphasizes the development of skills that enable people to grow their own food. For instance, when I asked Thompson-Curtis why farming was so important for poor Detroiters, she told me:

> Because you can totally depend on someone else, who at any given moment could cut it off! If you don't have a job, you don't have any, you don't have, if you live in an apartment, if you don't have a job—I'm using an apartment, because at least if I have a backyard I can grow me something. But if you don't have that access, and it might be illegal if I'm doing it, but I'm still going to do it. But if you don't have any access to the resources, or if you have the resources but you don't know what to do with them, it's just as bad. So, you know, the issue is with the need for resources, and to have the knowledge of what to do with the resources.[18]

Most striking, perhaps, is her analysis of paid labor. Rather than seeing paid employment as a route to independence, Thompson-Curtis describes it as representative of vulnerability and *dependence*, something that could be taken away at any time. Conversely, independent food production reduces dependence on unreliable capitalist wage-labor markets. People who can grow their own food may be somewhat less reliant on jobs that may disappear. Growing food can also give workers more leeway to leave jobs in which they are exploited, unfulfilled, or unhappy.

What is at stake for Black farmers in Detroit is life itself. Lack of access to healthy food leads to innumerable health problems, particularly diabetes and circulatory problems like high blood pressure. And these in turn lead precisely to what Ruth Wilson Gilmore defines as the essence of racism: "group-differentiated vulnerability to premature death," particularly in the context of urban austerity and divestment from public health systems, in Detroit and elsewhere.[19] In the words of Malik Yakini, the executive director of the Detroit Black Community Food Security Network, "Literally, that lack of access [to healthy food] is killing us."[20]

Feedom Freedom farmers define survival in broader and richer terms as well. On the one hand, they see securing the physical means to stay alive as a critical issue for most Detroiters. On the other, they also consistently assert that there is a difference between staying alive and surviving with one's full humanity intact—"really living," as Kezia Curtis puts it, as opposed to plodding on the treadmill of anxiety and just barely getting by that characterizes the economic life of many in Detroit.[21] The farm's understanding of work centers not just on surviving without a waged job but also on a sense that even the work that is available to most Detroiters devalues their humanity, their intellect, their creative capacity, and their dignity.

Thompson-Curtis was explicit about the relationship to land and nature and people's relationship to their work when she described to me the benefits of growing food and the small-business possibilities that farming offered:

> I think a lot of people are beginning to look at how they can work for themselves and do work that feels good, that feels like I'm making a contribution instead of just being like, "What am I doing this for?" You know, people are having work that feeds their spirit, their body. It feeds someone else. And you develop these relationships to your work. It connects you with the very thing that gives you life, which is food, which is the soil, which is the air, which is the water. I mean, it does. Look, I could just have me a little cart where I sell my vegetables. Or I could create this dish and just sell it, and make money from it. I mean, just enough to survive. That's what folks are saying—survive![22]

Thompson-Curtis begins and ends with work: working for oneself, and working to survive. But the heart of her argument is less about mere survival than about working with the natural world as a strategy for building a richer life. While acknowledging that working with soil and water is a way to provide for the biological needs of the human body, she suggests that it is also a way to provide a connection with a kind life force—that farming, and the connection with nature that it provides, feeds both the spirit and the body.

Moreover, it is not just a connection with nature that creates this spiritual dynamic. For Thompson-Curtis, satisfying work is about having a certain amount of autonomy: growers "can work for themselves," and their work has tangible purpose beyond themselves. Another essential component of these connections with nature, work, the body, and the spirit is caring for and feeding others. In her description of independent farm work in Detroit, Thompson-Curtis implicitly criticizes the nature of much of the work that is available to Detroiters: low wage, deskilled, boring—and, crucially, of little benefit to the community . She presents the idea of growing and selling food independently—whether produce or prepared dishes—as an alternative to waged jobs.

Thompson-Curtis also emphasizes the value of building a relationship with what one produces:

> I don't want to see everybody growing food and hauling it down the street to the store and selling it. No! Living off of it! Eating off of it! Understanding! Because people don't understand. Everybody wants to provide a processing space for folks to process food. They don't understand. Before you get off to racing off to market, experience it! So that it means something to you! So that you understand what it is that you're racing off to the market with to get that exchange of dollars. Get an understanding of what it is. How important it is, and what it means to keep growing—not just for the money. Because we're getting lost, once again. We've got to get this food to get this money to—okay—have you eaten any of the stuff you sold? No. So how do you know what's really coming out? Does their money taste all their green beans?[23]

Thompson-Curtis here makes an argument for an ethic of subsistence, as defined by Maria Mies: "all work that is expended in the creation, re-creation, and maintenance of immediate life, and which has no other purpose." Mies contrasts this with commodity production: "For subsistence production, the aim is 'life.' For commodity production it is 'money,' which 'produces' ever more money, or the accumulation of capital. For this mode of production life is, so to speak, only a coincidental side effect."[24]

Thompson-Curtis argues for subsistence, in the sense that she argues for work that fulfills basic needs. But her concept of subsistence also requires that producers develop a long-term relationship with their product, that they experience it and get to know it before "racing off to market." Her vision here not only argues for an economy in which people of color and poor people produce for themselves but also explicitly critiques the effects of alienation resulting from capitalist production.

Thompson-Curtis's ideas about the interrelationship between nature, work, and a meaningful meaning are an extension of a long tradition of Black environmental thought. Enslaved Africans brought with them ontologies that regarded the health of human communities as interconnected with the health of nature and nonhuman life.[25] However, Black people's relationship with the natural world in the United States has been profoundly fraught by the collective impact and memory of agricultural enslavement and racial terror. A tree, in Black poetry or Black music, is just as likely—or perhaps more likely—to evoke a lynching as a celebration of nature.

Yet Black people in general, and Black thinkers and activists in particular, also have a long history of seeing independent agriculture as a potential site of freedom. Even in the antebellum South, enslaved people gained some measure of control over their lives through the cultivation of small plots of land, hunting, fishing, and otherwise gathering their own food. After emancipation, many Black people (although certainly not all) placed their hopes for freedom in independent landownership and farming.[26] In the twentieth and twenty-first centuries, some radical Black movements have continued this focus on farming as a strategy for freedom. For instance, both the Nation of Islam and the Black Nationalist Pan African Orthodox Christian Church have explicitly included agricultural programs—indeed, they have bought land specifically to grow food—as an integral part of religious programs for Black liberation.[27]

For Feedom Freedom, agriculture represents the possibility of relying less on a job from an employer and on a food system that works against people's physical, mental, and spiritual well-being. It also represents a possibility of delinking from oppressive economic structures and of increasing collective self-determination.

SELF-RELIANCE FOR SELF-DETERMINATION

Feedom Freedom is part of a long trajectory of thought and action on how to create greater economic security, how to make do, and how to hedge against an economy in which one is considered expendable. However, its farmers theorize not just with an eye toward survival, in the sense of fulfilling the conditions necessary to remain alive, but also with respect to the ways in which acquiring the means of survival undermine or enhance one's full capacity as a human being. So the issue of being able to produce food for oneself and one's community entails, first, being able to garner the material security to eat, to live, and to survive; and second, being able, as Kezia Curtis puts it, to "truly live": to grow, to use one's creative capacities, and to build relationships with one's environment, with others, and with the spiritual.

Urban agriculture is often framed as a "white" thing, an issue for food purists and locavores.[28] But at Feedom Freedom, as well as in other Black-led urban agriculture in the city, we see an urban agriculture with a distinctly Black genealogy—an agriculture that emerged from the social and economic conditions experienced by Black people under racial capitalism. Their work grew out of longstanding Black traditions, brought north in the knowledge and skills of southern farmers. And their theorizing is rooted in long histories of Black political thought and movement building that asked how Black people might gain power and collective self-determination in an economy specifically structured against Black success. Feedom Freedom asks this question as well, and its farmers root their answers in the praxis of Black-led urban agriculture.

NOTES

1 See, for instance, *Urban Roots*, directed by Mark MacInnis (Tree Media, 2001); *We Are Not Ghosts*, directed by Mark Dworkin and Melissa Young (Bullfrog Films, 2012); "Becoming Detroit: Reimagining Work, Food, and Community," *On Being*, www.onbeing.org/program/becoming-detroit-grace -lee-boggs-on-reimagining-work-food-and-community/1060.

2 Michigan Public Act 101 (1988), Public Act 4 (2011), and Public Act 436 (2012), together known as the Michigan Emergency Management Law, enacted a system in which municipalities or school districts may be declared by the State of Michigan to be in a state of financial emergency. This declaration triggers the appointment of an emergency manager who takes charge of all financial matters. Because most government decisions have at least some financial implications, the emergency manager wields almost total power, rendering locally elected public officials impotent to make even the most basic decisions. The Emergency Management Law has been widely criticized as being racially biased because it so disproportionately affects Black people. More than half of African Americans in the state have lived under emergency management at some point since 2009.

3 Thomas J. Sugrue, *The Origins of the Urban Crisis: Race and Inequality in Postwar Detroit* (Princeton, NJ: Princeton University Press, 1996).

4 George Lipsitz, *The Possessive Investment in Whiteness: How White People Profit from Identity Politics* (Philadelphia: Temple University Press, 2006).

5 US Census Bureau, "Oak Park, Michigan, Quick Facts" (Washington, DC: US Census Bureau, 2010).

6 Quinn Klinefelter, "Mass Tax Foreclosure Threatens Detroit Homeowners," *All Things Considered*, March 30, 2015, www.npr.org/2015/03/30/396317153

/mass-tax-foreclosurethreatens-detroit-homeowners; Christine MacDonald and Joel Kurth, "Foreclosures Fuel Detroit Blight, Cost City $500 Million," *Detroit News*, June 25, 2015.

7   US Census Bureau, "Detroit, MI, State and County Quick Facts" (Washington, DC: US Department of Commerce, 2014).

8   Kezia Curtis, interview, 2012.

9   New Detroit, *Metropolitan Detroit Race Equity Report* (2014); US Census Bureau, "Detroit, MI, State and County Quick Facts."

10   Joe T. Darden and Richard Thomas, *Detroit: Race Riots, Racial Conflicts, and Efforts to Bridge the Racial Divide* (East Lansing: Michigan State University Press, 2013); David Sands, "Detroit Bus Service Cuts Take Effect, Frustrated Riders Voice Concerns," *Huffington Post*, March 2, 2012.

11   John Kuo, "Most Expensive Cities for Car Insurance," *Nerd Wallet*, February 3, 2014, www.nerdwallet.com/blog/insurance/2014/02/03/expensive-cities -car-insurance; US Census Bureau, "Detroit, MI, State and County Quick Facts," 2014.

12   Bureau of Labor Statistics, "Unemployment Rates for the 50 Largest Cities" (Washington, DC: US Department of Labor, 2014), www.bls.gov/lau/lacilg10 .htm.

13   James Boggs, *The American Revolution: Pages from a Negro Worker's Notebook* (New York: Monthly Review Press, 2009).

14   Richard Westmacott, *African American Gardens and Yards in the Rural South* (Knoxville: University of Tennessee Press, 1992); Monica White, "Black Farmers/Black Freedom," lecture at Detroit Public Library, June 15, 2013.

15   Jessica Gordon Nembhard, *Collective Courage: A History of African American Cooperative Economic Thought and Practice* (Philadelphia: Pennsylvania State University Press, 2014); Richard W. Thomas, *Life for Us Is What We Make It: Building Black Community in Detroit, 1915–1945* (Bloomington: Indiana University Press, 1992).

16   Myrtle Thompson-Curtis, interview, 2012.

17   Shannon N. Zenk, Amy J. Schultz, Barbara A. Israel, Sherman A. James, Shuming Bao, and Mark L. Wilson, "Fruit and Vegetable Access Differs by Community Racial Composition and Socioeconomic Position in Detroit, Michigan," *Ethnicity and Disease* 16, no. 1 (2016): 275–80.

18   Thompson-Curtis, interview.

19   Ruth Wilson Gilmore, *Golden Gulag: Prisons, Surplus, Crisis, and Opposition in Globalizing California* (Berkeley: University of California Press, 2008).

20   Jim Lynch, "Experts: Detroiters Cut Off from Healthy Food," *Detroit News*, August 17, 2011.

21   Wayne Curtis, interview, n.d.

22   Thompson-Curtis, interview.

23   Ibid.

24 Maria Mies, "Towards a Methodology for Feminist Research," in *Theories of Women's Studies*, ed. Gloria Bowls and Renate Duelli-Klein, 117–39 (London: Routledge and Kegan Paul, 1983).

25 Elizabeth D. Blum, "Power, Danger, and Control: Slave Perceptions of Wilderness in the 19th Century," *Women's Studies* 31, no. 2 (2002): 247–66.

26 W. E. B. Du Bois, *Black Reconstruction in America 1860–1880* (New York: Free Press, 1998); Kimberly K. Smith, *African American Environmental Thought* (Lawrence: University of Kansas Press, 2007).

27 Priscilla McCutcheon, "Community Food Security 'for Us, by Us': The Nation of Islam and the Pan African Orthodox Christian Church," in *Cultivating Food Justice: Race, Class, and Sustainability*, ed. Alison Hope Alkon and Julian Agyeman, 177–96 (Cambridge, MA: MIT Press, 2011).

28 Julie Guthman, "'If Only They Knew': The Unbearable Whiteness of Alternative Food," in Alkon and Agyeman, *Cultivating Food Justice*, 263–78.

CHAPTER SIX

REPLOTTING VALUE

Community Gardens and Bessie Head's A Question of Power

DOMINIQUE BOURG HACKER

For 27 years, I lived in South Africa, I had the experience of a Black South African—the poverty-stricken, slum-dweller; the feeling that there was no way in which you could look around and breathe and feel the air. . . . Black people had been so completely dispossessed that there was nothing there that Black people owned. Even the air choked you. Black people were totally dispossessed from ownership of land.

BESSIE HEAD, *BETWEEN THE LINES*, 1989

ESSIE Head often described her life in South Africa with expressions of rootlessness and dispossession. Her sense of alienation from land and community significantly shapes her writing. As Maxine Sample argues, Head wrote against South Africa's "stultifying environment" to create places that subvert restrictions and give space to men and women to "find themselves and transcend social and political boundaries."[1] Head's novels, stories, and nonfiction illustrate the interconnections between the dehumanizing system of South Africa's apartheid and the environment. Agriculture is significant not only in Head's writing but also in biographies of Head and critical discussions of her work. Jonathan Highfield notes that agriculture is often a metaphor for healing. Because her texts detail the trauma suffered by those living under repressive, patriarchal, colonial, and tribal systems but also envision possibilities for a more peaceful Africa, she has become one of the most prominent figures of modern African literature.

In her 1974 semiautobiographical novel A *Question of Power*, Head tells the story of Elizabeth, a South African refugee who has recently migrated to the small Botswana village of Motabeng with her young son. Dramatizing violent and chaotic conversations with two characters who appear to her in hallucinations, Sello and Dan, and their team of abusers, the text follows Elizabeth as she sifts and winnows through the human evil she experienced during apartheid.

The abusive and erratic dialogues with hallucinatory figures about the nature of good, evil, and power are punctuated by episodes in which Elizabeth participates in village life by working in and eventually directing the village garden. Elizabeth's participation in the garden allows her to see a southern African landscape for the first time as a welcoming space where people can come together. The role of the landscape in assuaging her suffering is pivotal, because, in the words of Anthony Vital, South African apartheid's "political geography has its roots in colonial spatial control, which also (if the 1913 Natives Land Act is recalled) amounts to a control of human populations with economic intent."[2] The South African apartheid government's bolstering of commercialized agriculture, combined with the reign of conservative racist environmentalism and the traditional Afrikaner "sense of cultural identity as *boernasie*," or "farmer nation," not only forcibly removed Africans from the environment but also barred their participation in imagining national environments.[3] *A Question of Power* directly engages with the material and imaginative effects of narratives of white ownership and legislation that silence black labor and presence.

Head's garden disrupts and reimagines South Africans' relationship to land in three ways that intertwine with her vision of a politically unified "brotherhood of man." First, in opposition to the South African literary tradition of the *plaasroman*, or the Afrikaner farm novel, which holds family and lineage as perquisites for landownership, Head venerates alternate forms of belonging as noble ways to connect to the land, and moreover suggests that "everyone knows *something* about vegetables."[4] Second, not only does the image of the community garden contest the *plaasroman*'s myth of familial ownership, but Head's narrative structure disrupts apartheid's political geography and invites black South Africans to imagine what the environment means to them. Third, by giving value to waste, Head's narrative undercuts apartheid discourses equating black people with rubbish and seeks to give black South Africans a proper and valued place in imagining the environment and defining their relationship with it.

As Christopher Warnes contends, "The fact that the word *boer* (farmer) remains . . . synonymous with Afrikaner powerfully suggests the role that the farm has played in the constructions of Afrikaner identity."[5] Between the 1920s and 1940s Afrikaner writers used the pastoral tradition to define their identity and sense of belonging. J. M. Coetzee's *White Writing: On the Cultures of Letters in South Africa*, which is one of the most comprehensive accounts of the *plaasroman*, explains how it became the dominant mode of Afrikaans fiction. Urbanization and economic depression, caused partly by growth in the mining industry and drought, created a class of poor and landless Afrikaners, and in response the *plaasroman* sketched the "ideal rural order."[6] The *plaasroman* provided a "transcendental justification for the ownership of land" at a time when the commercialization of agriculture was forcing farmers off the land.[7] The *plaasroman* used many different strategies to argue that ownership was based on generations of family labor, and in doing so it delegitimized any other form of ownership.[8]

In his reading of the prolific Afrikaans writer C. M. Van den Heever, Coetzee analyzes how the *plaasroman* establishes ownership. Van den Heever's novels picture famers paying for their farms with their blood, the bones they leave in the soil marking their lasting claim. Coetzee highlights how Van den Heever's farmers are "mystically bound" to the land, which becomes both a constant calling and a right that they cannot forsake. *Plaasroman* farmers describe their proprietorship as a marriage in which they must "love the farm, love this one patch of earth above all others." Thus the farmer comes to see his attachment to the farm beyond his individual self; his life "is the lineage."[9] The *plaasroman* works carefully to inscribe ownership in the land and tie it irrefutably to white Afrikaners. However, in legitimizing white claims, it erases black sharecropping or waged work on white-owned land.

The *plaasroman* remains significant not only because it characterizes the Afrikaner identity and environmental imagination but also because it is complicit with the emergence of apartheid.[10] In asserting that white farmers are the ideal stewards of the land, the *plaasroman* contributed to the South African government's vilification of black farmers during apartheid. For example, the government blamed soil erosion solely on the practices of black farmers. It subsequently prohibited black sharecropping and forced black farmers onto Native reserves, where farming practices were rigorously controlled.[11]

As Helen Tiffin and Graham Huggan argue in *Postcolonial Ecocriticism*, entitlement is the tension between imaginative possession and the laws that govern ownership.[12] Apartheid legislation intertwined the productivity of

DOMINIQUE BOURG HACKER

land with racist beliefs. Not only did the "capitalization of agriculture" disenfranchise and displace Africans, but apartheid policies also exacerbated the effects of the drought because of "inappropriate farming on marginal land" and increased soil and water pollution as "large commercial farms [used] huge amounts of pesticides."[13] All the while, the conservation ethic created laws and reserves that "alienated blacks from mainstream environmentalism."[14] Black South Africans were witnessing environmental degradation by the white farming industry while simultaneously being blamed for environmental destruction and barred from conservation, as well as from restoration activities like soil conservation or the enjoyment of "natural and recreational amenities."[15]

From Jan Rabie to Etienne van Heerden to J. M. Coetzee and Nadine Gordimer, white English- and Afrikaans-speaking writers have highlighted the problematic inscriptions of the farm in the *plaasroman* tradition and its contribution of racist ideologies to apartheid. Subsequently, critics have affiliated these writers with the "counterdiscursive plaasroman" or "counterpastoral" tradition.[16] Although Head's writing has not been associated with this tradition, I show that reading *A Question of Power* as writing against the *plaasroman* elucidates how Head invites black South Africans to imagine belonging, identity, and ownership outside apartheid's silences, removals, and divisions.

Much of the early scholarship about Head's writings used biographical details in order to draw parallels between her life and the lives of her protagonists. According to Sample, throughout the early 1990s, scholars performed "psychoanalytical" readings of *A Question of Power* and praised Head for the "psychological depth of the novel." In the late 1990s, critics began to read her as a political writer whose visions of inner personal struggles and peaceful, ideal communities could be interpreted as a "literature of protest."[17] Being read as a political writer links Head to other black South African writers in exile, like Dennis Brutus, Keorapetse Kgositsile, and Lewis Nkosi, whose texts also criticize the structural violence of apartheid. However, unlike these writers, Rob Nixon argues, Head's "stories are preoccupied with tensions between peasant women's agricultural authority and their subordination to local patriarchy, and with women's crimped sense of economic and social mobility" rather than with "the imaginative recuperation of a South Africa that is past and elsewhere."[18]

Head witnesses and documents agriculture throughout her work, from her detailed history of a Botswana village in *Serowe: Village of the Rain Wind* (1981) to her novels *When Rain Clouds Gather* (1968) and *A Question of Power* (1973), and her collection of short stories, *The Collector of Treasures* (1977).

When Rain Clouds Gather recounts how the English agronomist Gilbert Balfour works with South African exiles and local people, who have suffered at the hands of a corrupt tribal chief, to set up an agricultural collective and establish sustainable farming practices, supplanting the cattle and goat grazing that have exacerbated drought conditions in the region. The story "The Wind and a Boy," in *The Collector of Treasures*, details how agriculture organizes Tswana women's lives: "She was there all the time till the corn ripened and the birds had to be chased off the land, till harvesting and threshing were done."[19] Critics and biographers have highlighted Head's environmental themes and her concern for people's relationship with nature. Yet Highfield contends that none of these critics "look directly at the way agriculture and farmers are represented and the implications of that representation."[20] My analysis of *A Question of Power* examines Head's efforts to reimagine land and value outside apartheid ideologies.

In *A Question of Power*, Head highlights how anyone can find meaning in working the land. She invites Black South Africans to establish their identity in the environmental imaginary and thus changes the terms of their association with the landscape. On the day Elizabeth is to start work in the community garden, she thinks about how everyone is suited for this kind of labor because "everyman and woman is, in some way an amateur gardener at heart and vegetables are really the central part of the daily diet. . . . Everyone . . . knows *something* about vegetables . . . if their grandfather didn't grow a vegetable, then their aunt did." The repetition of *everyman* and *everyone* emphasizes that the ability and desire to cultivate are not bestowed on special groups by divine right. Elizabeth, who has no prior garden experience, is assigned to help out, and she learns from other students. Likewise, Elizabeth's belonging does not require payment with "blood, sweat and tears," unlike the dedication of Van den Heever's farmers. Elizabeth even resists the kind of threats that the village women encounter as they farm: "She cancelled totally the idea of being that kind of farmer who earned her year's supply of food in breakneck battles with dangerous wild animals." Simply living in a mud hut in Motabeng makes Elizabeth feel close to nature and incites "a great wonder about the soil and the food it produced."[21] Head's portrayal protests against the ideology of familial inheritance that supported the removal of black South Africans from participating in commercial or subsistence agriculture.

The novel provides many details of how the garden is prepared and cultivated. It follows Elizabeth's conversations with Small-Boy, one of the most knowledgeable local volunteers, as he closely describes fertilizing the garden: "I place three wheel-barrows of kraal manure on it and then broadcast

DOMINIQUE BOURG HACKER

one pound of chemical fertilizer in the proportions of two parts Nitrogen, three parts Phosphorus and four parts Potash. . . . I turn the soil once and deeply with a digging fork. I am careful to push the digging fork deep into the soil."[22] The watering system and the practice of planting out using seedling bags are described in the same detail. Recounting specific agricultural methods like this itself is an act of protest because it aims to educate readers. At the same time, the thorough description of garden labor stands in direct contrast to depictions of labor in the *plaasroman*. Coetzee notes that in many of Van den Heever's novels, workaday operations and tasks are left out of the narrative in favor of "timeless activities" such as plowing or reaping, which are seasonal and recurrent and allow Van den Heever to meditate on the farmer's mysterious love for his farm rather than the particular actions involved.[23]

By portraying the garden as a site of communal collaboration, in which volunteers can come and go and yet still lay claim to the space, Head's Motabeng Community Garden directly interrupts the *plaasroman*'s vision of ownership and belonging. *A Question of Power* features scene after scene of labor in the garden. Whereas in the *plaasroman* a claim to the land is based on an individual's birthright and willingness to pour blood and sweat into it, in the community garden the work is shared among a disparate group of individuals, with no prerequisite to participate. When Head portrays agricultural work in the garden, such as building a fence or preparing seedling bags, she depicts a flurry of work by many participants, and the work creates togetherness: "There was a tremendous clashing and banging of worktools all around as the students swarmed over the construction-works." Tom, an American; Kenosi, a young volunteer from Motabeng; and Elizabeth dig new trenches in the garden together: "Kenosi and Elizabeth worked behind [Tom's] pick, quickly scooping out the loosened earth with spades."[24]

When Elizabeth reflects on the work, she does not revel in the way that the labor has bound her and the other villagers to the land, as in the *plaasroman*. She does not speak about making her mark or about how their labor conveys ownership of the land. Instead, she talks about how it provides them with independence from South African commercial agriculture, which not only alienates black South Africans but also undernourishes them with "half-rotting orders of green vegetables." Working in the garden generates collective belonging; it is not necessary that laborers devote their lives to the landscape. Kenosi works in the garden, but he also works for the local industries wool project. Elizabeth leaves for seven months because of psychological distress, but her return to the garden is fairly seamless. Tom also leaves and returns several times. The garden invites *everyone* back: "Take me. Turn me into a one-acre plot of cabbage, green beans, carrots, beetroot, tomatoes, onions, peas, and lettuce."[25]

Head evokes a sense of belonging not unlike that of Coetzee's *Boyhood* (1997), an autobiography narrated in the third person. According to Jennifer Wenzel, Coetzee dramatizes "love of land without legal ownership."[26] The boy narrator realizes that his love of the farm is born not out of claiming ownership of it but rather out of the belief that the farm "belongs to no one" and "I belong to the farm."[27] Although he rejects capitalist and traditional Afrikaner forms of ownership, he still feels tied to the land.

Because *A Question of Power* has not been read against the *plaasroman*, Head's strategies for dismantling the farm novel's ideologies have not been compared to those of other counterpastoral writers like Coetzee. Reading Head in this context allows readers to understand more clearly what she is saying about belonging and environmental ethics in South Africa. While Coetzee asserts that the land lies beyond anyone's ownership, Head instead emphasizes that anyone can achieve a sense of closeness with the land.[28] Against the South African discourse of exclusivity, Head highlights how Elizabeth, who has never felt drawn to the landscape before, feels a part of it after living near it for a short time. Living in her mud hut next to the insects and the smell of "mouldy grass," Elizabeth feels that there is no distinction between human and animal life.[29]

There is no need to be wedded to the land in order to care for it or feel tied to it. Instead of using a metaphor of heteronormative love, Head simply describes the use of seedling bags to grow magnificent "cabbages, tomatoes, cauliflower and peppers" with "shimmering, green leaves." After their work digging trenches, Kenosi, Tom, and Elizabeth "prepared seedlings in plastic bags for transplanting into the trench-beds. Into each small plastic bag with its six inches of soil manure mixture they dropped four cabbage seeds. Eventually after a month, and gradual thinning, each bag would hold one gigantic cabbage seedling. They'd make holes with spades in the trench-beds, then cut away the plastic and place each seedling with its mould of earth into the holes. . . . All the seedlings grew [despite] the intense heat."[30]

The use of seedling bags is an effective technique for promoting seed germination in desert landscapes. The plastic bags protect seeds from being blown away. The gardeners marvel at the seedlings' success despite the climate. Rejecting the metaphor of marital relations as the only way for the land to prosper, Head also undercuts the association of the land with passive female sexuality awaiting male fertilization. However, Clare Counihan criticizes Head because by "circumventing the natural and idiosyncratic processes of flowering and pollination, the garden reproduces sterility." Since

Counihan reads the garden as a way for Elizabeth to stabilize her identity, including her sexual and gendered identity, the lack of metaphors about gender or female desire imply for Counihan that Elizabeth's new, healed identity is disembodied.[31]

Counihan is not alone in her criticism of Head's praise of modern Western, scientific agricultural techniques. Jonathan Highfield claims that while "women form the core of the workers who transform the agrarian community . . . European agricultural knowledge catalyzes those women. . . . Head's favoritism toward imported agricultural knowledge is problematic, particularly when the imported cabbages require an inordinate amount of water in a region where drought is part of the weather pattern."[32] Highfield suggests that Head's endorsement of European agricultural knowledge implicitly supports a history of colonization and undervalues local knowledge. He argues that this view has material consequences because, like the watering systems pictured in *A Question of Power*, the imported crops and techniques can damage landscapes.

These criticisms are important because Head portrays agricultural work in her fiction and nonfiction as an exemplary way to form community and claim belonging. Privileging authoritarian and European knowledge has the potential to contradict her aims. Yet by emphasizing scientific and nonlocal agricultural techniques, Head also writes against ancestral claims of belonging and good stewardship that can come only by way of inherited ownership.

Further, Head's garden in *A Question of Power* and the agricultural project in *When Rain Clouds Gather* are powerful images of protest that produce significant environmental imaginaries. Counihan and Highfield minimize the significance of this protest because they do not situate Head's writing as a response to South African cultural and material relationships to land, thus undercutting an important contextualization. Maureen Fielding reads the agriculture collective's reclamation of the land in *When Rain Clouds Gather* as a "healing gesture." She writes: "In South Africa . . . this reclamation is really a transformation of land that has been controlled by uncontrollable forces into land that can be managed by people who live on it."[33] In the context of South African apartheid capitalism and the narratives of ownership that buttressed it, Head's portrayal of practical communal cultivation imagines a different kind of value for the land: not property value or ancestral belonging, but value that derives from offering food security for the land's inhabitants.

Not only does the image of gardening disrupt the Afrikaner *boernasie* cultural identity, but the novel's structure also replots value. Critics often characterize *A Question of Power* by its themes of fragmentation.[34] Work in the garden is described intermittently throughout the narrative of Elizabeth's encounters with Sello and Dan. It appears when Elizabeth awakens, usually at the start of the day, but also at other unexpected moments. For instance, at one point Elizabeth is recounting her walk through the plots in the garden with Camilla, one of the Danish volunteers, but then the narrative quickly shifts back to Elizabeth's suffering as the brown-suited Sello and his companion, Medusa, predict her death. Then the narrative shifts back to the time when Elizabeth meets Kenosi and they begin working in the garden together. No all-encompassing image of the garden ever appears. Rather, it is described in a series of discontinuous moments: one describes the building of the fence, and another the planting or arranging of plots.

The semi-episodic structure works against rigid boundaries, whether around a garden or around and between communities. Gardens are about order and have long served as metaphors for ordering life, but Head's narrative structure replicates Elizabeth's gardening techniques. She plants in "holes, made when knotted roots of the thorn-bush had been dug out," not just in the neat and clean "streets" of the garden mapped out by Grahame, the English farm manager.[35] She also experiments with different plants and seeds, using the space available to her according to her own ideas. Head has described *A Question of Power* as a book that is "written in such a way that it invites people to fill in gaps and notes where the author has left blank spaces. There are actually blank spaces in the book where the reader walks in and fills in."[36] The novel's structure and the garden do not dictate order: rather, they encourage the work of imagining cultivation from multiple points of view.

For example, in the middle of the novel, when Elizabeth has been working at the garden for some time, Elizabeth meets Tom and tells him her ideas for the garden, mentioning that she and Kenosi need help "pick digging to construct deep beds." Then she is suddenly transported to a hallucination where she finds herself in "fields of pretty-looking flowers" that must have been "seen in the garden of Eden."[37] In the hallucination, Dan tells her about the nightmarish thoughts people have about abusing the helpless, and Elizabeth is reminded of her life in the slums of South Africa. Tortured, lonely women are figured as David facing a Goliath of evil. When the hallucination ends, the setting is once again Elizabeth's house, but time has passed. Before the hallucination, Elizabeth and Tom were eating together. After the hallucination, Elizabeth sees Tom walking on the road and being hailed by some village women.

The narrative fragmentation allows the reader to contemplate the nature of the ideas explored in the hallucination. Meaning is neither directive nor prescriptive.[38] Even though the hallucination incorporates floral, Edenic imagery, there is no direct link with the garden episodes. Elizabeth's hallucinations don't make sense of the garden episodes, and the garden episodes don't make sense of the hallucinations.

Hence space and place are open to interpretation, but more important, the boundaries between spaces and places are continuously crossed. The plot structure and the free-form nature of Elizabeth's garden release readers from the limitations imposed on them by apartheid, colonialism, and patriarchal societies. Head employs a similar technique in *When the Rain Clouds Gather.* As Sample observes, "Crossing thresholds and boundaries is part of the text's articulation of narrative situations [and] the movement through space . . . suggests a possibility for healing."[39] Rita Barnard, in her influential essay about Nadine Gordimer's *The Conservationist* (1973), similarly describes how Gordimer's novel calls attention to "apartheid's territorial schemes," which systematically "dumped" Black South Africans, dubbing them "surplus" people, into "dust and poverty" and then read that waste as "evidence that Black people are not farmers." By using the "discourse of rubbish," the apartheid government "justified exclusion without seeming to say anything about race, apartheid or any such ugly topic."[40]

For much of *A Question of Power,* the garden and the internal dialogue follow the kinds of boundaries marked by apartheid. When Elizabeth is in the garden, it is described as neat and ordered: the plants "shimmer," the air is perfumed, and it is peaceful. By contrast, the scenes of Elizabeth's internal strife are frantic, with Sello and Dan calling innumerable characters out of the shadows. Elizabeth at one point finds herself "deep [in a] cesspit . . . filled to the brim with excreta."[41] The hallucinations are mostly invisible to the rest of the villagers in Motabeng. However, the images of surplus and waste are not confined to Elizabeth's mind. Instead, Head renders waste and surplus beautiful and welcome in the garden, and thus the images work against the dichotomy of ownership and cleanliness versus waste and invisibility.

The image of the highly productive Cape gooseberry signals surplus: "One day, as she walked through her garden she noted thick mats of brown husks lying on the ground beneath the gooseberry bushes. With Kenosi, she harvested an enormous basket of berries." Elizabeth "at first" was in "sheer panic having so much fruit on her hands . . . it looked as if the harvest of ten pounds of fruit a week would continue for an indefinite period." Her panic is only momentary, however, as Elizabeth finds that she can easily incorporate the surplus into the local industries project. "The work had a melody." In a later scene, Elizabeth again makes light of the surfeit of gooseberries. Elizabeth and Kenosi "richly" sigh at the sight of "thousands and thousands of gooseberries," thinking "they'd have lunch and then pick the berries and start some of the jam-making in the afternoon." The surplus is not only manageable: it also provides Elizabeth with the greatest sense of hope she has experienced. This is one of the last scenes in the book. Using the gooseberries to provide a valuable product for the local industries store, whose profit is shared among the community, is a means of realizing her dream of black South Africans belonging. She falls asleep, her terrors kept at bay for the night by the touch of her hand on "her land. It was a gesture of belonging."[42]

Head's image of the community garden is not just a metaphor for Elizabeth's vision of the "brotherhood of man," which she arrives at after sifting through the visions of evil and power that Sello and Dan sling at her. Rather the Motabeng garden joins a political future with a materialized environmental future. As a utopia, the garden imagines an alternative to the divisions of apartheid. Diverse members of society who previously would have distrusted each other because of their status and beliefs—Eugene, an Afrikaner; Camilla, a Dane; and Tom, an American—all work together with the villagers, seeking a better understanding of each other. While gardens have long served as vehicles for hope, they are also about transforming space. The garden in A Question of Power democratizes knowledge of the environment and invites Black South Africans to participate in shaping the landscape. It argues that everyone has a claim to agriculture because everyone eats and is a part of nature, and the text dramatizes how empowering individuals with knowledge will help communities thrive.

Yet the problem of ownership remains unresolved. South Africa still struggles with land redistribution today: the deadline for the land reform process was moved from 2014 to 2025. This issue cannot be solved by inviting everyone to lay communal claim to the land. Not acknowledging disenfranchised black South Africans' claim to capital trivializes rural poverty and ignores the realities of capitalist dispossession and ongoing policies and practices of erasure. Head's dream is monumental in pitting its environmental imaginary against the *plaasroman* and apartheid geographies, but it is not complete. Nonetheless, her fragmented and compromised utopia strives to untangle land and people from racist ideologies. She envisions a different value for the land, one that is based on sustaining and sustainable practices for the community and the environment, and she invites black South

Africans to reimagine value in terms other than those proposed in capitalism and environmental conservationism. While *A Question of Power* cannot resolve problems of ownership or propose an ideal that can compensate for extraordinary experiences of loss, it nonetheless highlights the need to reformulate black South Africans' relationship to the land.

NOTES

Epigraph: Bessie Head, quoted in Linda S. Beard, "Bessie Head in Gaborone, Botswana: An Interview," in *Between the Lines: Interviews with Bessie Head, Sheila Roberts, Ellen Kuzwayo, Miriam Tlali,* vol. 1, ed. Craig MacKenzie and Cherry Clayton (Grahamstown: National English Literary Museum, 1989), 44.

1   Maxine Sample, "Space: An Experiential Perspective; Bessie Head's *When Rain Clouds Gather,*" in *Critical Essays on Bessie Head,* ed. Maxine Sample (Westport, CT: Praeger, 2003), 31.

2   Anthony Vital, "Waste and Postcolonial History: An Ecocritical Reading of J. M. Coetzee's *Age of Iron,*" in *Environment at the Margins: Literary and Environmental Studies in Africa,* ed. Byron Caminero-Santangelo and Garth Myers (Athens: Ohio University Press, 2011), 193.

3   Rita Barnard, *Apartheid and Beyond: South African Writers and the Politics of Place* (New York: Oxford University Press, 2007), 72.

4   Bessie Head, *A Question of Power* (London: Heinemann, 1973), 72.

5   Christopher Warnes, "'Everyone Is Guilty': Complicitous Critique and the Plaasroman Tradition in Etienne van Heerden's *Toorberg* (Ancestral Voices)," *Research in African Literatures* 42, no. 1 (2011): 123.

6   J. M. Coetzee, *White Writing: On the Cultures of Letters in South Africa* (Braamfontein: Pentz Publishers, 2007), 71; John Browett, "The Evolution of Unequal Development within South Africa: An Overview," *Living under Apartheid: Aspects of Urbanization and Social Change in South Africa,* ed. David M. Smith (Boston: George Allen & Unwin, 1982).

7   Coetzee, *White Writing,* 110.

8   Jennifer Wenzel, "The Pastoral Promise and the Political Imperative: The Plaasroman Tradition in an Era of Land Reform," *Modern Fiction Studies* 46, no. 1 (2000): 94.

9   Coetzee, *White Writing,* 86–89, 113.

10   Warnes, "'Everyone Is Guilty,'" 124.

11   William Beinart and Peter Coates, *Environment and History: The Taming of Nature in the USA and South Africa* (New York: Routledge, 1995), 66.

12   Graham Huggan and Helen Tiffin, *Postcolonial Ecocriticism: Literature, Animals, Environment* (New York: Taylor & Francis, 2010), 82.

13   Mark Butler and David Hallowes, "Power, Poverty, and Marginalized Environments: A Conceptual Framework," in *Environmental Justice in South Africa,* ed. David A. McDonald (Athens: Ohio University Press, 2002), 551;

Andrea Booth, Munyaradzi Chenje, and Phyllis Johnson, *State of the Environment in Southern Africa* (Harare, Zimbabwe : Southern African Research and Documentation Centre: International Union for Conservation of Nature; South African Development Commmunity, Environment and Land Management Sector Coordination Unit, 1994), quoted in Butler and Hallowes, "Power, Poverty, and Marginalized Environments," 63.

14   Farieda Khan, "The Roots of Environmental Racism and the Rise of Environmental Justice in the 1990s," in McDonald, *Environmental Justice*, 24.

15   Ibid., 22. Khan notes that "the conservation and education services provided by the Division of Soil Conservation and Extension in the Department of Agriculture were aimed solely at the white farmer" (21).

16   Warnes, "'Everyone Is Guilty,'" 124; Huggan and Tiffin, *Postcolonial Ecocriticism*, 97.

17   Maxine Sample, "Bessie Head: A Bibliographic Essay," in Sample, *Critical Essays on Bessie Head*, 133, 134.

18   Rob Nixon, "Rural Transnationalism," in *Text, Theory, Space: Land, Literature, and History in South Africa and Australia*, ed. Kate Darian-Smith, Liz Gunner, and Sarah Nuttall (New York: Routledge, 1996), 251.

19   Bessie Head, "The Wind and a Boy," *The Collector of Treasures* (London: Heinemann, 1977), 71.

20   Jonathan Highfield, "'Relations with Food': Agriculture, Colonialism and Foodways in the Writing of Bessie Head," in *Postcolonial Green Environmental Politics and World Narratives*, ed. Bonnie Roos and Alex Hunt (Charlottesville: University of Virginia Press, 2010), 103.

21   Head, *A Question of Power*, 72, 60.

22   Ibid., 74.

23   Coetzee, *White Writing*, 103.

24   Head, *A Question of Power*, 123, 124.

25   Ibid., 124, 112.

26   Wenzel, "Pastoral Promise," 111.

27   J. M. Coetzee, *Boyhood* (New York: Penguin, 1998), 96.

28   In "Hell of Desire: Narrative, Identity and Utopia in *A Question of Power*," *Research in African Literatures*, 42, no. 1 (2011), Clare Counihan argues that the garden allows Head to imagine an "ideal alternative" that "champions . . . egalitarian and universal humanism," but in doing so "eras[es] difference and [s]quash[es] . . . desire" (79). For Counihan, Head's garden problematically evacuates raced, gendered, and national identities "as the condition of admittance into [the] idealized future" (70).

29   Head, *A Question of Power*, 60.

30   Ibid., 124.

31   Counihan, "The Hell of Desire," 79–80.

32   Highfield, "'Relations with Food,'" 110–11.

33 Maureen Fielding, "Agriculture and Healing: Transforming Space, Transforming Trauma in Bessie Head's *When Rain Clouds Gather*," in Sample, *Critical Essays on Bessie Head*, 20.

34 Maxine Sample, "Artist in Exile," in Sample, *Critical Essays on Bessie Head*, 6.

35 Head, *A Question of Power*, 123, 203.

36 Head, quoted in Beard, "Bessie Head in Gaborone."

37 Head, *A Question of Power*, 114.

38 The narrative structure of *A Question of Power* stands in direct contrast to the narrative goal of the *plaasroman*. Coetzee contends: "The craft of the prototypical Van den Heever plaasroman must . . . lie in creating the preconditions for an epiphany, an eruption into words," a steady movement "towards the revelation of the farm as a source of meaning" (91). As Van den Heever's protagonists commune with nature, it validates their identity and the value of the land. Calling attention to how narrative writes the environment, *A Question of Power* emphasizes how pastoral and conservative ideologies inscribe proper ownership onto the land.

39 Sample, "Space," 33, 43.

40 Barnard, *Apartheid and Beyond*, 84, 72.

41 Head, *A Question of Power*, 113, 124, 100, 125, 53.

42 Ibid., 152, 153, 204, 206.

PART THREE

VULNERABLE EMBODIMENTS

CHAPTER SEVEN

DENORMALIZING EMBODIED TOXICITY

The Case of Kettleman City

JULIE SZE

T HIS chapter examines the connections between race, gender, and environment by focusing on one contentious moment in a larger case study of Kettleman City in California's Central Valley. Kettleman City is a small and predominantly Latino farmworker community that faces much industrial, air, and other environmental pollution. It is the site of the largest commercial hazardous-waste facility west of the Mississippi. Over the last decade, Kettleman City has been the focus of tremendous media and policy attention, following a cluster of births of babies with cleft palates and other birth defects. I examine Kettleman City in historical, racial, and spatial contexts to better understand how racial, gender, and spatial politics are connected in ways that make the causes of negative health impacts nearly impossible to prove, thus leading to the status quo, where racially disproportionate environmental and health impacts seem inevitable and naturalized.

Environmental and reproductive injustices are intimately interconnected. Here I examine the power of racialized images of motherhood and childbirth in the activist organizing strategy, specifically in counterweight to the highly technical knowledge about toxic exposures used by regulatory agencies and polluters. In her groundbreaking book, Stacey Alaimo argues that "the human is always the very stuff of the messy, contingent, emergent mix of the material world. . . . The body is enmeshed in social and material systems and systems of domination that are enacted in individual and community bodies, cultural representations, and modes of knowing and thinking."[1] She calls the messy mix of human bodies embedded with one other, with non-human creatures, and with physical landscapes *trans-corporeality*.

This chapter expands Alaimo's notion of trans-corporeality—the intermixing of humans and social systems with systems of political domination—with respect to racial ecologies. Looking at media coverage and at statements of residents from a listening session sponsored by the US Environmental Protection Agency, I argue that the Kettleman City cleft-palate controversy represents a meeting of reproductive and environmental justice in a racially specific manifestation of trans-corporeality. More than a new illustration of Alaimo's concept, the Kettleman City case is a salient example of racial ecologies because the controversy makes visible what is "normal," accepted, and political in the Central Valley. The activist politics of race, gender, and toxic exposure are constructed through the frame of motherhood and birth defects, which relies, in complicated ways, on normative ideologies of bodily health, even as activists challenge the social and economic structures that deny the bodily health of these women of color and their babies. The politics of gender and motherhood are mobilized by environmental justice activists in the context of anti-immigrant and antinatalist politics in California and beyond, in contrast to attempts by polluters and the state to reject the complex arguments about the cumulative impact of pollution that are advanced by activists.

In her study of controversies over pesticide drift, the sociologist Jill Harrison examines activism, policy, science, and the seeming paradox that pesticide poisoning is both pervasive and invisible. She opens with one of the high-profile cases in Earlimart, a small farmworker town in the Central Valley, where over 170 Spanish-speaking residents experienced nausea, respiratory distress, burning eyes and lungs, and dizziness because of a pesticide-drift incident. The emergency response personnel, who didn't speak Spanish, brought the most severely affected residents to the school, stripped them publicly, and sprayed them with hoses. An investigation revealed that metam sodium, a soil fumigant (and known carcinogen) was to blame.

Harrison shows how the pesticide industry and the state environmental regulatory agency offer a narrative that characterizes incidents like the Earlimart exposure as "accidental" and "exceptional." She argues that pesticide drift illustrates how the workings of "raw power" shift the burden of pesticide pollution to the bodies of the most marginalized and vulnerable residents.[2] Her articulation of raw power, and the pervasive and invisible normalization of environmental abuse of the most vulnerable populations, is directly relevant to the stories of the individuals and communities in Kettleman City.

The cleft-palate controversy demonstrates how a normalized state of pervasive environmental pollution and social inequality may be exposed and used by activists in ways that trigger attention from the state. Images of birth defects in babies powerfully communicate the effects of toxic exposures and bodily pollution on the most innocent and vulnerable victims. In Kettleman City, as in Earlimart, the raw power of environmental pollution, like racism, is met by community resistance.

The geographer Ruth Wilson Gilmore defines racism as the state-sanctioned or extralegal production and exploitation of group-differentiated vulnerability to premature death.[3] Pervasive and historical patterns of pollution exposure, toxic contamination, and environmental destruction are not accidental but rather embedded in systems of exploitation. These patterns are exacerbated by neoliberalism, which idealizes market, capital, and consumer subjectivities over communitarian notions of belonging or justice. Farmworker activism and the Kettleman City case are powerful examples of the environmental justice critique of separation: separation between bodies and environmental pollution, between labor and environmental issues, and between race, gender, and environmentalism. Here environmentalism is constructed as both the problem and the activism against racialized trans-corporeality. Attention to the complex relationship between race, class, gender, and environmental exposures, particularly with respect to motherhood, is a core component of antitoxics, environmental, and environmental justice activism.

GENDERED, RACIALIZED, AND ACTIVIST HISTORIES OF KETTLEMAN CITY

Since 2007, ten babies in Kettleman City have been born with deformities (chiefly cleft palates). Three died. The State of California initially withheld information about the number of cases; the data were garnered from the birth defects monitoring program run by the California Department of Public Health.[4] Community activism attracted media and government attention, including a study conducted by the Department of Public Health and the Environmental Protection Agency ordered by the governor of California, Arnold Schwarzenegger, and statements of concern from both of California's US senators, Dianne Feinstein and Barbara Boxer.[5]

Kettleman City has 1,500 residents, of whom 97 percent are Latino. Most are farmworkers. The average annual per capita income of the town is $7,300. The town is surrounded by agricultural fields and exposed to pollutants from runoff. Its drinking water has elevated levels of natural arsenic and benzene from the municipal wells.[6] It is also the recipient of sewage sludge from the city of Los Angeles.[7] In addition, residents are constantly exposed to diesel emissions from passing trucks on Interstate 5 and Highway 41 and airborne emissions from benzene and old oilfield operations. Residents report high rates of asthma, cancer, and miscarriages.[8]

Because the water is contaminated, residents buy costly water from a source half an hour's drive away. The situation is by no means unique.[9] Water samples from other Central Valley farm towns, such as Visalia, test positive for nitrates from fertilizers and cow manure from large dairy-farming operations. These samples also contain dibromochloropropane, a pesticide banned in 1977.

The Kettleman City cleft-palate cluster was identified in a health survey conducted by community and environmental groups. Local activism over the nearby hazardous-waste facility in 1982 is considered to be one of the foundations of the national environmental justice movement.[10] The landfill is owned and operated by a multinational corporation, Chemical Waste Management, Inc. (Chem Waste). It takes in over four hundred tons per year of hazardous waste, asbestos, pesticides, petroleum, and polychlorinated biphenyls (PCBs).[11] The company has been fined more than $2 million over twenty-eight years for violations such as the mishandling of PCBs, and most recently for not following proper quality-control procedures.[12]

In 2009, Chem Waste applied for a permit to expand, which was granted by the Kings County Board of Supervisors. Greenaction and El Pueblo para el Aire y Agua Limpio/People for Clean Air and Water filed a lawsuit to block the expansion.[13]

The cleft-palate controversy cannot be separated from the history of development and the social inequalities and racialized pattern of land use in the Central Valley. This is a society highly stratified by race, class, and immigration status. The land use and economic structure of the Valley render poorer and more vulnerable residents subject to greater pollution exposure. The social and environmental conditions of the Central Valley—the highest rates of air pollution in the country, high risks from water contamination, carceral landscapes, high poverty, high mortgage foreclosure rates, and low educational attainment—are not accidental but rather structural.[14]

California's Central Valley region is particularly vulnerable to environmental pollution because of its status as the most productive agricultural region in the world. The region represents 2 percent of the nation's farmland but is the site of the application of 25 percent of the nation's pesticides. According to Harrison, 90 percent of these aerially applied pesticides are liable to drift from the intended sites of application to other areas, including residential areas.

These injustices have not gone unremarked. The region is also home to a long and radical tradition of labor activism, dating back to the early twentieth century, and personified by Larry Itliong, a Filipino American, and Cesar Chavez and Dolores Huerta, Mexican Americans who led the United Farm Workers union in the 1960s. Much of the early activism for farmworker protection was focused on the effects of pesticides on maternal and fetal health.[15] In 1969 the California Rural Legal Assistance program (CRLA) and its general counsel, Ralph Abascal, filed a lawsuit on behalf of six farm workers who were exposed to DDT. Five of the six were nursing mothers: this was significant because DDT accumulates in breast milk. That lawsuit led to a ban on DDT.

Abascal and CRLA continued the struggle to protect farm workers from pesticide exposure, joining in a successful lawsuit twenty years later against the Environmental Protection Agency that led to an agreement to ban about 85 percent of the pesticides then in use. Yet the health effects of pesticide exposure on farmworkers and on developing fetuses still persist fifty years later.

Motherhood has long been a central component of environmental and antitoxics activism in the United States. In 1978, Lois Gibbs, a working-class white woman, discovered that her son's school in the neighborhood of Love Canal in upstate New York was built on top of a toxic waste dump. She was a leader in the successful effort to evacuate Love Canal, and her activism helped spur regulatory change at the US Environmental Protection Agency. The Love Canal protest helped to catalyze broad concern about exposure to toxics in the home, rather than in industrial workplaces. In the Central Valley, however, this distinction does not always hold, because in many poor Central Valley communities, homes are sited close to industrial agriculture. This lack of clear boundaries and separation is simultaneously a powerful metaphor for the lack of meaningful boundaries between mother and child during pregnancy. Likewise, attempts to protect developing fetuses from industrial pollutants are futile when their mothers are exposed to pesticides both at work in the fields and at home.[16]

Much of the public discourse around Gibbs focused on her identity as a mother and contributed to the perception that environmental activism was motivated by household exposures and threats to children's health. She was criticized in the press as a "hysterical housewife." This label has had continuing resonance. In 1984, a leaked report funded by the California Waste Management Board, called the Cerrell Report, noted that "one occupational classification has consistently demonstrated itself as a strong indicator of opposition to the siting of noxious facilities, especially nuclear power plants—housewives."[17]

The sociologist Tracy Perkins describes the gendered social construction of Lois Gibbs's experience as the traditional women's environmental justice narrative in which "apolitical women personally experience an environmental problem that launches them into a life of activism to protect the health of their families."[18] Perkins suggests that elements of this narrative conflate gender and motherhood: women are framed primarily as reproductive beings and assumed to see threats to their children as their most urgent political concerns. This gendered narrative of politicization, which focuses largely on white women, ignores the historical realities and complicated race and class politics at Love Canal and elsewhere. Perkins argues that this gendered narrative does not accurately depict the majority of the women she interviewed in her study of women organizers in the Central Valley, many of whom had become politically active through education, farmworker justice, and poverty issues.

However, the Kettleman City case complicates Perkins's findings, in part because the attitudes of women of color to motherhood and national belonging are different from those of white women.[19] The focus on connections between reproductive health and environmental justice is an example of a gendered relationship to race, place, and bodies. This relationship is not reductionist, biologically determined, or static. Kettleman City activists signify a return to the earliest roots of farmworker and environmental justice activism, shaped by concerns with social and political forces that disproportionately harm particular bodies—those of working-class women of color and their unborn children.

The Kettleman City case shows that discourses and experiences of motherhood, environmental exposures, and protection vary with class, citizenship, and geographic and social location. Whereas white middle-class mothers are seen as innocent and their children deserving of (environmental) protection from the state, working-class women of color and their children—particularly immigrants without legal citizenship—meet with different assumptions. Their insistence on their right to their experience of motherhood is not predicated on personal factors and biology (i.e., having a baby) as much as on placing that experience within a critique of racialized exposures from pollution that shape that experience. Last, their racialized trans-corporeality is not exceptional but exemplifies an important strand of environmental and reproductive justice activism.

In the past decade, environmental justice research has begun to take gender much more seriously as a category of analysis, focusing on the ways in which pregnant and lactating women's exposure to pollution makes toxic exposures and their health effects visible.[20] Miscarriages and birth defects are highly visible examples of the connection between reproductive and environmental injustice.[21]

Other examples of reproductive and environmental injustice in the United States are the occupational hazards faced by immigrant woman workers in computer and garment factories before this production largely moved out of the United States in the 1990s.[22] Occupational exposures include particular harms to the reproductive and nervous systems, which trigger elevated rates of miscarriages. Such exposures are not limited to large industries: recent media coverage of the reproductive effects of working in nail salons, where many workers are Asian immigrant women, show the pervasiveness of these problems. In response, community-based organizations and health professionals have designed programs to reduce such exposures.[23]

These examples of toxic exposures exemplify the racialized and gendered ways in which trans-corporeality is lived and experienced. While trans-corporeality is a broad *condition* of contemporary life (and a factor in premature death), the economic and environmental reality experienced by women of color and indigenous women cause them to suffer disproportionate burdens from global environmental pollution. The question here is not whether or how these populations "choose" the conditions of their life and labor. Rather, the racialized dimensions of trans-corporeality inevitably impose these burdens on their bodies, with reproductive consequences that lay bare the brutalities of the current economic and environmental system and histories of domination and violence.

In all these cases, arguments about reproductive and environmental justice are made in a context of anti-immigrant politics, anxieties about globalization, and the exodus of manufacturing jobs to other countries. These stories are part of a long history of the degradation of the bodies and environments of indigenous populations. Antinatalist attitudes toward indigenous and immigrant women create a context in which the health of their babies is always already politicized. Not only is the health of their children already precarious because of occupational exposures and particular pathways of bioaccumulation of toxic pollutants, but their children's very right to exist is challenged by anti-immigrant social movements and by long histories of settler-colonial states that have vigorously policed the health and reproductive life chances of women of color. Laura Briggs documents what she calls an expansive "reproductive politics" from feminism and racial justice traditions, in contrast to the reproductive politics advanced by business interests and government agencies. In one salient example, she details how "protection" from lead poisoning by an automobile battery manufacturer was the justification for excluding women (including those past reproductive age) from well-paid union jobs.[24] Defenders of mainstream environmentalism have also been complicit in these injustices. In the 1990s, a strand of the mainstream environmental movement conflated anti-immigration and population anxieties, arguing that immigrants to the United States use more of the planet's resources than they would in their sending countries and that they would contribute to overpopulation. This anti-immigration strand in mainstream environmentalism has a long history, starting with its connections to the eugenics movement. In tracing this history, Sarah Jaquette Ray suggests that environmentalist discourses draw on normative notions of body, wholeness, and health.[25] Her framework of "ecological othering" is useful, particularly when read alongside Julie Avril Minich's *Accessible Citizenships: Disability, Nation and the Cultural Politics of Greater Mexico* (2014). In her account of how corporeal images are used to depict national belonging, Minich argues that cultural representations conceptualize political community through images of disability, drawing on artwork, and literature from writers like Arturo Islas Jr., Cherrié Moraga, and Felicia Luna Lemus.[26]

It would be possible to argue that the Kettleman City mothers are relying on the old tropes of virtuous motherhood that have historically shaped mainstream environmental discourse. Their focus on birth defects can also be read as a troubling privileging of normative and idealized healthy bodies and a return to Ray's notion of disgust as a central mode of environmental politics, in which she challenges the normative ideology of healthy bodies as environmentally clean and virtuous. However, racialized trans-corporeality takes gendered, racialized, and disability studies critiques into account, simultaneously and intersectionally. The problem is not disgust and shame focused on babies with birth defects but the social, economic and environmental system that normalizes pollution exposure and whose effects are manifested in particularly visible fashion through human reproduction.

Recent activism around the Kettleman City cleft-palate cluster is a salient example of the relationship between race, gender, and labor—in both senses of the word—and between reproductive and environmental justice. The official study that was commissioned to investigate the cluster asked mothers to attempt to figure out the causes of the cleft palate and other birth defects, including enlarged heads, allergies, seizures, and defects in the corpus callosum.[27] The mothers (and their allies) objected to the framing of their personal exposures and behaviors as likely causes. Their testimony deflected focus away from individual factors and toward systemic ones such as outdoor pollution exposure, either from air or water. In the words of Maricela Alatorre, "You want to know if we ever smoked cigarettes or took drugs.... I'm telling you that if the dump is allowed to expand, we'll suffer more damage and illness. Why? Because we are poor and Hispanic. The people who issue those permits don't care about us getting sick from it because all they think about is money."[28]

These mothers conjoin their personal trauma with concrete political demands. At a listening session convened in Kettleman City with a number of agency representatives and elected officials, one mother, Daria Hernandez Lorenzo, said, "I'm here because my baby was born like this with his little face deformed and I ask you to not issue any more permits until an investigation is done."[29] This insistence on political critique and a focus on pollution as a cause of their personal tragedies are persistent. In the words of Magdalena Romero, the mother of America (one of the children who died), "Kettleman City to them is just a pigsty, but we are human beings and we have rights."[30]

For these mothers, and occasionally fathers, the visibility of the cleft palate and other birth defects is central to the way they stake political claims. Activists bring photos of their babies to political protests.[31] America's father tattooed a picture of his deceased child on his arm.

The prominent use of visual images is a key feature of environmental activism and, consciously or not, reprises the thalidomide controversy of the 1960s.[32] The images of damaged babies and cleft palates have visceral effects: they are self-consciously intended as a powerful political message. The pictures of the babies represent everything from personal anguish to political outrage. Centralizing these images serves to hold corporate polluters, and the social and environmental systems that support them, accountable for the harm.

Although the centrality of visual images and storytelling to activism assumes a close relationship between the image and the truth, scholars recognize that interpretation of these images and stories may be deeply contested. This tension was exemplified in the listening session in Kettleman

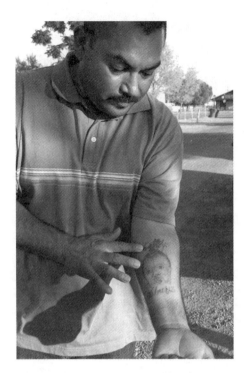

Alejandro Alvarez shows his tattoo in memory of his baby daughter, Kettleman City, California, July 18, 2009. Photo by Tracy Perkins.

City. According to one participant, Angela Borroyo, " Once upon a time, Kettleman City hills was pretty, beautiful green, clean air, everything was beautiful. . . . Right now, there's no business, everything's dead, everyone's sick. . . . Before, there were no allergies, Valley Fever. . . . It's not about a job, it's not about money, it's about life and babies." Borroyo paints a verbal picture of a landscape transformed by industrial siting. She outlines a stark choice between profits and health, and she argues that babies and human lives outweigh economic development.

Although the claim here is not explicitly racialized, Borroyo's assertion of the right to have babies, and of residents to live on their own terms in Kettleman City, is *itself* a racialized claim of politics and belonging. Others dispute this characterization on the basis of their own positionality and experience. One older, white community member, who lost her own child in 1958, commented, "We've always had Valley Fever [a damaging fungal infection endemic in the Central Valley] . . . It's not just Kettleman City, and it's not you against us. It's not brown against white, or black against white, or purple against green. It is people."[33]

Racialized trans-corporeality is both intimately connected to and an extension of the racial dimensions of global production and exploitation. Racialized motherhood and claims to bodily health in Kettleman City are not a simple reprise of virtuous motherhood but rather a radical claim to community and belonging. This section focuses on how racial trans-corporeality functions in addition to problem diagnosis, but in solution and theory building and knowledge production, in what is known in public health terms as "cumulative impact analysis." Traditional risk-exposure analysis looks at single sources, not the cumulative and interacting effects of multiple exposures. In other words, racial trans-corporeality and cumulative impact analysis connect things often seen as distinct (race, gender, and ecology in the former and different pollution exposures in the latter). This making of connections is a political stance as well, as a form of intersectionality.

As a result of community activism and media attention, the governor of California ordered the state Environmental Protection Agency (EPA) and Department of Public Health (CDPH) to conduct an investigation of the reported birth defects and the Kettleman City environment.[34] The study ruled out the toxic waste dump as a cause.[35] It found that "although the overall investigation found high levels of pollutants in the air, water and soil of Kettleman City, the comprehensive investigation did not find a specific cause or environmental exposure among the mothers that would explain the increase in the number of children born with birth defects in Kettleman City."[36] In essence, health investigators found the town's pollution levels to be on a par with those of similar communities elsewhere.[37] There was nothing unique about Kettleman City that could link the polluted air and landscape to the cleft-palate births.

Community activists blasted the study and, by extension, conventional measures of investigatory health research. According to Maricela Alatorre, a local activist and resident, the study involved no testing of blood or human tissue for pesticides.[38] She commented: "We're very, very disappointed. The state left us with a monster on the loose in town, and we don't know where it will strike next."[39]

The disappointment and fury the community members felt were not surprising. As scholars of environmental justice and public health have noted, traditional scientific practice is often at odds with community-based claims. Mainstream research methods require a high threshold of statistical significance, a large data set, and reproducible results. It is very hard by these measures to establish a causal link between environmental pollution and health effects.

In response, some public health scholars have developed tools and methodologies for assessing the cumulative impact of environmental and other hazards. The idea is that "racial or ethnic minority groups and low-income communities have poorer health outcomes than others [and are] more frequently exposed to multiple environmental hazards and social stressors, including poverty, poor housing quality, and social inequality."[40] Cumulative impact analysis recognizes multiple hazards and stressors with synergistic effects. Thus, individual biological susceptibility and social vulnerability to illness and birth defects are connected.

Cumulative impact research attends to social, health, and environmental vulnerabilities. It places community members at the center when setting research agendas, asking relevant questions, and collecting data. Working with environmental justice activists in Kettleman City and elsewhere in the Central Valley, public health and social science scholars have developed integrative methodologies that combine multiple factors: a cumulative environmental hazards index (CEHI), a social vulnerability index (SVI), and a health index (HI). Together these indexes form what some have called a cumulative environmental vulnerability assessment.[41] This form of assessment addresses the major shortcomings in the CDPH and EPA study on Kettleman City by reframing definitions of harm and vulnerability.

Cumulative impact research attempts to translate the elevated risk, the synergistic effects, and the interlocking effects of political, economic and ecological systems into terms that public health and regulatory agencies understand and can act on. This task is challenging and highly political. Racialized trans-corporeality is a starting point for activism as it moves into changing terrains of knowledge production.

CONCLUSION

In 2014, the California Department of Toxic Substances Control granted a ten-year permit for the landfill expansion in Kettleman City, promising residents, "You are safe."[42] Community members then filed administrative complaints of racial discrimination in the approval.[43] In August 2016, the state Department of Toxic Substances Control and the EPA announced an agreement with two environmental groups that ended the civil rights complaint. The state said it will take environmental justice factors into account when reviewing Chemical Waste Management's pending application to renew its operating permit and in reviewing any expansion application submitted within three years. The agreement also provided funds to improve public health and environmental quality in Kettleman City.[44] In addition, the Kings County Board of Supervisors approved a health survey to study the links between an area landfill and birth defects and disease, although some residents remain skeptical about the study, which is based on surveys funded by the polluting facility.[45]

The activism in Kettleman City was one important moment in an ongoing struggle for environmental and reproductive justice. Although the activists never used the terms *racialized trans-corporeality* or *racial ecologies*, these concepts can advance our understanding of environmental justice theory and social movement building. It connects the Kettleman City case to other examples of pollution that hit women of color and indigenous women particularly hard. The goal of environmental justice activists in Kettleman City and throughout the Central Valley is to *denormalize* existing environmental and social conditions of injustice and pollution by naming, showing, and highlighting conditions of racial trans-corporeality, and to bend the raw power of exploitation—environmental and otherwise—into new social and material realities.

NOTES

1   Stacy Alaimo, *Bodily Natures: Science, Environment, and the Material Self* (Bloomington: Indiana University Press, 2010).

2   Jill Lindsey Harrison, *Pesticide Drift and the Pursuit of Environmental Justice* (Cambridge, MA: MIT Press, 2011), 1.

3   Ruth Wilson Gilmore, *Golden Gulag: Prisons, Surplus, Crisis, and Opposition in Globalizing California* (Berkeley: University of California, 2007).

4   Eiji Yamashita, "Kettleman Birth Defect Cases Double," *Hanford Sentinel*, March 9, 2010.

5   Jacques Leslie, "What's Killing the Babies of Kettleman City?" *Mother Jones*, July–August 2010.

6   Louis Sahagun, "Grieving Kettleman City Mothers Tackled a Toxic Waste Dump," *Los Angeles Times*, April 1, 2010.

7   Mark Grossi, "Kettleman City Reaps Toxic Harvest of California Castoffs," *Fresno Bee*, January 2, 2013.

8   Jonathan London, Ganlin Huang, and Tara Zagofsky, *Land of Risk, Land of Opportunity* (Davis: UC Davis, Center for Regional Change, November 2011).

9   Carolina Balazs, Rachel Morello-Frosch, Alan Hubbard, and Isha Ray, "Social Disparities in Nitrate-Contaminated Drinking Water in California's San Joaquin Valley," *Environmental Health Perspectives* 119, no. 9 (2011): 1272–78.

10   Luke Cole and Sheila Foster, *From the Ground Up: Environmental Racism and the Rise of the Environmental Justice Movement* (New York: New York University Press, 2001).

11   Leslie, "What's Killing the Babies of Kettleman City?"

12   Louis Sahagun, "Toxic Waste Dump Ruled Out as Cause of Kettleman City Birth Defects," *Los Angeles Times*, November 23, 2010.

13   Ibid.

14   The social and environmental ills of the Central Valley and the resulting activism are the focus of recent research and public outreach projects, including Voices from the Valley (www.voicesfromthevalley.org), a collaborative, online outreach project involving university researchers and community members that highlights the photos and narratives of women environmental justice activists in the region.

15   Laura Pulido, *Environmentalism and Economic Justice: Two Chicano Struggles in the Southwest* (Tucson: University of Arizona Press, 1996).

16   Julie Sze, "Boundaries and Border Wars: DES, Technology and Environmental Justice," *American Quarterly* 58, no. 3 (2006) 791–814.

17   Cerrell Associates for the California Waste Board, "Political Difficulties Facing Waste to Energy Conversion Plant Siting," 1984, www.ejnet.org/ej/cerrell.pdf.

18   Tracy E. Perkins, "Women's Pathways in Activism: Rethinking the Women's Environmental Justice Narrative in California's San Joaquin Valley," *Organization and Environment* 25, no. 1 (2012): 76–94.

19   Ruby Tapia, *American Pietàs: Visions of Race, Death, and the Maternal* (Minneapolis: University of Minnesota Press, 2011).

20   Julie Sze, "Gender and Environmental Justice," in *Routledge Handbook on Gender and Environment*, ed. Sherilyn MacGregor, 159–68 (London: Routledge, 2017).

21   Ibid. Another issue is the elevated pollution in Arctic Native populations as a result of persistent organic pollutants (POPs). POPs are highly toxic, long-lasting, chlorinated organic chemicals, often from industrial sources, that can accumulate in animals and ecosystems thousands of miles away from their point of origin. Health effects of POP exposure include higher rates of infectious diseases and immune dysfunction and negative effects on neurobehavioral development and height. When a Nunavik midwife in the Arctic collected breast-milk samples from a "clean" environment as control samples for a study, researchers were surprised to find that these samples contained POP concentrations five to ten times higher than breast milk from women in southern Canada and among the highest ever recorded. David Leonard Downie and Terry Fenge, eds., *Northern Lights against POPS: Toxic Threats in the Arctic* (Montreal: McGill University Press, 2004).

22   The sociologists David Pellow and Lisa Park document the numerous hazards faced by computer production-line workers, mostly nonunionized,

low-income Asian and Latina immigrant women in Silicon Valley, California. D. N. Pellow and L. Park, *The Silicon Valley of Dreams: Environmental Injustice, Immigrant Workers, and the High-Tech Global Economy* (New York: New York University Press, 2003).

23 Julia Liou, Catherine Porter, and Thu Quach, "Policy Recommendations to Reduce Toxic Exposures for Nail Salon Workers," *AAPI Nexus: Policy, Practice and Community* 9, nos. 1–2 (2011): 43–50.

24 Laura Briggs, *How All Politics Became Reproductive Politics: From Welfare Reform to Foreclosure to Trump* (Berkeley: University of California Press, 2017).

25 Sarah Jaquette Ray, *The Ecological Other: Environmental Exclusion in American Culture* (Tucson: University of Arizona Press, 2013).

26 Julie Avril Minich, *Accessible Citizenships: Disability, Nation, and the Cultural Politics of Greater Mexico* (Philadelphia: Temple University Press, 2013), 3.

27 Leslie, "What's Killing the Babies of Kettleman City?"

28 Sahagun, "Toxic Waste Dump."

29 Official transcript of listening session, August 12, 2009, in author's possession (no longer accessible online).

30 Sahagun, "Toxic Waste Dump."

31 Ibid.; Leslie, "What's Killing the Babies of Kettleman City?"

32 Ibid.; Dunaway, *Seeing Green: The Use and Abuse of American Environmental Images* (Chicago: University of Chicago Press, 2015).

33 Listening session, August 12, 2009.

34 California Birth Defects Monitoring Program, "Birth Defects in Kettleman City," www.cdph.ca.gov/Programs/CFH/DGDS/Pages/cbdmp/documents/Birth%20Defects%20in%20Kettleman%20City.pdf, accessed December 3, 2017.

35 Sahagun, "Toxic Waste Dump."

36 California Birth Defects Monitoring Program, "Birth Defects in Ketteman City."

37 Sahagun, "Toxic Waste Dump."

38 Jesse McKinley, "In California, Birth Defects Show No Link," *New York Times*, November 22, 2010.

39 Sahagun, "Toxic Waste Dump."

40 R. Morello-Frosch, M. Zuk, M. Jerrett, B. Shamasunder, and A. D. Kyle, "Understanding the Cumulative Impacts of Inequalities in Environmental Health: Implications for Policy," *Health Affairs* 30, no. 5 (May 2011): 879–87.

41 Ganlin Huang and Jonathan London, "Mapping Cumulative Environmental Effects, Social Vulnerability, and Health in the San Joaquin Valley, California," *American Journal of Public Health* 102, no. 5 (2012): 830–32.

42 Louis Sahagun, "Waste Facility Allowed to Expand, Despite Community's Health Concerns," *Los Angeles Times*, May 21, 2014.

43 Lewis Griswold, "Kettleman City Activists Charge Racial Discrimination in Toxic Dump Approval," *Fresno Bee*, March 20, 2014.

44 Lewis Griswold, "State, Kettleman City Advocates Settle Dispute over Toxic Waste Landfill," *Fresno Bee*, August 10, 2016.

45 Eman Shurbaji, "Board of Supervisors Approves Kettleman City Survey," *Hanford Sentinel*, May 31, 2016.

CHAPTER EIGHT

HUMANIZING ANIMALS

Talking about Second Chances, Horses, and Prisoners

ERICA TOM

THE horse stood still. He was a chestnut thoroughbred, a gelding with streaks of fly spray beneath his eyes, gleaming where the man had wiped his face. The prisoner, a Latino man, gave another light tug on the lead rope. He paused, as if flipping back through mental notes on his horsemanship lessons—he was new to the Second Chances Horse Program. He moved to the other side of the horse and asked him to move forward again, but the gelding wouldn't budge.

I watched the prisoner and the chestnut gelding. The man kept looking into the horse's eyes, searching for an answer. Why wouldn't he go back to the pasture? Did the horse not understand what he was asking? An experienced horsewoman, I looked the length of the horse, thinking perhaps that he was favoring a hoof or injured in some way. Then I looked down. I smiled and spoke sideways to the instructor. "He's *reee*laxed."

"Hm?" He turned. "Oh." He paused. "*Ha*, yeah."

The horse's penis was dropped, erect, and he was whacking it against his stomach. Engorged, it made only the slightest noise under the rustle of leaves and the tractor in the distance. *Thwack, thwack, thwack.* The horse started ejaculating, his penis wobbling up and down and side to side, spraying, as he finally began to walk. The prisoner hadn't seemed to notice: it often takes time for humans to learn to read the entire equine body, instead of focusing on the face. He walked the gelding down the road, taking off his halter and securing the pasture gate. He patted him softly on the cheek. The horse nuzzled the man's hand briefly before flipping his head at the flies and turning to join the herd.

Sweating from too many layers on a hot summer day, I pulled at the damp armpits of my cardigan and smiled to myself. Many people had warned me to cover up, for fear that the sight of a young woman's skin might spark a frenzy of sexual deviance in the incarcerated men I was to interview. They were, after all, prisoners—men (so many of them black and brown) locked up ostensibly because of their deviance, their lack of humanity, their animality. The men I met at the Second Chances Horse Program were kind to me. They were generous with their time, their knowledge, and their stories. The horse was the only one exhibiting oversexual behavior. A symbol of strength, freedom, and beauty in the United States, equines are often elevated above humans: their animality is often left out. This sexual expression, this masturbating chestnut gelding, disrupted prisoner stereotypes and reinforced a basic element of what it means to be an animal—human or otherwise.

For racehorses at the end of their careers, the ability to be retrained determines their fate. An ex-racehorse with a kind eye who is keen on children might become a schooling horse for a training stable. An ex-racehorse with good conformation and coordination might become a competitive jumper. An ex-racehorse that finds herself in the hands of a rescue organization might live out her years with no more asked of her than ornamenting a pasture, accepting carrots from small children. An ex-racehorse with too many injuries or psychological issues from the rigors of the racing industry might go to the kill lot. To be of use is a horse's best chance at living.[1]

To be of use is a cross-species issue. Among humans, those categorized as unfit for or not of use to society are often locked up. Prisoners, especially men of color, are viewed as deviant by mainstream America, as lacking the desire to be of use. Those who do not "redeem" themselves by learning to make themselves "useful" while incarcerated may face longer prison terms and increased difficulty when or if they are released. Ex-racehorses, no longer able to run or earn income for their owners, are all too often thrown away—left to starve or sold at kill lots.

In 1982, these two disregarded populations were brought together for the first time. The Thoroughbred Retirement Foundation (TRF) and the Wallkill Correctional Facility (WCF) in upstate New York joined forces to establish the Second Chances Horse Program (SCHP), teaching prisoners how to take care of horses.

The relationship between horse and human is a fraught one. First hunted for their meat and hides, horses then carried humans across continents and into war. They were forced to plow fields and build cities. The relationship

ERICA TOM

is ever changing, characterized by negotiation, domination, and intimacy.[2] Humans' own struggles of dominion over one another have long been bound up with their categorizations of other species. Likened to apes, black people were denied membership in the human species by whites. Despite centuries of racial struggle, black- and brown-bodied people's fight for inclusion in humanity continues.[3] I use this phrase because black- and brown-bodied people have been relegated to subhuman status; however, it implies a devaluation of nonhuman animals, a speciated hierarchy of worth. The category of humanity and the concept of humaneness require problematizing. How can we talk about equality, about valuing the lives of all human beings, alongside valuing the lives of nonhuman animals?

THEORETICAL FRAMEWORK: CONSTITUTIVE
CATEGORIES AND MUTUAL AVOWAL

As an educator working with horses, I have long explored the benefits that working with horses can have for humans. I have discussed how training horses can encourage a more expansive understanding of the body in the classroom, for both teachers and students, and I continue to be interested in the empowering possibilities of horse-human interactions—specifically in how the articulation of this cross-species relationship is entangled in both bolstering and breaking down categories of race and species.[4] This chapter is directly informed and inspired by Claire Jean Kim's book *Dangerous Crossings: Race, Species, and Nature in a Multicultural Age*.[5] Employing an intersectional approach, Kim argues for a multioptic vision, a "reorientation toward an ethics of mutual avowal, or open and active acknowledgment of connection with other struggles." Examining an "ethics of disavowal," Kim demonstrates how prioritizing the interests of oppressed human *or* nonhuman animals is a "false choice," one that disavows the struggle of one group in order to bolster the situation of the other. This approach is blind to the intricate way in which power "traverses and binds the taxonomies of race and species."[6]

Kim's project demonstrates that avowal does not foreclose critique. She analyzes the controversy over Michael Vick's conviction for his involvement in dog fighting by encouraging animal advocates to acknowledge not only the pain and mistreatment of the pit bulls that were exploited but also "that white people clamoring for a Black man's (violent) punishment can never, ever be a race-neutral narrative." She likewise encourages an ethics of avowal for those fighting racism, urging them to resist the "reflexive moves of asserting human superiority and reducing animal advocacy to anti-Black racism."[7] Embracing an ethics of avowal requires those on both sides of the argument to deeply consider the multiple issues at stake, acknowledging the connection between the exploitation and oppression of human and nonhuman animals.

THE SECOND CHANCES HORSE PROGRAM

The Bureau of Land Management and the Thoroughbred Retirement Foundation (TRF) have joined with prisons to create vocational opportunities for prisoners to learn to care for and work with horses. The Second Chances Horse Program focuses on the care of ex-racehorses.[8] Some of the programs created in correctional facilities provide vocational training for the prisoners, where they might earn a certificate in the Groom Elite Vocational Program or learn how to shoe a horse. Established in 1984, the SCHP was the first program of its kind in the United States.[9] It was created for the benefit of both horses and humans.

Animal programs can address basic needs that are not often met inside prisons, such as exposure to daylight, access to open space, and contact with other living beings. In her writing on solitary confinement, Lisa Guenther observes that holistic approaches to caring for prisoners require us to think of them not just as humans, but as *human animals*—as whole beings. This shift may also move society toward Kim's ethics of avowal (if only linguistically at first) as we break down the binary of human and animal.

Animal programs inside prisons attend to the basic need for contact and connection with other living beings, without shifting the culture and ideology of prisons. They remain places where it is deemed unsafe to have prisoners develop relationships with other human animals. In this context, nonhuman animals are offered up as both spiritually elevated and sacrificial animals. Research supports the positive effect of relationships between nonhuman animals and prisoners.[10] Media coverage, from newspaper articles to YouTube videos, extols the Second Chances Horse Program as helping prisoners develop discipline, patience, and empathy. The same message echoes: SCHP saves horses *and* prisoners.

Positioned as healers, horses inside prisons serve to reinforce the necessity of the institutions themselves. Articles in the *New York Times* about the SCHP emphasize the function of horses as teachers. Supporters and staff posit that ignored and discarded ex-racehorses engender empathy in the prisoners who learn to take care of them. Prisoners are viewed stereotypically, cast as ideal students for education in empathy because they are without compassion, do not trust, and cannot be trusted.

A representative success story in this kind of coverage is that of Jay Schlei-fer, a former Wallkill inmate, who is now an alcohol and substance abuse counselor with the New York Department of Correctional Services. Schleifer claims, "Working with the horses saved my life.... Around them I could let my guard down. I could be myself. I could also learn from them ... about love, trust and caring. And I also realized how much in common we had. We were all in pretty bad shape and we might have been beaten down, but we were definitely not out. Together, we could all make it."[11]

Schleifer isn't the only prisoner to convey this sense of connection.[12] Many prisoners quoted in these articles observe that they are able to be themselves, and better themselves, with horses. This finding is supported by research on human-animal bonds and is central to the growing field of equine-assisted learning (EAL) and therapy practices.

EAL programs serve many populations. Across these programs, the rhe-toric is consistent: horses are healers; horses are nonjudgmental; horses are mirrors of their environments; horses help humans become better people.[13] Many of theses programs indeed benefit participants. However, these stories can also bear deeply problematic assumptions about race.

During my two-day visit to the SCHP in September 2015, the vocational instructor, Jim Tremper, a tall white man with bright eyes and a warm, gruff voice, was both my research subject and chaperone, hardly leaving my side. When I asked him about his philosophy of working with horses and prison-ers, he told me about his own change of heart. Growing up in rural New York, Tremper had learned that when you wanted a horse to do something, "there wasn't a question." Although the treatment of horses wasn't cruel, a harmonious relationship with the horse wasn't the central goal.

Soon after Tremper became the vocational instructor at the newly founded SCHP, he received a horse-training video in the mail from a man named Monty Roberts. Part of what some call a revolution in horsemanship, Roberts is seen as a practitioner of a new model of horse training called natural horsemanship.[14] Although training methods vary, the defining approach is based on ethology. People work with horses as partners, utiliz-ing paralinguistic techniques that trainers like Roberts have translated from the body language of horses.[15] The core belief that humans should approach horses with the horses' best interest in mind, and with compassion and patience, is important in many equine-assisted learning and equine reha-bilitation centers, including the SCHP.

In her book *Thinking Animals: Why Animal Studies Now?*, Kari Weil investigates the question of knowability across species.[16] How much can humans know about other animals? The poet, philosopher, and animal trainer Vicki Hearne believes that training enables us to begin understanding another being only insofar as we ourselves are willing to be understood. Humans have long pointed to language as the capacity that separates human animals from nonhuman animals and makes humans superior. However, Weil directs us to Hearne's interest in destabilizing hierarchies of knowledge: "Horses stand as rebuke to our knowledge because they seem to know us better than we can ever know them."[17] Natural horsemanship, EAL, and rehabilitation programs echo Hearne's assertion that horses know us. We cannot hide ourselves from them. Weil observes: "We may know animals in ways they cannot—we may know their breeds, their color, their weight, their names, their 'histories'—but they may also know us in ways that we cannot know because they know the world and us by other means."[18] This knowledge by other means (means beyond our human-animal language and systems of knowledge) is a crucial element of the horse-human relationship.

During my visit, the bonds between prisoners and horses were evident: a prisoner slipped into a pasture to identify the horse that had altered his life, and that horse began walking toward the prisoner of his own volition, pushing his nose into the man's hands, expecting and receiving affection.[19] Ex-racehorses, whose fates once depended on how fast they could run, now have a place to live peacefully without physical or psychological stress.

HUMANIZING ANIMALS: TALKING ABOUT RACE, GENDER, AND REDEMPTION

The horses taught me how to love.

NOËL JIMÉNEZ

He is sitting across from me, underneath a black walnut tree. He sits up straight for a few moments, then leans forward, hands on his knees. I begin by asking his name and where he is from: "Noël Jiménez. The Bronx. New York." I ask him how he came to work with the horses and how the work has affected him. He smiles shyly at me, his teeth as white as the teardrop tattoo, under his left eye, is black. He begins to share his story.

Since childhood, people had been telling Noël he needed to control his anger. His family. His friends. Counselors. Other prisoners. He couldn't hear them. However, with the horses it was different. Without spoken language, Noël says, the horses speak clearly: "[The horses] show me, they don't tell me." Noël explained that when people tried talking to him it never stuck. He made a motion with one hand toward his ear, the other hand continuing the motion on the other side of his head. But the first day he came to the

Chance, one of the lead horses at the Second Chances Horse Program,
visits with Noël Jiménez. Photo by Erica Tom.

SCHP, the horses *showed* him. He walked into a pasture: the horses walked
away from him. Noël told Tremper, the instructor, that the horses must have
a problem with him. Tremper asked Noël how he felt. He looked at me as he
recounted his answer: "I'm in prison, how do you think I feel?" Tremper told
him if he wanted to be able to work with the horses, he would need to at
least start talking to the horses. "I asked him for help. I tried to approach
the horses positive. I was going through a lot and I was bringing it out. Talking to them. Waiting for them to come to me. I knew I had to be sincere,
they can hear it from the tone of your voice."

Tremper told him that the horses didn't know what he had done to be in
prison: they only knew how he was being in that moment. This rhetoric constructs the horses as mirrors. Located as instinctual, nonjudgmental, trans-
parent reflections of their environments and the people who interact with
them, horses are unmediated manifestations of "truth."[20]

Noël tells me that the horses changed him for the better. I asked if he
could give me an example. Noël smiled and told me that his sister couldn't
believe how he had changed; she couldn't believe that horses had made his

change possible. He explained, "My sister has had a lot of anger at me . . . for being locked up." And for a long time, he shrugged it off: "You know, like, 'She got issues.'" It wasn't until he saw himself reflected in the horses that he could see what she had been telling him. When he came out to the fields angry, the horses walked away. This allowed him to assess himself, to accept that he needed to make some changes, without feeling the weight of his sister's judgment. Though the horses might have been telling him the same thing as his sister, he could hear them when he could not hear her. Because horses are understood as instinctual, detached from human social issues, their reactions are read as objective and trustworthy. As many practitioners of natural horsemanship and those working in EAL programs claim, horses can't lie.[21] Noël explained that as he talked to the horses, he relaxed and shifted his body language, an aggressive stance falling away for an open one. And one day, Chance, a sociable gelding described by several prisoners as the lead horse, walked over to Noël. He waited patiently, and Chance reached out and touched him. After that, he fell in love with horses. Noël claimed he "changed."

Programs like the SCHP function within the mainstream discourse and ideology that characterizes prisoners as less than human and requires them to "make good." These redemptive narratives require that prisoners identify themselves as lacking empathy and other "human" traits so that they can take advantage of the "opportunity" to demonstrate "value" to society, such as being useful to horses.

These stories do not disrupt prisoner stereotypes. These stories are useful to prisons. Yet these stories also illuminate a basic human-animal need. Noël described how much he came to love the horses and how they showed him how to love. How exactly they showed him this love he couldn't articulate. This seems the case in other prisoners' stories as well; however, it always appears to be clearly connected to the acceptance and affection prisoners receive from the horses. Standing in the pastures with the horses calm under the blue skies, listening to the trees rustle and a splash in the water trough, feeling the warmth of the sun and relief of the breeze, it's a peaceful place; one of the dark bay horses walked over to me, expectant for my hands on his face. I ran my fingers over his eyes where the flies gathered. I felt the feeling I always experience when a horse chooses to share space with me, asks me for affection—*love*. Can you imagine how someone might feel "changed" by the gentle nuzzle of a beautiful thousand-pound animal, whether or not they need changing? Can you imagine how you might feel?

Before I was allowed to enter the SCHP, I had to agree to a long list of rules. Arriving that morning, a question arose that I hadn't thought of before:

I asked if I could shake the hands of the prisoners when I met them. The employee wondered aloud why so many visitors to the prison asked this question; clearly there is anxiety about contact between prisoners and other people, at least on the part of visitors.[22] I was told that there were no strict rules about handshakes. If I wanted to shake hands, and if a prisoner offered his hand, it wasn't a problem.

I was also allowed to take photographs of prisoners if, after sharing with them why I was there to interview them, they signed consents. Most men signed the consents; some men did not. And I was aware that even those who did sign may have done so because they wished to appear cooperative to the staff at the prison. It was a unique opportunity to be with and listen to these men inside this program, so I took advantage of the time to take these photographs—at the time not knowing what would emerge from them. I chose to share these photographs in this chapter, and I have shown them in several educational settings, because of what is visible. They show affection, camaraderie, and love. Images are powerful tools. These images are meant to place a positive, compassionate vision of incarcerated men in the minds of all who view them.

Billy Douglass embraces Boodles, a horse that nearly died of starvation as a foal. Photo by Erica Tom.

These photographs capture the physical contact and intimacy between prisoners and horses. Prisoners lean against the thick torsos of the horses; they run their palms across their muzzles; they rub sleep from the eyes of the horses; they throw their arms around the horses' necks, embracing them. And the horses return these touches. They stand patiently leaning their necks into a hug; they nod their heads up and down against a palm on their foreheads; they nudge the backs of the men for attention; they nose the pockets of prisoners (hoping for a starlight mint, which several men bring from commissary). Reading through articles, listening to videos, parsing interview notes, each time a prisoner says that the horses taught them how to love or made them feel loved, I think of my time observing the prisoners at the Second Chances Horse Program, taking these photographs, and what was captured: the contact and intimacy between horse and human.

Does working with horses, building caring relationships with them, benefit prisoners? Research indicates that it does. Looking beyond prisons, to equine-assisted learning programs that serve people of all ages—whether foster children, CEOs, veterans, or teachers—spending time with horses appears to have a positive impact on just about everyone. What would the United States look like if we stopped supporting the massive prison-industrial complex? What would the United States look like if we prioritized the basic human animal needs of all people—emotional and physical care, access to safe space, light, and socialization—in our health and education systems?

CONCLUSIONS

The instructor and prisoners at the SCHP watch over the health of the fifty-some retired race horses, preparing grain and supplements for the older horses, like Birthday Surprise, a thin bay gelding, who is standing strong at thirty-five years old. At the close of my two-day observation it seemed apparent that whether the horses are physically recovering from a racing injury or emotionally and psychologically healing from abuse, Jim Tremper and the prisoners ensure the horses' health. Unlike other rescues that stress retraining and adoption, with the financial support of the TRF and the cost saved by partnering with the WCF, in the SCHP there isn't a push to repurpose the horses. Thoroughbreds retired from the track and rescued from abandonment, abuse, or starvation can live out their lives in peaceful pastures.

The prisoners walk these pastures in pairs, carrying supplements for the oldest horses, who answer the call of the sound of pouring grain with whinnies. As I observed the health and well-being of the horses, as I watched the men handle the horses with skill and care, as I listened to the stories of the prisoners, I saw the simple joy that emerged in the relationships between the horses and the prisoners. I experienced my own joy in interactions with the prisoners, as I felt they shared genuinely and generously with me.

However, despite the undoubted good that this program creates—giving prisoners access to the outdoors and to contact and intimacy with the horses, and providing a caring home for old, injured, or abused racehorses— it also poses dangers to both horses and humans. The discourse of empathy that emerges in the media, as well as in my fieldwork, can be read as heartwarming stories of men making good. However, in what has been described as the era of the New Jim Crow, to speak of prisoners is implicitly to speak of blackness and of poverty. Michelle Alexander warns us that the "color-blind public consensus" creates a new, invisible caste system through housing policies and legal actions that function together to subjugate nonwhite people, particularly black men. The prison-industrial complex takes part in the making of race. As intersectional analysis has demonstrated, race is bound to class, just as it is bound to species. To be a black man is to be associated with the lower classes and with crime. Alexander asserts, "This process of being made a criminal is, to a large extent, the process of 'becoming' black.'"[23]

When people view my photos and hear the stories these men told me, they ask, "Do you think they were telling you the truth?" This impulse saddens me. Yet it is unsurprising. In mainstream America, images of black- and brown-bodied criminals are normalized as neutral representations of a biological reality instead of a manifestation of institutionalized racism. This colorblindness ignores the fact that contemporary society is entwined with, and is a product of, the deep history of racism. Prisoners, and those framed as lawbreakers, are seen as people who inherently lack the empathy and the desire to contribute to society that are required for decent treatment by society, and specifically by law enforcement. Recent media coverage of the shooting deaths of unarmed black men and the subsequent Black Lives Matter movement belie the claims of a postracial America.[24]

Prisoners like Noël, who claim that horses teach them about love and patience, are acknowledging that they previously lacked love and patience, reinforcing the stereotype that prisoners are incarcerated because they lack these qualities. Such narratives may blind us to the public policies that put a disproportionate number of black and brown men (and poor people) in prison and that make it nearly impossible for them to find employment and retain housing on release, difficulties that put them on a fast track back to incarceration.

With the use of horses in therapy and educational programs, we must also consider that the framing of the horse as a healer can sometimes de-animalize the horse. It may deflect attention from the industries that supply horses to these programs and from the continuing need to better the lives of equines in America. While safety measures were implemented in horse racing after the year 2000, following highly publicized deaths of both horses and humans, the continuing frequency of accidents and injuries indicates the need for further changes. The cooperative nature of the horse should not blind us to seeing it as a full animal being, with complexities, needs, and desires.[25]

Despite the conflation of blackness and criminality that they demonstrate, these prisoners' stories may allow us to develop an expanded and inquiring vision of relationships between humans and other animals. What happens when humans who are incarcerated, whose bodies have only been understood as dangerous and derogatorily "animal," are conceived of as full animal beings with complexities, needs, and desires? What happens when these incarcerated humans are allowed to be outdoors, to experience nature, to touch and be touched by another animals? These stories show how these programs provide the basic need for access to safe, open space, to feel the sunshine and shift of seasons. These stories show how these programs meet the basic need for physical and emotional relationships, the need to feel the intimate connection to another animal being. These stories illuminate the failure of incarceration. The stories show that humans and other animals, beyond the prison walls and the racetrack, are able to thrive in environments where basic needs can be fulfilled.

These programs highlight the importance of talking about prisoners and horses, about humans and other animals, without valuing one above the other. Kim's theoretical intervention in animal studies and American studies encourages ways of thinking about these questions that allow for the avowal of all beings. The academy, the government, the media, and mainstream America still need to find a language of mutuality—a way of talking that can change culture and policies. Yet, as I turn to the stories of these prisoners, it seems that they are already talking about themselves and other animals with an ethics of avowal. Prisoners spoke of connection, of common experiences. Jay Schleifer told me that among the horses, he could let his guard down and be himself. Noël helped prisoners new to the program learn how to care for the horses; he was protective, telling the new participants, "If you're not here to be about the horses, then you shouldn't be here." Even as they struggle in a racist system that diminishes their possibilities for health and happiness, in their stories they avow the lives of their equine companions.

Noël, who has now been released, is grateful to the horses for the change he feels they facilitated in him. Hoping for a chance to stay out of prison, to make good, he also hopes for the well-being of horses. I too hope that Noël has the chance to stay out of prison, but I know that it will require more than hope. I know that it will require more than Noël's desire to "make good." It will require access to safe, open space; it will require the opportunity to develop physical and emotional connections with humans and other animals. Noël's survival in America requires that others see him as a being worthy of care. Our shared survival requires that we recognize one another as human animals—living with regard for, and with, other animals and life on the earth.[26]

Michael Wilkins and Quantity, an ex-racehorse recovering from a broken leg, hang out together across the fence. Photo by Erica Tom.

1 Those in the horse industry use the phrase "kind eye" to describe the expression of a horse thought to exhibit a positive frame of mind and personality.

2 Relatively new evidence suggests that humans may first have domesticated horses for riding as well as for their milk. See Alan K. Outram et al., "The Earliest Horse Harnessing and Milking," *Science* 323, no. 5919 (2009): 1332–35. For more on domestication, codomestication, and the human animal–nonhuman animal relationship, see Edmund Russell, *Evolutionary History: Uniting History and Biology to Understand Life on Earth* (New York: Cambridge University Press, 2011), and Stephen Budiansky, *The Covenant of the Wild: Why Animals Chose Domestication* (New Haven: Yale University Press, 1999).

3 During the Jim Crow era, men of color were ascribed the animal qualities of aggressiveness and menace. The trope of the dangerous black man continues today.

4 Erica Tom and Mira-Lisa Katz, "Pasture Pedagogy: Reflections from the Field on Embodied Learning," in *Moving Ideas: Multimodality and Embodied Learning in Communities and Schools*, ed. Mira-Lisa Katz (New York: Peter Lang, 2013). This article concerns the effect of horse training on my embodied and multimodal approaches to teaching college composition. Working with horses engendered social growth and the breaking of gender norms for a young woman I mentored at a mustang rescue.

5 Claire Jean Kim, *Dangerous Crossings: Race, Species, and Nature in a Multicultural Age* (New York: Cambridge University Press, 2015). In addition, the work of Kari Weil and Natalie Corrinne Hansen has been particularly influential on my thinking concerning race, sex, and species. See Weil, *Thinking Animals: Why Animal Studies Now?* (New York: Columbia University Press, 2012), and Hansen's "Humans, Horses, and Hormones: (Trans)Gendering Cross-Species Relationships," *Women's Studies Quarterly* 36, nos. 3–4 (Fall–Winter 2008): 87–105.

6 Kim, *Dangerous Crossings*, 20, 283.

7 Ibid., 278.

8 See the Thoroughbred Retirement Foundation's website, www.trfinc.org.

9 TRF currently has nine partnerships with correctional facilities across the United States, from Massachusetts to California.

10 For overviews of how companion animals can help humans, see Christian Deaton, "Humanizing Prisons with Animals: A Closer Look at 'Cell Dogs' and Horse Programs in Correctional Institutions," *Journal of Correctional Education* 56, no. 1 (March 2005): 46–62; Sue-Ellen Brown, "The Human-Animal Bond and Self Psychology: Toward a New Understanding," *Society and Animals* 12, no. 1 (2004): 67–86. See also Temple Grandin (with

Catherine Johnson), *How Animals Make Us Human: Creating the Best Life for Animals* (New York: Houghton-Mifflin Harcourt, 2009); Earl O. Strimple, "A History of Prison Inmate-Animal Interaction," *American Behavioral Scientist* 47, no. 1 (2003): 70–78; Froma Walsh, "Human-Animal Bonds, I: The Relational Significance of Companion Animals," *Family Process* 48, no. 4 (December 2009): 462–80.

11 See the Maryland Department of Public Safety and Correctional Services website, www.dpscs.state.md.us/rehabilitation.

12 Mike Wise, "Partners, Horse and Man, in Prison and Pasture," *New York Times*, August 10, 2003; Robert Lipsyte, "Backtalk; It's Not a Winner's Circle by Any Means, but It'll Do," *New York Times*, October 29, 1995. Other *New York Times* articles point to prisoners who have developed deep relationships with horses. Lipsyte describes a prisoner, Rafael Cepeda, feeding an apple to a horse, saying he loves the horse and the horse understands him. Mike Wise writes that Efrain Silva "wept openly in front of his fellow inmates" when he was told that his favorite horse, Creme de la Fete, had been euthanized. Another prisoner Tony Garner, observed: "I'm an ex–drug addict, I had low self-esteem. This makes you feel like someone. Taking care of an animal— they're like children, dependent—brings out your empathy."

13 Other equine-assisted education and therapy programs include the Equine Assisted Growth and Learning Association (www.eagala .org), the Equine Experiential Education (www.e3assoc.org), and the Equine Guided Education Association (https://egeassociation.wordpress .com/about).

14 See Robert M. Miller and Rick Lamb, *A Revolution in Horsemanship and What It Means to Mankind* (Guilford, CT: Lyons Press, 2005).

15 Scholarship has only recently begun to look at the practice of natural horsemanship. See Lynda Birke, "'Learning to Speak Horse': The Culture of 'Natural Horsemanship,'" *Society and Animals* 15 (2007): 217–39.

16 Kari Weil, *Thinking Animals: Why Animal Studies Now?* (New York: Columbia University Press, 2012). In this canonical book in a burgeoning field, Weil engages philosophical questions that form the base of theoretical animal studies. Across literature and art, she considers how "animals are good to think with," invoking thinkers from Jacques Derrida to Donna Haraway, from Vicki Hearne to Giorgio Agamben, and suggests new ways of thinking animals.

17 Weil, *Thinking Animals*, 11.

18 Ibid.

19 From my field notes. Prisoners often show affection by scratching and petting the horses in ways that mimic equine grooming behavior. In *The Mind of the Horse* (Cambridge, MA: Harvard University Press, 2013), Michel-Antoine Leblanc explains that while equine mutual grooming can serve a hygienic function, it is also an important aspect of social relationships.

20   See Miller and Lamb, *A Revolution in Horsemanship*; Erica Tom, "Gender and Power in Narratives of 'Natural Horsemanship': The Production of 'Prey-Identified Masculinity,'" *Humanimalia: A Journal of Human/Animal Interface Studies* 7, no. 1 (Fall 2015).

21   The notion that horses cannot lie is often cited by those working with horses in educational and equine therapy settings as well as equestrians, particularly in the natural horsemanship community. See Chris Irwin (with Bob Weber), *Horses Don't Lie: What Horses Teach Us about Our Natural Capacity for Awareness, Confidence, Courage, and Trust* (New York: Marlowe, 2001).

22   This is perhaps unsurprising given how prisoners and prisons are depicted in the mainstream media: prison films constitute an entire genre.

23   Michelle Alexander, *The New Jim Crow: Mass Incarceration in the Age of Colorblindness* (New York: New Press, 2012), 13, 200.

24   According to Angela Davis, "The term 'prison industrial complex' was introduced by activists and scholars to contest prevailing beliefs that increased levels of crime were the root cause of mounting prison populations. . . . Those who utilize the term prison industrial complex contest that the development of prisons and the push to keep them filled with people is ruled by 'ideologies of racism and the pursuit of profit.'" Angela Davis, *Are Prisons Obsolete?* (New York: Seven Stories Press, 2003), 84.

25   It is also important to acknowledge that this project does not call for the freedom of all horses but rather accepts the subjugated status of the horse in American culture. Further work might call such normalized notions into question, considering the wild horses currently under protection of the government and the potential rewilding of horse populations.

26   Donna Haraway writes about a complex notion of *regard* as active looking: "To have regard for, to see differently, to esteem, to look back, to hold in regard, to hold in seeing, to be touched by another's regard, to heed, to take care of. This kind of regard aims to release and be released in oxymoronic, necessary, autonomy-in-relation." Donna Haraway, *When Species Meet* (Minneapolis: University of Minnesota Press, 2007), 164.

CHAPTER NINE

THE ECOLOGICAL BOUNDARIES OF MEXICAN MIGRANT WOMEN'S LABOR IN EMPALME, SONORA, MEXICO, 1940–1960

ANA ELIZABETH ROSAS

THE structure of the mid-twentieth-century US-Mexico guest worker program, commonly known as the Bracero Program, mobilized Mexican women to migrate throughout Mexico in search of employment opportunities that would make it feasible for them to meet the financial obligations and pressures of raising a family as abandoned heads of household. Many men failed to return from contract labor in the United States. Empalme, Sonora, was one of the Mexican border towns most heavily transited by prospective braceros (contract laborers). Without US or Mexican government protections in place, these women learned to abide by this town's inhumane boundaries for the sake of their families.

In October 1947, Teresa Ramirez, the abandoned wife and mother of four daughters, was among the Mexican women who migrated to Empalme, Sonora, where she worked for eight months selling blankets, pillows, and shoes to laborers awaiting selection for the Bracero Program in Empalme. On returning to her home in San Martin de Hidalgo, Jalisco, she assumed that town residents would be receptive to her because she had sent remittances home throughout her absence and had returned in order to continue to care for and support her family. Instead, her former friends and peers avoided her. Her family was not invited to neighborhood gatherings, and she was forced to wash and iron clothes for lower rates than other women in order to attract business. She recollected that town families did not accept her as "a mother, neighbor, employee, or client. Their rejection was unbearable. Working at this program-selection center town had come at a high price."[1]

Like Ramirez, other abandoned women who asserted new roles as migrant female heads of household were ostracized by residents of their home-towns for migrating to towns with Bracero Program selection centers and laboring among predominantly migrant Mexican men. Such alienation compelled Ramirez to return to Empalme.

The Bracero Program resulted from an agreement between Mexico and the United States to supply Mexican workers to alleviate US labor shortages during World War II. It began on August 6, 1942, and was terminated on December 31, 1964. Through the program, an estimated five million Mexican men were contracted to work on railroads, harvesting crops, and in forestry throughout the United States. The men who participated in this program were separated from their families in Mexico for indefinite periods of time and faced exploitative program conditions and terms.

When the Bracero Program was launched in Mexico, the Mexican government accepted responsibility for managing selection centers for prospective workers in Baja California, Districto Federal, and Veracruz. At these centers, candidates were required to undergo chemical baths, chest X-rays, psychological profiling, and serological tests for venereal disease at the hands of the US Immigration and Naturalization Service (INS), the US Employment Service (USES), and officials of the Mexican and US public health services (MPHS and USPHS). Successful applicants boarded trains bound for agricultural labor camps throughout the US Southwest and Pacific Northwest to undergo yet another selection process at the hands of US agricultural growers' association representatives. The men who passed this second round of selection were issued a temporary contract allowing them to plant and harvest cotton, fruits, and vegetables in the United States.

As demand for braceros in the United States grew, Mexican government officials tactfully reconceptualized the process and the selection sites. By demonstrating successful management of the program selection centers, they hoped to persuade the US government to finance the construction of additional centers throughout Mexico. These would serve the Mexican government's interests by recruiting unemployed Mexican men while keeping those deemed ineligible for the program closer to their hometowns instead of attracting them to overcrowded areas close to the US-Mexico border. Empalme was considered the perfect location for developing a model selection program, a generative example of building boundaries within borders while simultaneously reinforcing those borders. These new boundaries took the form of agreements, attitudes, policies, and rules, sanctioned and enforced by the governments of both nations, to control the employment, migration, parenting, and settlement of women and men throughout Mexico.

The implementation of these boundaries transformed the social worlds, bodies, and spirits of Mexican women and men. Mexican rural and border towns alike became dependent on Mexican women's labor for housekeeping, vending, and caretaking. Transnational labor often required Mexican men to separate from their families and endure unsanitary, unsafe, cramped, and stressful employment and living conditions and exploitative terms of employment. It separated both men and women from their families and deprived them of a healthy day-to-day sociality and quality of life.

The burden fell most heavily on Mexican migrant women. These new boundaries were designed and implemented to orient and discipline their physical existence, employment opportunities, family arrangements, social relationships, living conditions, and, in consequence, their humanity. The welfare and rights of Mexican migrant women were sacrificed for the sake of supplying labor needs and enforcing the US-Mexico border.

Historians of the Mexican American and Mexican immigrant experience during and after World War II have yet to consider how Mexican migrant women negotiated their transition to becoming heads of their households in a system that relied on and reinforced their exploitation and marginalization.[2] As Mae Ngai has shown, the US government's discourse on undocumented Mexican immigrant women's activity in bracero agricultural labor camps characterized them as likely to engage in prostitution and undocumented immigration.[3] This view of these women's experience completely overlooked the full extent of Mexican migrant women's labor, vulnerability, and exposure to the realities of the Bracero Program. Historicizing the gendered conditions and terms of the program, and specifically its operation in the town of Empalme, brings to light the pivotal role of Mexican migrant women's labor and migration in the program. The Mexican government increasingly depended on Mexican women's labor and their accommodation of its new boundaries to offset the emotional, financial, and physical costs of the Bracero Program. These boundaries required Mexican women to accept public scrutiny of and restrictions on where and how they could labor, live, socialize, and raise their families. It transformed many of them into sole heads of household.

My in-depth consideration of Mexican migrant women's experience in Empalme is informed by oral history interviews with these women and their families and government records of the program.[4] Not only did the boundaries established by the Bracero Program shape the experience of Mexican immigrants to the United States, but they also paved the way for much internal and gendered turmoil in Mexico.

A MOST MARGINALIZED MIGRATION

From the inception of the Bracero Program in August 1942, impoverished Mexican women were expected to accommodate their bracero relatives' absence by cooking and selling food, washing and ironing clothing, cleaning homes, and harvesting crops. They were expected to labor fourteen to sixteen hours a day, seven days a week, with very little time to spare to raise their children, care for their elderly parents and grandparents, or tend to their own health and welfare. Laboring simply to keep their families and themselves from starving became commonplace. By March 1944, many women were facing the reality that their bracero relatives had failed to write to them or to return after the expiration of their labor contracts. Thus the program exposed them to the risk of losing what little they had, growing deeper in debt, and seeing their children suffer from malnutrition. Employment opportunities for women without skills had grown scarcer. Women were unwilling to pay other women for products and services they could provide for themselves. The work available was too poorly paid to enable them to support their families: on average, each of these women was responsible for three children and two other adults. As a result, women between the ages of twenty and thirty-four, many of them in charge of households, migrated to program selection-center towns in search of employment.

Some women who did not migrate depended on their parents, in-laws, and extended families to supplement their earnings. Family members felt partly responsible for their female relatives, especially during long-term family separations and bracero negligence. Relatives feared for abandoned women's safety, honor, and reputation and the implications for their own reputation and livelihood.

Mexican women were often discouraged from unaccompanied and unsupervised internal migration because it challenged traditional, gendered family values. These women's independence, mobility, and labor implied that they were living and working in dishonorable conditions without their families' guidance and support. Hence Empalme was a minefield for Mexican migrant women, making them vulnerable simultaneously to the border-enforcement prerogatives of the Mexican and US governments, the advances of migrant men, and exploitation and marginalization at the hands of local women and men.

CONSTRUCTING GEOGRAPHICAL
BOUNDARIES IN EMPALME

The Mexican government capitalized on Empalme's long-standing international role and history to develop a model for managing Mexican immigration to the United States. They failed, however, to anticipate how the Bracero Program would affect Mexican migrant women desperate for wages.

Beginning in 1933, the Mexican government had promoted Empalme as Mexico's gateway to the United States. Although Empalme is approximately one thousand miles from the US border, its railroad system facilitated commerce and transportation from Mexico's interior to the United States. It catered to *cruzadores* (border crossers) as they made their way to their final destination. Its residents were used to working in bars, banks, marketplaces, theaters, and makeshift eateries catering to large groups of itinerant men. Mexican government officials assumed that because the town was equipped with a transportation system and its residents were receptive to travelers, the tide of braceros and women migrants would prove manageable.

In the summer of 1948, Empalme's Bracero Program selection center opened its doors, but it could not accommodate the many thousands of Mexican men who had traveled and crowded into the town to await program selection. Realizing that the town was unprepared to cater for migrants on this scale, the government suspended the center's operation in order to reorganize it.

The influx of migrant men troubled Empalme residents, who resented the construction of Bracero Program selection facilities close to marketplaces and homes. Although they prided themselves on a long history of accommodating *cruzadores*, they protested that prospective braceros were not travelers: they were men who were impoverished and had been unfairly treated. If they grew desperate, they would assault and steal from residents. Residents feared that this migration would lower their quality of life and expose them to the constant and demeaning scrutiny of US program selection-center personnel.

The Mexican government ignored these concerns. It accommodated the Bracero Program through its management of the built environment, local business, employment and rental agreements, and the Bracero Program contract. Candidates could be expected to comply with the program's rules and boundaries, since their livelihood depended on it, but the government also expended considerable energy and resources on enforcing compliance among other migrants and town residents.

Empalme's selection center was divided into areas with distinct purposes, and the surrounding marketplace into separate sectors. An official waiting area adjacent to the selection center's inspection facility housed thousands of prospective braceros registered on municipal recruitment rosters, who awaited program inspection with letters of recommendation in hand.[5] It was important to house these men separately from town residents to determine how many prospective braceros were eligible to fill US labor quotas. Assembled and lined up by hometown, men might wait six to ten hours before being inspected. By placing prospective braceros in this waiting area, Mexican government officials strove to instill order and conformity with their management of this environment and program.[6]

The selection center also contained large areas for conducting mass medical, psychological, and physical examinations. Mexican men were crowded into these rooms, asked to undress, and expected to comply with the English-language instructions and procedures of the US physicians in charge. Then each man was showered with toxic disinfectant chemicals and escorted to a lunch area. After a warm meal, successful candidates were transported to the train station to board trains heading for the United States. Men who did not pass the examination or comply with instructions were escorted out of the selection center and denied a contract.

Other measures were enacted to enforce order in Empalme. Prospective braceros, who often waited for weeks before being admitted to the selection-center facilities, needed food and supplies. The Mexican government allowed resident and migrant women to sell blankets, clothing, food, and drinks in the marketplace outside the selection center. The material needs of the prospective braceros offered abundant but extremely competitive opportunities for vendors. The rules of the marketplace were strict and designed to enforce gender segregation. Women had to wear clean clothes to work every day and could not bring their children. Male relatives or friends were allowed to accompany them only when setting up or storing their stands. The Mexican government opposed visible semblances of family among thousands of men, while the US government sought to maintain clear distinctions between female market vendors and prospective braceros. Stripping families of the right to work together in the marketplace was an integral dimension of the boundaries framing migrants' physical presence, employment, and interactions.

Similar practices applied in other towns with Bracero Program selection centers. The rules transformed the traditional ambiance and dynamics of the surrounding marketplaces. In Empalme, the marketplace was revamped to provide affordable meals to the groups of men awaiting inspection.

Security guards were hired to prevent brawls between prospective braceros, other customers, and female vendors. Protecting female vendors against assault or theft was not a priority: instead, security personnel were ordered to arrest drunk or violent prospective braceros. Violation of marketplace regulations would result in expulsion from the area. The Mexican government enforced a selective and strict sense of spatial awareness and order in and around the selection centers.

Beyond the marketplace, Empalme catered to transient men with bars, brothels, hotels, pool halls, and taverns. Mexican government officials required business owners to pay a registration fee but decided that they did not have the resources or the local support to prosecute the myriad crimes associated with the entertainment sector: instead it simply restricted these trades to an area approximately two miles away from the selection center.

Empalme residents and migrant women felt alienated by these boundaries, which undermined their family relationships and sense of honor. Displaced migrant women had made it far more difficult for locals to earn a living wage. Migrant women working in the marketplace sector worked long shifts under increasingly inhumane conditions for low wages. These women were employed to clean large dining areas and prepare vast quantities of food with inadequate ingredients and supplies. They were expected to work under the scorching sun for hours without a break and often were not paid on time. In addition, customers were suspicious of their intentions and routinely interrogated them about their family background and personal lives. The Mexican government overlooked such declines in the quality of life in Empalme and continued to frame its management of the town's selection-center facilities and sectors as serving the local and national interest.

GENDERED BOUNDARIES

Cristina Rodriguez, a nineteen-year resident and Empalme marketplace vendor, was frustrated with the selection-center security personnel.[7] Rodriguez blamed her marginalization, and the increasingly restrictive and gendered marketplace regulations, on recently arrived migrant women and men. The distribution of women and men without protections against sexual harassment and low wages made it increasingly difficult to abide by the Mexican government's rigorous rules and boundaries. She hoped that the Mexican government would launch a campaign against migrant women's settlement, as she was tired of competing with so many newly arrived women while earning little and encountering substantial government harassment. Rodriguez also resented not being allowed to defend herself or appeal when she and other resident women were accused of criminal activity by selection-center security personnel.

Rodriguez recollected that such boundaries strained her marriage. Her husband was ashamed of her. He and their children helped her prepare and set up her merchandise, but they were not allowed to help her cater to thousands of Mexican men in a competitive marketplace. Her husband's inability to earn enough to enable her to quit and leave Empalme was viewed by town residents as emasculating. He and his wife worked in separate venues to support and educate their children in a local economy transformed by the influx of migrant women and men and the boundaries created to uphold program imperatives.

Jacqueline Mejia, a migrant woman who sold food in the marketplace, complained that to earn a living wage, marketplace vendors had to set up their assigned vending areas by 5:00 a.m. to coincide with the selection center's hours of operation.[8] Mejia opposed working under the rules and terms dictated by the selection center. She feared that people were free to disrespect her and pay as little as they wanted to. Although the Mexican government did not pay her or afford her any protections, she was required to have large orders of food ready for sale to prospective braceros in accordance with selection-center demands. The government justified such management as necessary for meeting US criteria for operating the center.

Mejia was most troubled by the expectation that women vendors should project and inspire order. It was not enough to cater to prospective braceros sixteen hours a day: women had to "look clean and honorable." Selection-center personnel fined "dirty or scantily clad" business managers, cooks, merchants, and vendors working in the adjoining marketplace.[9] The rationale was that women projecting a poor or provocative appearance and demeanor would give rise to sexual attacks and prostitution. Moreover, it was important for the selection center and nearby market to project an air of cleanliness and respectability in order to distinguish it from the lawless entertainment district. Nonetheless, throughout the twenty-two years of the Bracero Program, the government claimed that it did not have the resources to protect women from prospective braceros' sexual harassment. Thus the Mexican government selectively downplayed its authority and power when implementing and facing the consequences of the Bracero Program.

Such policies and practices compelled women and men in Empalme to develop their own gendered hierarchies of belonging. Longtime women residents worked together to protect their livelihoods and autonomy, taking advantage of migrant women trying to do the same. Residents hired recently arrived migrant women to work poorly paid early-morning and late-evening shifts, the times when fellow vendors left to care for their own families.

Maribel Alvarez's experience as a migrant working in Empalme's marketplace reveals how her gendered sense of belonging was contingent on resident women's needs and official boundaries. A group of five vendors pooled their resources and hired her to tend and clean their business premises and homes so that they could get home to cook, clean, and care for their families. Alvarez explained to her relatives that "I had to be very accommodating and overlook much." She was expected to work all types of jobs at all hours of the day for a reasonable wage. She shared with them that she had to settle for "eating a bowl of beans and a few tortillas, but it is worth it." She also stressed the value of her labor to them: "I am sending you a few pesos, so that you can get back on your feet. In our hometown I can't do this, working among our people."[10]

Migrant women in Empalme usually shared apartments in buildings designated specifically for their occupancy. As part of the effort to suppress prostitution, women seeking housing in these buildings had to provide proof of employment and details of their family history. Married women were preferred, as their migration was assumed to be driven by family obligations.

Despite the invasiveness of the apartment rental applications and agreements, migrant women abided by this ecological boundary. It was safer to live in these closely monitored apartment buildings than to live and work in the underground entertainment district, where criminal activity was rarely prosecuted. These women did everything within their power to avoid laboring and living in or near this district.

Despite the restrictions and indignities, female relatives, wives, and widows of braceros continued to migrate to Bracero Program selection-center towns. In October 1950, Victoria Hernandez moved to Empalme because she could not support her daughters and mother working in San Martin de Hidalgo. After working for five years in the marketplace outside the selection center, she brought her daughters to Empalme and settled with them in the town.

Through selling goods in the market and cleaning resident vendors' homes and lots, Hernandez and three other migrant female vendors saved enough to rent a stand in the marketplace. Working longer shifts brought in more money, but not enough for Hernandez to support two households. She missed her daughters badly. Meeting her emotional and financial obligations to them enabled her to persevere under the town's restrictions and regulations.

Additionally, Hernandez's daughters were emotionally alienated and ostracized in their hometown, where residents insisted that even remittances and their grandmother's care would not prevent their eventual migration *pa' el rumbo de los contractados* (to the place where braceros go).[11] She knew that living and working with her daughters by her side and enclosed in Empalme's maze of boundaries would prove difficult, but she believed that it would facilitate a desirable family transition. Negotiating boundaries alongside similarly marginalized women would inspire her daughters to aggressively pursue an education and to learn a well-paid, skilled trade.

On arriving in Empalme, Hernandez's daughters began by sharing a room in a five-story apartment building with two other migrant vendors, attending school with other vendors' children, and helping Hernandez set up and store merchandise. They worked cleaning other vendors' homes on weekends to help their mother pay for their school tuition and send remittances to their grandmother, who was too sick to accompany them. Their teachers, fellow students, and neighbors supported the family. Migrant and resident women who confronted similar challenges for the most part cooperated to avoid drawing negative attention to their family arrangements. After all, Empalme's boundaries, intended to project a sense of order, did not accommodate migrant women or their families on humane terms.

CONCLUSION

The end of the Bracero Program in December 1964 did not deter migrant women from migrating to and resettling in Empalme and other sites of selection centers. Because men still aspired to emigrate to the United States, these towns still had a population of migrant women and men to cater for. Mexican migrant women, many of them heads of households, still sought full-time employment to support their families. Mexican women's undocumented immigration to the United States had also significantly increased.

Ironically, the boundaries of the selection centers also outlived the Bracero Program, particularly those governing the housing and employment of migrant women and, increasingly, their children in Empalme. These boundaries became critical to the development of internal migration and settlement arrangements that energized women to move past depending solely on their migrant relatives and their extended families in their hometowns when facing the consequences of the Bracero Program. However, the migrant women who labored in Empalme's marketplace sector also remember most clearly how these boundaries made it extremely difficult for them and others, especially their children, to move into and out of these towns.

The conceptualization and management of migrant women by the US and Mexican governments did not create humane conditions and terms for these women to labor or raise families, but they did create employment opportunities that, with or without the Bracero Program, offered better options than the poverty and ostracism women faced in their hometowns. Victoria Hernandez recollects that raising her daughters by her side, parenting them wherever possible, was the most responsible response to the rejection and boundaries shaping their lives.[12] Women like Hernandez continued to opt for migration and employment opportunities that enabled them to live and work with their children. These women went to extraordinary lengths to protect their children from the emotional, physical, and economic turmoil of the Bracero Program.

NOTES

1 Author's oral history interview with Teresa Ramirez, Los Angeles, July 2004.
2 Jose Alamillo, *Making Lemonade out of Lemons* (Urbana-Champaign: University of Illinois Press, 2007); Deborah Cohen, *Braceros: Migrant Citizens and Transnational Subjects in the Postwar United States and Mexico* (Chapel Hill: University of North Carolina Press, 2011); David Fitzgerald, *A Nation of Emigrants: How Mexico Manages Its Migration* (Berkeley: University of California, 2009); Ernesto Galarza, *Merchants of Labor: The Mexican Bracero Story; An Account of the Managed Migration of Mexican Farm Workers in California, 1942–1960* (Charlotte, NC: McNally and Loftin, 1964); Juan Ramón García, *Operation Wetback: The Mass Deportation of Mexican Undocumented Workers in 1954* (Westport, CT: Greenwood Press, 1980); Garcia Matt, *A World of Its Own: Race, Labor, and Citrus and the Making of Greater Los Angeles, 1900–1970* (Chapel Hill: University of North Carolina Press, 2003); David G. Gutierrez, *Walls and Mirrors* (Berkeley: University of California Press, 1995); Kelly Lytle Hernandez, *Migra! The History of the U.S. Border Patrol* (Berkeley: University of California Press, 2010); Mae M. Ngai, *Impossible Subjects: Illegal Aliens and the Making of Modern America* (Princeton, NJ: Princeton University Press, 2004); Stephen Pitti, *The Devil in Silicon Valley* (Princeton, NJ: Princeton University Press, 2003); Zaragosa Vargas, *Labor Rights and Civil Rights* (Princeton, NJ: Princeton University Press, 2004).
3 Ngai, *Impossible Subjects*, 136–45.
4 Gonzalo Hurtado, *El manejo de Empalme y el Program Agricola entre México y Los Estados Unidos* (Empalme, Sonora, Mexico: Impresora Publica, 1947).
5 Ibid.

6   Ibid.
7   Author's oral history interview with Cristina Rodriguez, Tulare, California, June 2002.
8   Author's oral history interview with Jacqueline Mejia, Los Angeles, July 2003.
9   Ibid.
10   Author oral history interview with Maribel Alvarez, Los Angeles, July 2003.
11   Author oral history interview with Victoria Hernandez, Los Angeles, July 2003.
12   Author oral history interview with Victoria Hernandez, Los Angeles, June 2002.

PART FOUR

ORGANIZING RACIAL AND ENVIRONMENTAL JUSTICE

CHAPTER TEN

MĀORI OPPOSITION TO FOSSIL FUEL EXTRACTION IN AOTEAROA NEW ZEALAND

ZOLTÁN GROSSMAN

I N most Western countries, Indigenous priorities have been largely ignored or marginalized within white-led environmental movements. But in Aotearoa New Zealand, Māori have gained powerful leadership in the opposition to foreign corporate deep-sea oil exploration. Their resistance has grown primarily through cross-cultural organizing anchored in the power of the 1840 Treaty of Waitangi between Māori and Pākehā (European settlers).

Opponents view deep-sea oil drilling as a threat to fisheries, beaches, tourism, marine mammals, and climate stability and fear that a massive oil spill would overwhelm the country's economy and the government's capacity for cleanup. Despite interest in oil revenues from a few Māori leaders, growing numbers of Māori are beginning to view oil drilling as a challenge to treaty rights and proclaiming that "Aotearoa Is Not for Sale." Indigenous climate-justice activists around the world have increasingly sought to collaborate with non-Native partners, as in the Idle No More and Standing Rock movements, but on their own terms that prioritize their own cultural identities and political self-determination.[1]

I visited Aotearoa for two months in 2015, as part of my study-abroad class "Native Decolonization in the Pacific Rim: From the Northwest to New Zealand" (cotaught with my colleague Kristina Ackley), at the Evergreen State College in Olympia, Washington.[2] We joined fifteen of our undergraduate students, half of them Indigenous, in the journey to visit Māori and Pasifika (Pacific Islander) communities throughout the North Island and to conduct research projects comparing Pacific Northwest treaty rights and tribal sovereignty to the Treaty of Waitangi and Māori self-determination.[3]

I interviewed two dozen North Island Māori and Pākehā involved in the movement in the East Cape, Waikato, Northland, and Auckland regions. My main question was, "How does the Treaty of Waitangi, or Te Tiriti o Waitangi, contribute to collaboration between Māori and Pākehā communities in confronting the fossil fuel industry, and how does this collaboration strengthen the popular understanding of treaty rights as benefiting all New Zealand citizens?"

I was not so much interested in the pros and cons of fossil-fuel development, or the scant Māori support for oil drilling, as in Māori relationships with environmental organizations and the local relationships between Māori and Pākehā neighbors. My recent book *Unlikely Alliances* focuses on similar Native and non-Native rural collaborations in the United States (such as the Cowboy Indian Alliance against the Keystone XL pipeline and Pacific Northwest alliances to stop coal and oil terminals).[4]

New Zealand has recently become an important center in "Blockadia," as Naomi Klein describes places where frontline residents are blocking fossil-fuel development.[5] The Treaty of Waitangi has become a powerful tool to protect the coastal environment, in much the same way that Pacific Northwest treaties help protect salmon habitat. I wanted to learn how the treaty-based resistance contributed to the decisions of giant oil companies to leave Aotearoa.

TREATY WARS AND ENVIRONMENTAL CONFLICT

The 1840 Treaty of Waitangi was signed by Māori rangatira (chiefs) to safeguard their tino rangatiratanga (self-determination) in the face of British colonization. The multiple Māori versions of the treaty retained self-determination and limited the British to kawanatanga (governance), but in the English version, the Crown claimed full sovereignty over the entire country. Even the English version, however, guaranteed Māori chiefs the "full exclusive and undisturbed possession of their Lands and Estates Forests Fisheries and other properties" and never involved the Māori cession of offshore lands.

Only a few years after the treaty signing, settlers began to violate its terms, and the Crown responded to Māori resistance by confiscating the chiefs' lands. As war raged in Taranaki in the early 1860s over British land confiscations, one of the first oil wells in the world (and the first in the British Empire), was drilled on the New Plymouth foreshore in 1865.[6] A century later, in the 1960s and '70s, extensive oil and gas fields were developed onshore and offshore in Taranaki, making the district the New Zealand equivalent of Texas or Alberta. Māori iwi (tribes) and hapū (subtribes) were alarmed by the subsequent contamination and could do little to stop it, but they tried to mitigate the effects by measures such as diverting pipelines from their urupā (cemeteries).[7]

Public awareness of threats to the ocean environment increased in the 1980s, as Greenpeace blockaded French tests of nuclear weapons near the Māori original homeland in Polynesia. The retributive French bombing of the Greenpeace boat *Rainbow Warrior* in Auckland Harbour in 1985 left one person dead.[8] In the same year, the Waitangi Tribunal was empowered to address violations of the treaty since 1840.

Pākehā support for land returns and Māori cultural and language revitalization grew concurrently with environmental consciousness. The Treaty of Waitangi was officially embedded into most environmental legislation. The 1991 Resource Management Act required governments to consult on both onshore and offshore development with tangata whenua (people of the land), meaning that under the treaty Māori have to be informed of any plans in their fishing grounds.[9]

THE FORESHORE AND SEABED ACT

The confluence of Pākehā support for Indigenous rights and environmental protection was severely tested in 2004, when a South Island hapū planned to farm mussels in Marlboroughs Sound. Because the Treaty of Waitangi never ceded ownership of the foreshore and seabed, or tākutaimoana, to the Crown, the Court of Appeals ruled that Māori could seek customary title. The media and the conservative National Party raised hysterical fears that if the Labour government of Helen Clark allowed Māori iwi to assert rights to harvest shellfish, they could also restrict public access to beaches, an integral part of New Zealander (or Kiwi) identity.

In reality, as the Pākehā treaty workers Moea Armstrong and Tim Howard pointed out, the iwi never intended to prevent other Kiwis from having a "picnic at the beach" but sought to protect the beaches and safeguard their own access to them under the Treaty of Waitangi. Armstrong compared Māori title over the area as even benefiting Pākehā, in the same way that hospitals' concessions to create large rooms for visiting Māori whānau (extended families) also benefited Pākehā families. She asserted, "It upsets the mainstream discourse, but if it's good for Māori, it's good for everybody. . . . Māori sovereignty is good for all New Zealanders."[10]

Yet most Pākehā, including many environmentalists, sympathized with the government position, and Helen Clark's Labour government passed the

Foreshore and Seabed Act to unilaterally extend Crown control beyond the tidal line.[11] Māori raised strong objections to what amounted to the largest single land confiscation in their history, even if it was mostly land underwater. A hīkoi (march) of forty thousand people in Wellington involved one-tenth of the entire Māori population, with a handful of Pākehā allies.[12] But they didn't get what they wanted.

In angry response to the act, top Māori leaders left the Labour Party to found the new Māori Party. The government's strategy pitted Māori and Pākehā against each other, appealing to deep settler anxieties, or in the words of Mike Smith, to the "colonial fear of being pushed into the sea . . . sent back in ships."[13] Armstrong saw the government's "massive treaty breach" as an "insidious" strategy "to take it back to us versus them."[14]

So it was a surprise to many Pākehā environmentalists that almost immediately after the act's passage, mining and oil companies began registering to make claims out in the seabed, with the government issuing its first mineral, oil, and gas prospecting permits within two months.[15] The government began to arbitrarily set the twelve-mile territorial limit as the start of a "treaty-free zone." At the same time, the government criminalized climate-justice activists in Taranaki and elsewhere, even targeting them as "terrorists" in 2007 police raids that primarily targeted Tūhoe sovereignty activists.[16]

It quickly became clear to Māori that the government had acquired title to the foreshore and seabed in order for corporations to extract resources (such as iron sands and oil) without allowing Māori either a voice in the process or a cut of the revenue, but most Pākehā did not hear or believe this claim. The government's particularist game of divide and conquer put at risk a universalist Māori-Pākehā defense of the ocean environment from resource extraction.

MINING PRECEDENT

Whatever the government's intentions, Māori and Pākehā began to join in resistance to seabed mining. When Trans-Tasman Resources proposed to dredge the seabed for iron sands off Taranaki in 2005, it encountered fierce opposition.[17] Farther north on the Waikato coast in Raglan, Angeline Greensill of Tainui Hapū ki Whaingaroa shared information with the local Pākehā community that she had acquired in company consultations and called a public meeting on her hapū land (the scene of an iconic 1978 land rights confrontation) to form Kiwis against Seabed Mining (KASM).[18]

According to KASM's president, Phil McCabe, the whole North Island coastal community got behind the opposition, concerned that the sediment

ZOLTÁN GROSSMAN

wastes would harm fishing, surfing, blue whales, and other marine life. In 2014, the Environmental Protection Authority ruled against the project and a similar project off the coast of the South Island. McCabe concluded that "every stretch of coastline is loved and valued" despite differences over control of the seabed, and that Pākehā can effectively defend the coast only in conjunction with Māori.[19] A similar alliance of Māori and Pākehā neighbors later took on the Mangatawhiri coal mine project in North Waikato.[20]

In spring 2010, a new mining conflict erupted when the new National Party government proposed to open high-value conservation estate lands to mining, the equivalent of permitting mining in US national parks. Incensed that their favorite weekend destinations could be polluted by gold mining wastes, as many as forty thousand people marched in Auckland, this time nearly all of them Pākehā environmentalists (including Greenpeace activists) with a handful of Māori allies. Less than two months later, the government backed down on its plans. As Steve Abel of Greenpeace observed, Māori have been "fighting these various struggles . . . for years, and forty thousand Pākehā march . . . and get what they want straight away. Two messages were sent to the Māori community, which were 'make it about the environment, people care about the environment,' and 'get the big environmental NGOs on your side, and you're going to increase the power of what you can do.'"[21]

At exactly the same time, the Deepwater Horizon blowout spilled oil into the Gulf of Mexico. Thousands of vessels and nearly fifty thousand responders were deployed against the eighty-seven-day leak, which was situated too deep to cap quickly. In June 2010, when the New Zealand government began to issue permits to companies to explore for oil in even deeper waters, Māori and Pākehā environmentalists immediately mobilized. In TV news coverage, the first permit signing literally shared the split screen with the Deepwater Horizon disaster. While the existing Taranaki wells were only 125 meters deep, the new permits were for drilling at depths of two thousand to almost three thousand meters, in a country with only three small oil skimmers and several hundred responders to handle a spill. A leak on the scale of Deepwater Horizon would devastate New Zealand's marine-based economy and require decades for recovery.[22]

PETROBRAS

The deep-sea oil conflict provided new opportunities for building cross-cultural alliances and direct action. The first came when a five-year permit was issued to the Brazilian state oil company Petrobras to search for oil in the sprawling Raukumara Basin off East Cape. This is the homeland of Te-Whānau-ā-Apanui, one of the few iwi to still control nearly all of its ancestral territory. As a tribe that had never had their land confiscated, they were little concerned about the Foreshore and Seabed Act until the government granted the oil permit without consulting the iwi (even though New Zealand had just signed the UN Declaration on the Rights of Indigenous Peoples). Iwi leaders told Petrobras it had "no consent" to be in their territory and would be evicted. Apanui counsel Dayle Takitimu recalled that the iwi developed a multipronged strategy, starting with spiritual ceremonies as the "backbone," expanding to political engagement with the government (which quickly failed), legal cases to generate media attention and damage the company's brand, and finally direct action to physically block the seismic survey ships.[23]

Apanui put out a karanga (call) for assistance to other iwi and the global public and were met with silence, except by Greenpeace New Zealand, "the first and only people in this country that put up their hand," according to Takitimu, to stand with the tribe. As a tribe that had always closely guarded its land and been suspicious of outsiders, Apanui felt a "certain amount of trepidation" in working with any non-Māori group.[24] Greenpeace had a mixed reputation in Indigenous circles because of a global history of opposing and then being neutral on Native fur and whale harvests, supporting and then withdrawing from Native environmental justice work in the United States, and, more recently, placing climate action signs on the Nazca sacred site in Peru.[25]

But what happened with Greenpeace New Zealand was quite different. In the 1990s, it had worked in a limited way with Māori on campaigns against toxic chemicals and workplace exposure, although not in a sustained reciprocal relationship.[26] The breakthrough came in the Petrobras battle when Mike Smith, a Māori activist and filmmaker (noted for symbolically chopping down a colonial pine tree on Auckland's One Tree Hill), applied and was hired for a key job at Greenpeace. His only previous exposure to Greenpeace had been to kick their activists out of restricted tribal meetings. Although he was from a northern tribe that was their historical enemy, Apanui trusted Smith because of his reputation, and he served as the "pivotal" link to the Greenpeace "big machine" on the front line.[27]

Takitimu said that Smith was "able to act as the broker or the bridge between Greenpeace and us, interpreter sometimes. . . . He, I suppose, culturally interpreted things for them that they may not have understood." The relationship was not smooth at first, as the tribe made decisions slowly through its intergenerational leadership, and Greenpeace was sometimes too decentralized and hypersensitive to criticism. But the relationship deepened as the confrontation with Petrobras escalated, and Greenpeace helped with communication, media work, data crunching, and a blockade at sea.

When Greenpeace asked Apanui for permission to conduct the blockade, it deferred to tribal leaders to develop protocol for the flotilla that respected tribal tikanga (customs) in the majority-Māori region, such as honoring the rāhui (closure) of the area in case of a drowning in the community and not causing harm on the water (unlike the activist group Sea Shepherd's ramming of boats). Instead of drafting a memorandum of understanding, the two groups decided to have the relationship develop organically, making the Greenpeace activists comfortable with marae (Māori community) culture, and letting "our kids and their kids grow up together on the front line."[28]

In April 2011, the Greenpeace flotilla was greeted with a gathering of six hundred people, the largest such greeting in the region since Captain Cook's 1769 landing.[29] For forty-two days, seven protest vessels and an Apanui fishing boat played a cat-and-mouse game with a Petrobras seismic survey ship, trying to divert it from its required straight course. A New Zealand Navy warship and police special-tactics boat were called in to deal with the protests, in an insult to a tribe that had sent many men to fight in the Māori Battalion of World War II and a reminder of Brazil's military junta history that troubled even Petrobras executives.[30]

The Apanui skipper Elvis Teddy was arrested soon after parking his fishing boat in front of the survey ship in an "expression of mana in our waters." As the tribal leader Rikirangi Gage told the ship, "We won't be moving. We'll be doing some fishing."[31] Apanui used the conflict to build better relationships with nearby Pākehā fishing and tourism businesses and with the neighboring Ngati Porou iwi.[32] Ngati Porou was less unanimous in its opposition to oil exploration, but many remembered that a 2002 oil leak from a ship that ran aground off Gisborne had had residual effects that lasted many years.[33]

As the Petrobras battle raged, the Māori Party did not take a position, and it had become part of the pro–fossil fuel National Party government. New legislation replaced the Foreshore and Seabed Act with the Takutai Moana Act, which declared the seabed to be public space and allowed tangata whenua to prove customary title only within a prescribed time limit and by proving uninterrupted customary use.[34] Some leaders in the Māori Party and Iwi Chairs Forum did not oppose the drilling at the time because they wanted their people to have a share in the revenue. Hone Harawira, a Māori activist who was then a member of Parliament, founded the Mana Movement as an alternative party for Māori who objected to the government's sale of assets to foreign interests, and along with the Green Party, it became a key voice in the resistance to oil drilling.[35]

Opposition to drilling intensified in October 2011, when the ship *Rena* ran aground and leaked near Tauranga, causing a relatively small spill that was the nevertheless the country's worst maritime disaster. In December 2012, Petrobras relinquished its exploration permit, and the anti-oil movement had its first major victory.[36]

The movement left important legacies along the East Coast (Te Tairāwhiti), according to the Ngati Porou educator Tina Ngata, including community projects concerned with renewable energies, food sovereignty, and water monitoring. When the Canadian company TAG Oil proposed natural-gas hydraulic fracturing (fracking) near Gisborne in 2013, a strong alliance developed between local Māori and Pākehā to prevent it.[37] Similar fracking had already contaminated groundwater in Taranaki.[38] According to the Gisborne community organizer Marise Lant, the company withdrew, claiming that it had found only unsafe pockets of gas. The New Zealand Energy Company also relinquished its East Cape onshore permit in 2015.[39] Lant asserted, "We've never given up land. We've always had it, and fought tooth and nail for it. . . . Land is who we are."[40]

ANADARKO

The second front in the deep-sea oil fight expanded the Māori-Pākehā collaboration to the entire country. The focus quickly turned in 2013 to the east coast of the South Island and the Waikato region on the west coast of the North Island, where the Texas-based company Anadarko was granted new permits for seismic testing and drilling by the new energy minister, Simon Bridges (himself Māori). In the South Island town of Kaikoura, with an economy based on ecotourism—particularly whale watching and a seal colony—many saw Anadarko's drilling in the Pegasus Basin as a threat to the environment and their livelihoods. Residents around Dunedin in the Otago region, famous for its penguins, mobilized against drilling in the Canterbury and Great South Basins.[41]

The dominant iwi in the South Island, Ngāi Tahu, had acquired a prominent financial role in the tourism industry through its treaty settlements. The Ngāi Tahu chairman Mark Solomon was moved by a US photojournalist's presentation on the Gulf of Mexico spill and came to view the oil industry plans as a threat. In January 2013, he invited Anadarko and Bridges to attend a consultation and invited the Greenpeace representatives Smith and Abel to sit with him at the meeting.[42] Solomon reported that Anadarko "tried to restrict who we had on the marae. My response was you do not tell the tangata whenua who they have on their marae. . . . They came, incredibly nervous, both the ministry and Anadarko."[43] Steve Abel of Greenpeace recalled that Solomon was "brilliant" in inviting Anadarko to return only so that he could explain to them the Māori concept of kaitiakitanga (guardianship) over the land and sea. Ngāi Tahu had not protested against the company but instead used its authority to withhold its consent.[44]

In order to prevent a repeat of the Petrobras blockade, Bridges declared an "Anadarko Amendment" banning protesters from coming within five hundred meters of an oil-industry vessel and proposed to end public comments on the oil projects. Both moves raised a firestorm of objections that these moves would violate the right to dissent. In May 2013, in "Hands across the Sands" gatherings, thousands of citizens to formed lines on iconic beaches in Kaikoura, Raglan, and other areas to show their support for a clean-energy future.[45]

When Anadarko sent out an exploration ship to drill in the Taranaki Basin off Raglan, Greenpeace sent a flotilla of six boats to confront the vessel, and for five days it defied the Anadarko Amendment without any arrests. Up to five thousand people participated in "Banners on the Beach" protests on West Coast foreshores to support the flotilla.[46] In a repeat of the seabed mining alliance, Angeline Greensill gathered Raglan Māori and Pākehā on the former golf-course land that her mother, Eva Rickard, had recovered twenty years before, where they have now built a campground and kōhanga reo (Māori language preschool). As the kaitiaki (guardian) of the land, the hapū brought to bear its previous experience in defeating TV towers, wind turbines, oyster farms, and other development on its sacred ground.[47] After a flotilla confronted Anadarko's drill ship off the coast of Otago in February 2014, the company ended its drilling, claiming that its tests had not found oil.

STATOIL

The third front in the deep-sea oil conflict brought the fight into the homeland of Māori sovereignty. The Norwegian state oil company Statoil was granted exploration blocks in the Reinga Basin of the Tasman Sea off Northland, the semitropical peninsula northwest of Auckland. Northland (Te Tai Tokerau) was the region where Māori chiefs declared their independence in 1835 and signed the Treaty of Waitangi five years later. Some of its beaches, capes, and islands serve as the sacred "pathway of the dead" on spirits' journey to and beyond the northern tip of Aotearoa. Northland is a heavily Māori region to this day, and its Māori and Pākehā residents have long been neglected in government economic policies, which tend to promote only seasonal tourism.

After Statoil approached hapū rūnanga (councils) in August 2013, a grassroots (or "flax roots") cry quickly went out: "Waiho Papa Moana" (Leave the ocean alone). Māori and Pākehā had worked together on previous environmental challenges, such as mining, prison construction, restoring river flows, opposing an oil refinery, and reaching accords on the comanagement of fisheries. But Māori support for Pākehā-led environmental causes was only rarely reciprocated, and in most areas their social circles tended not to intersect.[48]

By November 2013, 300 hapū representatives met at a marae in Ahipara in the Far North (Te Hiku o Te Ika) and declared unanimous opposition to Statoil and its plans for seismic testing.[49] An Ahipara organizer, Rueben Taipari Porter, said, "It's not just Māori, it's Pākehā that are feeling those emotions that they're not being listened to, that the government is imposing their laws down on us just to shut us down."[50]

Much of the opposition in the Kaitaia area centered on the Transition Town movement, which was planning for a community affected by climate change, and the Far North Environment Centre, where both Pākehā and Māori served on the board.[51] A former board member, Mike Finlayson, observed that farmers and fishermen were joining the opposition to Statoil and that more Pākehā now realized that the Treaty of Waitangi "is a document that would protect" the sea.[52] The center's director, John Kenderdine, asserted, "I'd much rather have Māori in charge of the foreshore and seabed because it would be communally owned."[53] Te Hiku Media in Kaitaia broadcast news and talks by Statoil opponents on TV and radio, in both Māori and English.[54] Taipari saw that Pākehā were starting to value the protocol and tikanga of Māori and in turn offered "beneficial resources, political knowledge, capital, social networks, and social media. . . . We're now decolonizing around the environment."[55]

Throughout 2014, the Greenpeace organizer Mike Smith helped spread the movement from the Far North throughout the homeland of the Ngāpuhi (the country's largest iwi).[56] In November 2014, the Waitangi Tribunal ruled that the tribe had never surrendered its sovereignty to the Crown.[57] The small network was galvanized by three hīkoi against Statoil, from Cape Reinga in the far north to Auckland in September 2014, and to the Waitangi treaty commemorations in February 2014 and 2015, with Pākehā participation.[58] At the end of the 2014 hīkoi, the antimining activist Tim Howard became the first Pākehā to be asked to participate in the pōwhiri (welcome) at Te Tii Marae in Waitangi, telling the audience, "We would like to be the Pākehā you signed the Tiriti with." A talk in the same room by Prime Minister John Key was greeted with Māori protests against oil drilling.[59]

Two Pākehā residents of Herekino, Gary Little and Asta Wistrand, had first joined with Māori residents of Kaitaia who rallied against drug use and sexual abuse in the community and followed their Māori neighbors into opposing the "existential threat" of Statoil. Little had originally favored the Foreshore and Seabed Act, feeling in 2004 that Māori were "going to take away my right to go down to the beach and . . . go fishing. . . . I see things in a different light now, and the Act could have been the start of the erosion of New Zealanders' rights." When Little joined the Statoil resistance, he thought, "I was starting to feel what the colonizers had done to the Māori, that if in some small way I can help to ease that burden, I'll carry this thing through. . . . We were able to get on the wagon that the Māori were driving, and it made us feel good to be there."[60]

The couple were asked to join the two hīkoi to Waitangi, experiencing the tikanga and manākitanga (hospitality) of the marae that hosted them. On one relay of the march, the couple were even asked to carry the Tino Rangatiratanga flag as a symbol of treaty partnership. Wistrand commented, "I don't have a problem with Māori sovereignty. I think they'd probably treat us a whole lot better than the outfit that we've got in Parliament now."[61]

Opponents raised fears of a link between the intense seismic pulses from the survey ships, "like sonic booms," and a series of mysterious whale and dolphin beachings and strandings, and deaths of seals, that occurred along the coastline.[62] The Māori oceangoing waka (canoe) *Haunui* issued a warning to the survey ship *Amazon Warrior* that new oil drilling would exacerbate climate change.[63] In December 2014, protesters at a dozen beaches throughout the country staged "Heads in the Sand" protests to dramatize the government denial of climate change implicit in issuing the oil permits. Statoil resisters used other creative cultural tactics in their campaign, such as an Ahipara reggae festival, to raise awareness.[64] A children's ballet in Kerikeri pulled a huge black tarp over the audience to symbolize the effects of an oil spill on marine life. A Kerikeri organizer, Barbara Belger, observed that cultural approaches "make Pākehā more comfortable in joining all this . . . I compare it to a marriage, if you manage to work through difficulties."[65]

In the beautiful Hokianga Harbour region, the Rawene community organizer Lorene Royal organized an Opononi flotilla protest against Statoil in January 2015. Schoolchildren greeted the hīkoi to Waitangi with a massive haka dance at the ferry landing in her hometown. She had felt the "odd one out" in her own majority-Māori community because most residents were "in survival mode" and affected by "delayed development" in jobs and infrastructure. Her Pākehā friend Ketana Saxon, a treaty worker from Waiotemarama, challenged fellow Pākehā to move beyond treaty workshops and build relationships with Māori through opposing Statoil. They both agreed that the culturally based protests had shifted the anti-oil movement from a Pākehā core to Māori leadership.[66]

The groups also began to connect the Statoil resistance to the growing opposition to the Trans-Pacific Partnership (TPP) Agreement, which they said would threaten New Zealand sovereignty in much the same way that the English version of the Treaty of Waitangi undercut Māori self-determination. A March 2015 anti-TPP rally in Whangarei was opened with karakia (prayer) by a Māori kaumātua (elder) and a Pākehā Christian minister. Taipari, then a Mana Party parliamentary candidate, told the rally that Statoil "didn't know one bloody thing about the North. They barely found their way without GPS. They tell you you're poor, living in a land of scarcity—what a load of crap. We're all from here—Māori and Pākehā—we all chose to live here. Tell them how rich we are."[67]

Catherine Murupaenga-Ikenn, of the Ahipara Komiti Tākutimoana (tasked with protecting the Far North foreshore and seabed) pointed out that kotahitanga (unity) "transcends Māori people. Kotahitanga means that if aliens are coming from outside to Planet Earth . . . you'd all come together, black, white, yellow, whatever, to protect the Earth. So the alien now is Statoil . . . the alien now is climate change." But she added a caution: "This is Aotearoa, this ain't any other country. . . . There was a Tiriti, which we signed in good faith, as an internationally legal binding contract. . . . You cannot walk in front of us, but we really want you to walk beside us. Because we know it's the only way; we're only 15 percent of the population, . . . so we need you as much as you need us. We need each other; that's kotahitanga."[68]

CONVERGENCE

Kotahitanga was in full display on March 29, 2015, when as many as four thousand New Zealanders converged in Auckland to protest a petroleum industry summit promoting oil drilling off Aotearoa. They heard speakers from Greenpeace, KASM, Te-Whānau-ā-Apanui, and the American singer-songwriter Michael Franti.

The protesters brought hundreds of drums that they beat in unison in the canyon-like chasm by the SkyCity event center. The buildings provided a perfect echo chamber for the slow, repetitive drumbeats, evoking the loud

ZOLTÁN GROSSMAN

booms that marine mammals hear during seismic testing for oil. The Big Oil representatives inside the center must have heard the thunderous reverberations, which were intended to make them reflect on possibly becoming the next oil company to be kicked out of New Zealand.

Only eleven years earlier, the streets of New Zealand cities had reverberated with Māori protests that the treaty had been violated and their stewardship of the foreshore and seabed had been extinguished. And five years earlier, a mainly Pākehā crowd had loudly denounced plans for mining. But in this hīkoi, Māori and Pākehā marched and drummed together to protect the ocean and beaches from the harm that had been set in motion by the Crown confiscation of the seabed. This time, they carried signs affirming the power of treaty rights, and of the vitality and resilience of Māori society, to protect the environment for everyone. The protest showed that Māori have retained a distinct parallel identity and leadership within the anti-oil alliance, rather than being subsumed within a non-Native environmental agenda.

Dayle Takitimu observed that "more and more Pākehā New Zealanders have realized everything's for sale, and that probably the Māori or the treaty trump card might be the only thing that stops that as its final hurdle, if you can't reason with the government on other economic or environmental grounds. They're starting to see the treaty relationship and Native worldview as a safety net, whereas before it's always been presented as a threat."[69]

THE STRUGGLE CONTINUES

In May 2015, the Ahipara Komiti Tākutaimoana announced it would bring a Waitangi Tribunal claim to stop deep-sea oil drilling.[70] As New Zealand hosted the official signing of the TPP agreement in February 2016, six Auckland iwi refused to perform the pōwhiri welcome ritual for the TPP delegates.[71] Hundreds of activists blockaded the 2016 oil summit to protest the opening of new exploration blocs by the National Party government.[72] None of the new blocs were located in deep water, a fact that perhaps testified to the pressure placed on the government by the treaty-based alliance of Māori and Pākehā. Statoil finally pulled out of Northland in October 2016, but its seismic survey ship *Amazon Warrior* (which activists nicknamed "The Beast") remained active off the eastern seaboard and Taranaki, where it faced renewed opposition.[73]

The National Party government fell in October 2017, replaced by a coalition of the Labour Party and the populist New Zealand First party, in partnership with the Green Party. The new government, led by Prime Minister

Jacinda Ardern, signaled that "our future is not in fossil fuels."[74] Anadarko pulled out of New Zealand entirely in November 2017.[75] Māori leaders met for a climate change summit in March 2018.[76] The annual oil summit was also blockaded in Wellington.[77]

The change in government may offer new opportunities for protection of the marine environment, in collaboration with coastal Māori.[78] Tony Fala, a Pasifika community activist in Oil-Free Auckland, had predicted in 2015 that more Pākehā "will listen very respectfully because the treaty is part of the consciousness now. . . . It's very much a part of awareness that this is an Earth issue, the treaty is an Earth issue. It's an ecological issue as much as a political and historical one."[79]

NOTES

1   Naomi Klein, "Dancing the World into Being: A Conversation with Idle No More's Leanne Simpson," *Yes!*, March 5, 2013; Jenni Monet, "Climate Justice Meets Racism: This Moment at Standing Rock Was Decades in the Making," *Yes!*, September 16, 2016.

2   "Native Decolonization in the Pacific Rim: From the Northwest to New Zealand," class report and student projects, Evergreen State College, 2015, http://academic.evergreen.edu/g/grossmaz/NZ2015.pdf.

3   This was the second of three classes we have taken to Aotearoa New Zealand between 2011 and 2018.

4   Zoltán Grossman, *Unlikely Alliances: Native Nations and White Communities Join to Defend Rural Lands* (Seattle: University of Washington Press, 2017).

5   Naomi Klein, *This Changes Everything: Capitalism vs. the Climate* (New York: Simon & Schuster, 2014).

6   Sorell Hoskin, "Moturoa Black Gold: 'The Good Oil,'" Puke Ariki, 2004, http://pukeariki.com/Learning-Research/Taranaki-Research-Centre /Taranaki-Stories/Taranaki-Story/id/371/title/moturoa-black-gold-the-good -oil.

7   Interview with Mike Smith and Hinekaa Mako, Auckland, February 18, 2015.

8   David Robie, *Eyes of Fire: The Last Voyage of the Rainbow Warrior* (Auckland: Asia-Pacific Network, 2005).

9   "Resource Management Act 1991," Parliamentary Counsel Office, New Zealand Legislation, www.legislation.govt.nz/act/public/1991/0069/48.0 /DLM230265.html.

10 Interview with Moea Armstrong and Tim Howard, Whangarei, March 11, 2015.

11 "Foreshore and Seabed Act 2004," Parliamentary Counsel Office, New Zealand Legislation, www.legislation.govt.nz/act/public/2004/0093/latest /DLM319839.html.

12 Aroha Harris, *Hīkoi: Forty Years of Māori Protest* (Auckland: Huia Publishers, 2004).

13 Smith and Mako interview.

14 Armstrong and Howard interview.

15 New Zealand Petroleum and Minerals, *Online Exploration Database*, 2015, https://data.nzpam.govt.nz.

16 Matt Rilkoff, "Couple Sure Raids Case Will Collapse," *Taranaki Daily News*, July 9, 2011.

17 Interview with Phil McCabe, Raglan, March 3, 2015.

18 Interview with Angeline Greensill, Raglan, March 4, 2015.

19 McCabe interview.

20 Interview with Jeanette Fitzsimons, former New Zealand Green Party coleader, Auckland, March 4, 2015.

21 Interview with Steve Abel, Auckland, March 12, 2015.

22 Green Party of Aotearoa New Zealand, "Green Party Launches Plan to Protect Our Beaches from Oil Spills," July 27, 2014, https://home.greens.org .nz/press-releases/green-party-launches-plan-protect-our-beaches-oil-spills.

23 Interview with Dayle Takitimu, Auckland, April 7, 2015.

24 Ibid.

25 Cavan Sieczkowski, "Greenpeace Offends Peru with Nazca Lines Stunt," *Huffington Post*, December 12, 2014.

26 Abel interview.

27 Takitimu interview.

28 Ibid.

29 Greenpeace New Zealand, "Deep Sea Oil Campaign Timeline," 2015, www .greenpeace.org.nz/deep-sea-oil-campaign-timeline.

30 Takitimu interview.

31 Greenpeace New Zealand, "Deep Sea Oil Campaign Timeline."

32 Takitimu interview.

33 Interview with Marise Lant, Gisborne, March 21, 2015.

34 "Marine and Coastal Area (Takutai Moana) Act 2011," Parliamentary Counsel Office, New Zealand Legislation, www.legislation.govt.nz/act/public /2011/0003/54.0/DLM3213131.html.

35 Mana Movement, "Environment and Energy Policy," www.mana.org.nz /environment_energy.

36 Greenpeace New Zealand, "Deep Sea Oil Campaign Timeline."

37 Interview with Tina Ngata, Gisborne, March 20, 2015.

38 Climate Justice Taranaki, "Fracking Factsheet," 2012, https:// climatejusticetaranaki.files.wordpress.com/2011/04/cjt-fracking-factsheet -15aug2012.pdf.

39 New Zealand Energy Corporation, "New Zealand Energy Relinquishes East Coast Permit," press release, May 21, 2015.

40 Lant interview.

41 Smith and Mako interview.

42 Abel interview.

43 Kaituhi Mark Revington, "The Risk and Reward of Offshore Mining," Te Rūnanga o Ngāi Tahu, January 22, 2014, http://ngaitahu.iwi.nz/our_stories /risk-reward-offshore-mining.

44 Abel interview.

45 Greenpeace New Zealand, "Deep Sea Oil Campaign Timeline."

46 Bronwen Beechey, "New Zealand: Protests Target Deep Sea Drilling," *Green Left Weekly*, November 25, 2013.

47 Greensill interview.

48 Armstrong and Howard interview.

49 "Taikaha: Indigenous Māori Delegation to Norway from Aotearoa New Zealand," May 2015, www.scribd.com/document/264775353/Taikaha-Briefing -Paper-Norway-Delegation-may2015.

50 Sophie Lowery, "Anti-oil Hīkoi Nearing Waitangi," *3News* report, February 5, 2014.

51 Interview with Pat Davis and Cheryl Toka, Kaitaia, March 9, 2015.

52 Interview with Mike Finlayson, Ahipara, March 9, 2015.

53 Interview with John Kenderdine, Awanui, March 10, 2015.

54 Interview with Ngawai Herewini and Peter-Lucas Jones, Kaitaia, March 10, 2015.

55 Interview with Rueben Taipari Porter, Ahipara, March 9, 2015.

56 Smith and Mako interview.

57 Paul Chapman, "New Zealand's Maori 'Did Not Cede Sovereignty to Britain,'" *Telegraph*, November 14, 2014.

58 Greenpeace New Zealand, "Deep Sea Oil Campaign Timeline."

59 Armstrong and Howard interview.

60 Interview with Gary Little and Asta Wistrand, Herekino, March 9, 2015.

61 Ibid.

62 Mike Dinsdale, "Answers Being Sought for Whale Strandings," *Northern Advocate*, September 18, 2014.

63 Greenpeace New Zealand, "Deep Sea Oil Campaign Timeline."

64 Ibid.

65 Interview with Barbara Belger, Kerikeri, March 10, 2015.

66 Interview with Lorene Royal and Ketana Saxon, Rawene, April 2, 2015.

67 Rueben Taipari Porter, speech to anti-TPPA rally, Whangarei, March 7, 2015.

68 Interview with Catherine Murupaenga-Ikenn at anti-TPPA rally, Whangarei, March 7, 2015.

69 Takitimu interview.

70 Tepara Koti, "Te Ahipara Komiti Tākutaimoana Attempt to Stop Statoil," *Māori Television*, May 22, 2015, www.maoritelevision.com/news/regional/te -ahipara-komiti-takutaimoana-attempt-stop-statoil.

71 Mihingarangi Forbes, "Iwi Refuse to Perform TPP Pōwhiri," *Radio New Zealand News*, February 2, 2016.

72 PMC Editor, "Climate Change Protesters Blockade Oil Summit in Auckland's Sky City," *Asia Pacific Report*, March 21, 2016.

73 "Norwegian Oil Giant Statoil Pulls Out of Northland," *Northland Age*, October 18, 2016; Te Ikaroa, "NZ Maori Opposition to Statoil to Be Discussed at UN," *Scoop*, June 6, 2017.

74 John-Michael Swannix, "No More Petroleum Block Offers?," Newshub, October 21, 2017, www.newshub.co.nz/home/election/2017/10/no-more -petroleum-block-offers.html.

75 Paul McBeth, "Anadarko Pulls Out of Oil Exploration in NZ," *New Zealand Herald*, November 28, 2017.

76 Hui Ahuarangi, "Māori Call for Climate Action," *Scoop*, March 26, 2018.

77 Katarina Williams, Ged Cann, and Hamish Rutherford, "Protesters Blockade Petrol and Gas Exploration Conference in Wellington," *Stuff*, March 27, 2018.

78 James Shaw, "Green Party Announces Plan for Largest-Ever Marine Mammal Sanctuary," Green Party of Aotearoa New Zealand website, August 29, 2017, www.greens.org.nz/news/press-release/green-party-announces-plan-largest -ever-marine-mammal-sanctuary.

79 Interview with Tony Fala, Auckland, March 29, 2015.

CHAPTER ELEVEN

A BRIEF HISTORY OF ASIAN AMERICAN ACTIVISM AND WHY IT MATTERS FOR ENVIRONMENTAL JUSTICE

SUNNY CHAN

A SIAN Americans face multiple stereotypes in the arena of environmental justice activism. Before I began my research, I was hard-pressed to think of any prominent Asian American voices in the environmentalism movement and, through tacit ignorance, I did not really question the common misconception that Asian Americans do not experience the same environmental racism that other, "more disadvantaged" minorities do. Through my research, I found that these assumptions about Asian Americans being neither much interested in nor much affected by environmental injustice are not just harmful stereotypes: they are active falsehoods.

In 2004, the scholar Julie Sze pointed out that Asian American contributions to the environmental justice movement "have not been well documented in the literature, or well recognized by the wider environmental justice community," despite an ostensible mandate for the environmental justice movement to embrace racial diversity.[1] More than thirteen years after her groundbreaking article came out, little more has been written on the subject. Because of the specific historical context of activism by Asian immigrants in America, as well as the environmental racism they continue to face, Asian Americans bring unique approaches to environmental justice. The cultural heritage of Asian Americans is indispensable to the environmental justice movement, and it is vital that their contributions no longer be ignored.

Here I detail the efforts of the Asian Pacific Environmental Network (APEN) to draw attention to and raise awareness about the current work being done by Asian Americans. The documents I analyze from the APEN website have a double textual life, as artifacts in and of themselves and as narratives of actions that lend themselves to close reading.

My decision to choose close reading and literary analysis for studying these works is inspired by the ecocritic Rob Nixon's astute observations about the nexus of environmentalism, oppression, and literature. In *Slow Violence and the Environmentalism of the Poor*, Nixon points out that the harmful effects of problems such as climate change pose a "representational challenge": how to make something visible when its effects are too slow-moving and too diffuse for the unaided human eye to perceive.[2] For Asian Americans, the slow violence of cumulative toxicity is compounded by institutional racism that began centuries ago. Through the narratives embedded in the APEN website, I illuminate not only how Asian Americans have been constructed in understandings of environmental justice but also how they tell their own stories as actors rather than mere objects in the movement. To properly understand the significance of my archival materials, however, we must first situate them in the broader contexts of environmental racism and Asian American history.

ENVIRONMENTAL RACISM AND ITS HISTORY IN AMERICA

The term *environmental racism* emerged in the late 1980s to refer to an issue that dovetailed with the growing environmental justice movement in America. Legal scholars Marianne Lavelle and Marcia Coyle identify a study done by the United Church of Christ (UCC) in 1987 as a landmark in establishing environmental racism as a reality in America.[3] The UCC's Commission for Racial Justice, led by Benjamin F. Chavis Jr., produced *Toxic Wastes and Race in the United States: A National Report on the Racial and Socioeconomic Characteristics of Communities with Hazardous Waste Sites*, which found that a "disproportionate number of racial and ethnic persons residing in communities with commercial hazardous waste facilities is not a random occurrence, but rather a consistent pattern." This report tested the statistical associations not only of toxic-waste dumping sites with the race of nearby residents, but also of the dumping sites with socioeconomic status in the form of mean household income, and the mean value of owner-occupied homes. It found the association between race and dumping sites to be stronger than any other association and calculated that the probability of this association occurring by chance was less than one in ten thousand.[4]

This 1987 report found that three out of every five Black and Hispanic Americans and approximately half of all Asian/Pacific Islanders and

American Indians lived in communities with uncontrolled toxic waste sites.[5] The study looked specifically at *uncontrolled* toxic waste sites. The creation and safe disposal of toxic wastes is itself a significant environmental problem, and it is of course important to look toward better practices that reduce the very production of toxic waste in the first place. However, the situation this study addressed is not a simple case of "not in my backyard," in which nobody wants treatment facilities near them and the dominant group happens to have the power to put them in the neighborhoods of minorities. This is toxic-waste dumping, with no real attempts to control for the resulting health hazards. Although this study was conducted in 1987, APEN has found that Santa Clara County, which has the second largest Asian/Pacific Islander population of all counties in California, still has the largest number of ongoing Superfund sites anywhere in the United States.[6] The attitude that ethnic communities are just as disposable as the toxic waste dumped on them persists to this day.

Following the UCC study, investigators began to discover more sites of undeniable environmental racism. Lavelle and Coyle, in their investigative analysis for the *National Law Journal*, found a striking imbalance between white and minority neighborhoods in the US Environmental Protection Agency's enforcement of environmental laws. In analyzing twenty-eight pollution cases that were brought to prosecution, they found "a 506% disparity in fines under the US Resource Conservation and Recovery Act." The actual fines charged were "306% higher in white than in minority areas, $239,000 compared to $59,429."[7] There is a clear racial component in what Lavelle and Coyle call the "unequal protection" against environmental hazards that white communities experience, often regardless of whether the communities are wealthy or poor. Making a similar reference to the equal protection clause of the US Constitution's Fourteenth Amendment, Robert Bullard incisively argues for a holistic approach to racial justice and environmentalism. The burdens of poor environmental practices are localized to people of color, "yet the benefits are generalized across all segments of society. . . . Over the years, disparities have been created, tolerated, and institutionalized by local, state, and federal action."[8]

Like other researchers before him, Bullard finds that environmental racism is a systemic issue facilitated and maintained by institutional authorities. Historically, resistance against environmental racism also entailed resistance against government and corporate policies. Because activists against environmental racism work in a style different from the more conventional approaches of environmental conservation, it has been easy to overlook their actions as not environmental in scope. The urban planning professor Raquel Pinderhughes states that "African Americans, Latinos, Asians, and Native Americans have long been concerned about environmental issues, but they have conceptualized their concerns as community, labor, economic, health, and civil rights issues rather than as 'environmental' issues."[9] One recent example is the 2010 documentary *A Village Called Versailles*, directed by S. Leo Chiang. It is about the Vietnamese residents of New Orleans East who settled there as refugees in the 1970s. Because the close-knit enclave of about eight thousand people kept to itself and avoided interactions with local government, when Hurricane Katrina hit, their viewpoints were left out of the redevelopment process. When they discovered that the authorities planned to use the area surrounding Versailles as a dumping ground for toxic debris, the Vietnamese American community came together to strike back.

While *A Village Called Versailles* obviously documents the moment of a community's coming into political consciousness, the residents' resistance against racist and classist government and corporate incursion is also a clear example of Asian American contributions to the environmental justice movement. Yet the promotional materials, reviews, and even library categorizations of this film overwhelmingly focus only on its depiction of racial politics: where mentions of environmentalism are present at all, they are secondary.

Largely excluded by mainstream conceptions of environmentalism, minorities have nonetheless found ways to engage in activism in order to address the environmental concerns of their own communities. Being excluded from the mainstream and resorting instead to multiple local actions is a familiar pattern in the history of Asian American civil-rights activism.

THE HISTORY OF ASIAN AMERICAN
ACTIVISM IN AMERICA

Asian Americans bring a long history of strategic resistance to the fight against environmental racism. Since the first large-scale arrival of people from Asia to the United States in the nineteenth century, Asians have been systematically disenfranchised through government policy and legislation such as the 1882 Chinese Exclusion Act, which explicitly rejected Asians from American citizenship despite the reality that their labor and presence were crucial to the country's development. The strategies that Asian Americans developed to protest the state's harmful incursions into their lives, therefore, tended to challenge the status quo rather than work within it.

The famed ethnic studies scholar Gary Okihiro claims that the significance of Asians in America "rests in their opposition to the dominant paradigm, their fight against 'the power,' their efforts to transform, and not simply reform, American society and its structures."[10] Despite stereotypes of Asian immigrants as amenable and servile, both Okihiro and the historian Sucheng Chan document an extensive history of active resistance against an oppressive and exploitative state structure. This history includes the landmark 1903 Oxnard Strike, when the Japanese-Mexican Labor Association joined together for union action on California sugar-beet farms; the Supreme Court cases, such as *Gong Lum v. Rice* (1927), that challenged the exclusion of Asian students from "whites only" public schools; the Japanese American draft resisters in World War II who drew attention to the injustice of internment; and the Third World Movement student protests in the 1960s that led to the establishment of ethnic studies departments in American universities. These alternative approaches to resistance arose out of a history of exclusion from mainstream life.

Although Asian Americans have since asserted their voices in many arenas of public policy, they remain underrepresented in the mainstream environmental movement. For example, in a recent report titled *The State of Diversity in Environmental Organizations*, the noted environmental justice researcher Dorceta E. Taylor surveyed 191 environmental nonprofit organizations, 74 government environmental agencies, and 28 leading environmental grant foundations. She found that no organization with a budget over $1 million has a president who is a member of an ethnic minority and that while Asians hold 19 percent of the science and engineering jobs in America, they hold only 3 percent of the staff positions in conservation organizations.[11] Other prominent forms of mainstream environmental organizing that involve working with existing structures, such as land-acquisition conservancy or political parties, have also not been major sites of Asian American activity for multiple reasons, including a comparatively small population, fewer established legacy funds, and a different historical relationship to private land ownership.

Despite the history of resistance activism I have sketched out above, the most common stereotype of Asian Americans continues to be that of the docile model minority. The persistence of this stereotype is partially a result of racism, but increasing class stratification inside the Asian American community also leads some people to turn away from pan-ethnic solidarity, as the socioeconomic advantages of being accepted as a model minority pragmatically benefit certain classes of Asian Americans. This is not to suggest that class stratification is only a recent phenomenon. As Viet Thanh Nguyen's in-depth analysis of the history of the category of "Asian American" shows, class cleavages have been a source of tension in the community for a very long time.[12] Attitudes toward Asian Americans tend to be generalizing: if some members of the group have a particular characteristic, then all of them must share it. This lack of nuance obviously does not reflect reality. High rates of college graduation and median income in Indian, East Asian, and Filipino Americans compared to other racial groups, including the white majority, demonstrate that there is an extremely wide range of variation among other Asian ethnic groups.[13] Therefore, although Asian Americans may form coalitions based on common experiences, one of those experiences is facing the problem of being seen as a homogeneous group by other parties, including the state when dealing with Asian Americans' environmental needs.

When Asian Americans are treated as a monolithic category that has uniformly attained class benefits, disadvantaged groups within that category are often overlooked for social services. According to Yen Espiritu and Paul Ong, "The welfare state bureaucracy treats all Asian Americans as a single administrative unit in the distribution of economic and political resources."[14] In the case of environmental justice, socioeconomically disadvantaged Asian Americans face the double burden of the troubling statistical truths of environmental racism, as documented by the UCC and subsequent studies, and of a false perception that they need no assistance because they are an advantaged race. Thus, pan-ethnic organizing, which may be cast as being "only" about racial politics, can actually also be about environmental justice, about creating conditions where Asian Americans can recognize the differential effects of environmental racism on members of their community while also organizing pan-ethnically to effect change.

The relationship between the environmental justice movement and the Asian American movement at large can therefore be imagined as a mutually beneficial one. For all the strategies of resistance that Asian Americans have refined over their long history in this country, the environmental justice movement can, in return, provide a rallying call that reestablishes solidarity. This relationship is already readily observable, because Asian Americans have been active in the environmental justice movement since its inception. APEN's online materials showcase the diversity as well as the efficacy of Asian American strategies in the fight against environmental injustice. Recognizing their contributions benefits the environmental movement as a whole.

APEN came into being precisely because of the exclusion of Asian Americans from the mainstream environmental movement. Their underrepresentation was turned into a condition of possibility for unification. APEN was first conceived of during the People of Color Environmental Leadership Summit held in Washington, DC, in 1991, where it was noticed that among six hundred activists of color, fewer than thirty were Asian Americans. Jack Chin, one of the founders and a steering committee member, says that those few people "felt it was imperative we stick together because Pacific Islanders and Asian Americans have not been represented to the degree they should be."[15] The government's disregard of class stratification and of the diversity of environmental needs among Asian Americans means that government policies often do not correspond to working-class Asian American realities, and a lack of Asian Americans in management positions in major mainstream environmental organizations results in representational gaps. APEN therefore continues the nineteenth-century Asian American tradition of working outside established institutions to address the needs of the community, using such techniques as grassroots organizing, pan-ethnic solidarity, strategic political alliances, and litigation.

Officially established in 1993, APEN focuses on the unique needs of the Asian American community in relation to environmental racism. Because of Pacific Rim immigration patterns that have led to a high number of Asians settling in Silicon Valley and the San Francisco Bay Area, APEN began in California, but it has since established chapters in New York and New Jersey as well. Since, as Sze points out, "almost half of the Asian Pacific Islander population has lived in the United States for 20 years or less," language and cultural assimilation barriers are particularly significant among this population.[16] Such barriers leave them vulnerable to exploitation by companies with poor environmental ethics. The journalist and scholar Gwen Shaffer documents the case of a Silicon Valley electronics worker who became alarmed after finally learning the word *toxic* in an English-language class because she realized that for the past two years her desk at work had been right next to a barrel labeled "toxic."[17]

Another issue affecting the Asian American population is overrepresentation in the high-toxicity electronics and garment industries. Assembly workers in Silicon Valley, 43 percent of whom were Asian at the time of Shaffer's inquiry, were exposed to toluene and other solvents used in circuit-board production, which are strongly linked to a higher rate of miscarriages. Similarly, dry-cleaner operators, 60 percent of whom were of Korean descent, were exposed to the carcinogen perchloroethylene. According to the APEN website, in 2002, 53 percent of all textile and apparel workers in the San Francisco Bay Area were Asian women, and 28 percent were "Asian men working under unhealthy conditions due to overcrowding, poor ventilation and lighting, fire hazards, and daily exposure to chemicals such as formaldehyde and other dye preservatives."[18] More recently, two *New York Times* articles have demonstrated that workers in nail salons are regularly exposed to reproductive toxins and carcinogens such as dibutyl phthalate, toluene, and formaldehyde.[19] In New York City, the metropolitan area with by far the largest number of nail salons per capita in America, these workers are overwhelmingly Asian and Hispanic. In addition, 70 to 80 percent of the salons in the city are Korean owned.[20]

APEN works on three levels: direct organizing at the grassroots level for specific community needs, building networks among disparate Asian Pacific Islander populations for pan-ethnic solidarity, and working with various other organizations to effect change at the state and national levels. Examples of each include the Laotian Organizing Project (LOP) in Richmond, California, the Power in Asians Organizing initiative (PAO), and the Asian Pacific American Climate Coalition (APACC). These smaller, more focused groups are all gathered under the parent organization of APEN, which provides guidance, support, publicity, and community access. In addition to organizing, APEN also engages in litigation when it may be more effective than other tactics.

The LOP, which began in 1995, focuses on the effect that the Laotian community can have on their local environment. Members of this project live in neighborhoods surrounded by more than 350 industrial and toxic hazard sites, which expose their home, school, and work environments to dangerous levels of lead, pesticides, and other chemical wastes.[21] Because the majority of the Laotian population are relatively recent immigrants (arriving in the 1970s), the LOP functions in a similar way to the mutual-aid associations started by the first Asian immigrants to America to assist members in navigating language, cultural, and economic obstacles. Since the earliest arrival of Asian immigrants to America, according to Sucheng Chan, "the ability to form associations, along with their repeated efforts to resist oppression, enabled Asians to carve a place for themselves in a host society that did not welcome them."[22] These associations include the Chinese *huiguan* (district associations, eventually amalgamated into the Chinese Six Companies) and clan associations, which provided aid for newcomers—such as temporary lodging, clothing, credit, and letter- and money-sending services—and care of the sick and poor. Similarly, the Japanese immigrants had *kenjinkai* (prefecture associations) as well as a Japanese American trade association, established in 1940. Korean immigrants formed the Chinmok-hoe (Friendship Society) in 1903 and the Kongnip Hyop-hoe (Mutual Assistance Society) in 1905. Asian Indians established the Sikh organization Khalsa Diwan in 1912 and a nonsectarian Hindustani Welfare Reform Society in 1918.[23]

In Richmond, low-income African American, Latino, and Asian residents face the highest environmental hazard risk. The Laotian refugee community is additionally marginalized because of linguistic isolation and lack of access to information and services. Following a major chemical explosion at Chevron's Richmond oil refinery in 1999, it became obvious that many of the area's residents were poorly informed about emergency safety procedures, such as the shelter-in-place protocol. In response to this incident, the LOP campaigned to implement a multilingual emergency phone-alert system. Contra Costa County's first-ever Laotian emergency messages marked the LOP's first major campaign victory.[24] LOP continues to work with members to identify the needs of the Laotian community and provide mutual aid in areas neglected by other organizations.

The sense of community among Asians has been based not only on mutual aid but also on broader experiences of racial struggle. Asian American pan-ethnic organization has always been closely tied to workers' rights and the labor movement, which have in turn been closely tied to industries with high environmental impact. In Hawai'i before World War II, for example, the Hawaiian Sugar Planters' Association (HSPA) upheld a system that exploited both ethnic workers and the environment through corporate agricultural practices. HSPA defeated a strike by Japanese farm workers for higher wages by pitting parts of the community against each other. Having learned from this experience, Japanese and Filipino workers in Honolulu banded together to form a massive coalition. Although HSPA retained control, historians deem the 1920 strike significant because it was one of the first major strikes in America to be based explicitly on a racial affiliation between workers of different national origins.[25] It paved the way for future pan-ethnic alliances in Hawai'i as well as in the continental United States.

Following in this tradition, APEN's Power in Asians Organizing initiative (PAO) was launched in 2002 to bring together various Asian ethnic communities in Oakland, California. Like the LOP, PAO aims at organizing a population that is largely composed of recent immigrants in low-income households. Unlike the Laotian project, however, PAO focuses on strategically uniting several communities with shared challenges to effect change. In the diverse neighborhoods of Oakland, which include large numbers of

Vietnamese, Chinese, Laotians, Cambodians, and Filipinos, PAO uses multilingual services to reach "folks who have not been previously engaged in the civic process."[26] Rather than having one particular leader for their projects, PAO has multiple leaders who speak different languages and can therefore unite different populations who would otherwise find it difficult to form alliances. Once again, the focus is on the rights of those deliberately excluded from the protection of the state: APEN found that the Asian population in Oakland experiences higher than average rates of toxic exposure at work and at home and also lacks access to decision makers.

Fortunately, PAO is not only an example of pan-ethnic organizing but also an example of success. When a semiconductor manufacturer in Oakland called AXT, Inc., was discovered to be knowingly exposing workers to criminally high levels of arsenic from 1998 to 2003, the company fired its workers, 90 percent of whom were Chinese immigrants, and moved the factory to Beijing.[27] When the workers were left to deal with the specter of cancer and without any recourse, PAO drew on the experience of all of its members to help the workers organize and demand a settlement with AXT. They succeeded in establishing a lifetime medical monitoring fund for over two thousand poisoned workers. Although this example may be interpreted by some as primarily a labor dispute, in the broader context I have been sketching out, it is better understood as a clear case of activism to combat environmental racism.

APEN effects change not only locally but also at the state and national levels. APACC is APEN's most recently launched initiative, created "in an effort to ensure that Asian Pacific American communities are at the forefront of advancing solutions to climate change." APACC tries to organize Asian Americans as a swing voting bloc in order to effect changes to government policy as well as to gain more representation in the meetings where these policies are written. APACC strongly supported Assembly Bill 1405 for funding to go to communities affected by climate change, for example, but they were troubled by the absence of Asian American community leaders at the table when defining which communities would need this funding. Based on APEN's own research, they find that "four out of five APA voters in California consider themselves environmentalists."[28] The defining goal for APACC, therefore, is to harness the civil power of a potentially large segment of the population in order to influence climate legislation at the state and eventually the federal level.

In 2010, APACC successfully campaigned to get Asian voters to vote no on Proposition 23, which proposed to indefinitely delay environmental regulations such as greenhouse emission reductions and which was colloquially called the "Dirty Energy Prop" by its opponents. By using a trilingual phone bank, as well as twenty-five thousand pieces of mail in Chinese and English and ads in every major Chinese newspaper in the Los Angeles and Bay areas, APEN was able to achieve a 68 percent turnout rate among the fourteen thousand Chinese voters they identified, and thereby helped to defeat Proposition 23 on November 2, 2010.[29]

APEN also uses litigation in the fight against environmental racism. Since the earliest days of Asian immigration to America, plaintiffs have used lawsuits to challenge both the state and private corporations: between the years 1882 and 1943, when official Chinese exclusion policies were in effect, the *Federal Reporter* records over 1,100 cases involving Chinese plaintiffs or defendants.[30] These legal battles often involved access to resources and a clean and sustainable quality of life, which are arguably environmental justice issues. Nayan Shah's study of San Francisco's historic Chinatown, for example, reveals a common white supremacist belief that "Chinese workers and servants were injecting disease into the white middle-class home," which resulted in "increased vigilance in regulating Chinese work sites and workers" such as Chinese laundries, "the most visible symbol of the Chinese presence in the local economy." In 1886, the Supreme Court case of *Yick Wo v. Hopkins* referenced an 1885 raid in which San Francisco authorities arrested nearly two hundred Chinese laundry workers on the pretext of enforcing "cleanliness." Yick Wo was a laundry proprietor who had received certifications from the health officer and fire warden but was arrested regardless. In response, "the Tung Hing Tong Association, the Chinese laundry guild, hired attorneys to submit a habeas corpus petition to the courts. A parallel case was mounted in the federal courts in the name of Wo Lee on grounds of habeas corpus." The court ultimately ruled in favor of both Yick Wo and Wo Lee, recognizing their arrests as an attempt to give monopolistic power to majority-owned laundry companies through the manipulation of widespread racial anxieties among the white population, which saw Asian immigrants as contaminants. Justice Stanley Matthews ruled that the ordinances were "arbitrarily enforced" to "discriminate against all Chinese operators pursuing their harmless and useful occupation while eighty others who were not Chinese were permitted to carry on the same business under similar conditions."[31] This historical example demonstrates once more the importance of labor collectives in Asian American mutual aid, but, even more important, it shows a disingenuous attempt to use public health and environmental concerns against Asian Americans unjustly. This is another form of environmental racism. True environmental justice involves resisting such forms of discrimination and instead addressing environmental concerns for the protection of all groups equally.

APEN carries on this legacy of legal action. In 2014, it joined with several other environmental groups to file a suit against the energy infrastructure company Kinder Morgan and the Bay Area Air Quality Management District (BAAQMD) to stop trains from carrying highly flammable Bakken crude oil over rails running directly through several Richmond neighborhoods that house tens of thousands of people.[32] The language used by APEN to announce their involvement in the lawsuit emphasizes that APEN does "not take legal action lightly" and joined this lawsuit specifically to support "an ecologically sane and economically just world."[33] Unfortunately, this lawsuit was later dismissed by the San Francisco Superior Court on the grounds that it was filed too late.[34] Nevertheless, as the pioneer generations of Asian Americans have shown, losing court cases in a system stacked against them is not indicative of inaction. Sucheng Chan has argued that there is value in continuously engaging in litigation even when cases are lost, because they are at least keeping the issues alive in current discourse.[35]

APEN's activities show that traditional patterns of Asian American activism are not only still prevalent but also in many cases still effective. All of these efforts and programs are compiled on APEN's website in a in one long, clickable timeline titled "Mission, Vision and History."[36] This visual presentation emphasizes the connection of APEN's activism to the past, with each event forming part of a larger historical narrative. This effect is supplemented by the photograph chosen to accompany this page: an older Asian woman smiles at the baby she is holding, while the baby looks straight into the camera. The passage of time and its consequences are symbolized by this image of an older generation that passes their victories, the lessons they have learned through failure, and the tactics they have accumulated over time on to younger generations.

CONCLUSION

Problems such as global climate change can often feel too big to deal with, causing defeatism before people even begin to act. But the history of Asian American activism shows that fighting local injustices by every available means can be a powerful and effective tactic of resistance. By targeting local, fixable instances of environmental racism in California neighborhoods and across the United States, APEN's cumulative efforts lead to a vital net effect. Sze argues that "Asian immigrant communities have been crucial in expanding definitions of environmentalism and in advancing the legal and community-based activist approaches for environmental justice."[37] Although resistance often inherently opposes the state, all of APEN's actions can also be thought of as expanding the democratic process in a positive way.

As environmental crises become more common and more urgent for reasons such as climate change and the rapid expansion of corporate powers, it becomes ever more necessary to use multiple prongs of attack in the fight against environmental degradation and its effects. The time is ripe to recognize the importance of Asian American activist strategies of resistance, litigation, grassroots direct action, mutual aid, and pan-ethnic solidarity to the environmental justice movement. These are approaches learned from a broader history of social and political exclusion since the days of the earliest Asian immigrants to America. The environmental activism of Asian Americans has been there all along, but operating in the background, below the radar. Their ongoing achievements are not only significant but also proof of the effectiveness of ethnic-specific approaches. These can no longer be ignored if the environmental movement truly wants to address issues that face all communities.

NOTES

1   Julie Sze, "Asian American Activism for Environmental Justice," *Peace Review* 16, no. 2 (2004): 150.

2   Rob Nixon, *Slow Violence and the Environmentalism of the Poor* (Cambridge, MA: Harvard University Press, 2011), 8.

3   Marianne Lavelle and Marcia Coyle, "Unequal Protection: The Racial Divide in Environmental Law," *National Law Journal* 15, no. 3 (1992). 567–88.

4   Benjamin F. Chavis Jr. et al., Commission for Racial Justice, "Toxic Wastes and Race in the United States: A National Report on the Racial and Socioeconomic Characteristics of Communities with Hazardous Waste Sites" (New York: United Church of Christ, 1987), 15.

5   Ibid., xiv. This study used population statistics and racial categories from the US Census Bureau.

6   Asian Pacific Environmental Network, "Environmental Justice and API Issues," http://archive.apen4ej.org/issues_api.htm, last modified 2002. Superfund sites are areas where, under the Comprehensive Environmental Response, Compensation, and Liability Act of 1980 (CERCLA), two main categories of actions have been authorized for cleaning up contamination by hazardous substances. The two categories are removal (designed to address short-term threats to health and environmental safety) and remediation (designed to reduce long-term risks). For more information, see US Environmental Protection Agency, "Superfund," www2.epa.gov/superfund, accessed April 9, 2016.

7   Lavelle and Coyle, "Unequal Protection."

8   Robert D. Bullard, *Unequal Protection: Environmental Justice and Communities of Color* (San Francisco: Sierra Club Books, 1994), xv–xvi.

9   Raquel Pinderhughes, "The Impact of Race on Environmental Quality: An Empirical and Theoretical Discussion," *Sociological Perspectives* 39, no. 2 (1996): 239.

10 Gary Y. Okihiro, *Margins and Mainstreams: Asians in American History and Culture* (Seattle: University of Washington Press, 1994),155.

11 Dorceta E. Taylor, *The State of Diversity in Environmental Organizations: Mainstream NGOs, Foundations, and Government Agencies*, Green 2.0, 2014, http://vaipl.org/wp-content/uploads/2014/10/ExecutiveSummary-Diverse -Green.pdf.

12 Viet Thanh Nguyen, *Race and Resistance: Literature and Politics in Asian America* (New York: Oxford University Press, 2002), 144.

13 C. N. Le, "Socioeconomic Statistics and Demographics," Asian-Nation: The Landscape of Asian America, www.asian-nation.org/demographics.shtml, last modified 2015.

14 Yen Espiritu and Paul Ong, "Class Constraints on Racial Solidarity among Asian Americans," in *The New Asian Immigration in Los Angeles and Global Restructuring*, ed. Paul Ong, Edna Bonacich, and Lucie Cheng (Philadelphia: Temple University Press, 1994), 315.

15 Jack Chin, quoted in Gwen Shaffer, "Asian Americans Organize for Justice," *Environmental Action* 25, no. 4 (1994).

16 Sze, "Asian American Activism," 149.

17 Shaffer, "Asian Americans Organize for Justice."

18 Asian and Pacific Environmental Network, "Environmental Justice & API Issues."

19 Sarah Maslin Nir, "Perfect Nails, Poisoned Workers," *New York Times*, May 8, 2015.

20 Sarah Maslin Nir, "The Price of Nice Nails," *New York Times*, May 7, 2015.

21 Pamela Chiang and Maria Kong, "Fighting Fire with Fire: Lessons from the Laotian Organizing Project's First Campaign," *IssueLab*, June 6, 2001, www .issuelab.org/resource/fighting_fire_with_fire_lessons_from_the_laotian _organizing_projects_first_campaign.

22 Sucheng Chan, *Asian Americans: An Interpretive History* (Boston: Twayne Publishers, 1991), 63.

23 Ibid., 75.

24 Benjamin Pimentel, " Multilanguage Warning System: Contra Costa Will Expand Telephone Disaster Alerts," *San Francisco Chronicle*, September 29, 1999.

25 Chan, *Asian Americans*, 86. See also Huping Ling and Allan W. Austin, *Asian American History and Culture: An Encyclopedia* (New York: Routledge, 2015), 259; Edward D. Beechert, *Working in Hawaii: A Labor*

History (Honolulu: University of Hawaii Press, 1985), 196–202; and Masayo Umezawa Duus, *The Japanese Conspiracy: The Oahu Sugar Strike of 1920* (Berkeley: University of California Press, 1999).

26 Asian Pacific Environmental Network, "Direct Organizing: Power in Asians Organizing," http://archive.apen4ej.org/organize_pao.htm, last modified 2008.

27 Chris Thompson, "Biting the Hand That Poisoned Them," *East Bay Express*, September 7, 2005.

28 Asian Pacific Environmental Network, "Asian Pacific American Climate Coalition," http://archive.apen4ej.org/movement_api.htm, last modified 2010.

29 Asian Pacific Environmental Network, "Civic Engagement," http://apen4ej .org/what-we-do/civic-engagement, last modified 2014.

30 The number of cases was counted by Sucheng Chan and reported in *Asian Americans*, 90. The *Federal Reporter* is an American case law reporter, a series of books containing judicial opinions from a selection of courts. During this time frame, the *Federal Reporter* covered decisions from the Commerce Court of the United States (abolished 1913), Court of Appeals of the District of Columbia, the Court of Claims, United States circuit courts (abolished 1912), United States courts of appeals, and United States district courts. Because this is not a complete list of courts in the United States, this count likely underestimates the actual total number of cases.

31 Nayan Shah, *Contagious Divides: Epidemics and Race in San Francisco's Chinatown* (Berkeley: University of California Press, 2001), 64, 65.

32 Christin Ayers, "Lawsuit Filed over Fracked Oil Trains in the Bay Area after KPIX 5 Report," *CBS SF Bay Area*, March 28, 2014, http://sanfrancisco .cbslocal.com/2014/03/28/lawsuit-filed-over-fracked-oil-trains-in-the-bay -area-after-kpix-5-report.

33 Asian Pacific Environmental Network, "Challenging Crude-by-Rail," http://apen4ej.org/challenging-crude-by-rail, last modified 2014.

34 Joshua Chin, "Lawsuit Seeking to Stop Rail Shipments of Bakken Crude Oil Dismissed," *Richmond Confidential*, September 11, 2014.

35 Chan, *Asian Americans*, 100.

36 Asian Pacific Environmental Network, "Mission, Vision & History," http://apen4ej.org/who-we-are/mission-and-vision, last modified 2014.

37 Sze, "Asian American Activism," 149.

CHAPTER TWELVE

"ES UNA LUCHA DOBLE"

Articulating Environmental Nationalism in Puerto Rico

CATALINA MAÍRE DE ONÍS

T HE Vía Verde (Green Way) gas pipeline signals both the presence of energy colonialism and the power of progressive, grassroots mobilizing. Defeated in 2012, the one-hundred-mile-long *gasoducto* would have stretched across Puerto Rico's Big Island (three times the size of Rhode Island), threatening endangered species, heritage sites, and human health, as well as furthering dependency on imported fossil fuels.[1] News accounts characterized the project and opposition to it as "el próximo Vieques" (the next Vieques). In leading protests against Vía Verde, the community organization Casa Pueblo was careful to avoid presenting the campaign as one motivated by political sovereignty, given the divisive disagreements over Puerto Rico's status as a US unincorporated territory, which many claim positions the archipelago as a de facto colony. Instead, the group framed its organizing efforts using a strong environmental nationalism that emphasized the preservation of Puerto Rican culture and land. This strategy effectively mobilized large numbers of Puerto Ricans throughout the archipelago and in the contiguous United States, who rejected the dystopian present and future that the pipeline represented.[2]

Known as the Isla del Encanto (Island of Enchantment), Puerto Rico is touted in dominant colonial discourses as a tropical paradise. While the archipelago indeed boasts much beauty, it also is burdened with interrelated economic and ecological crises. The utopian mirage of an enchanted island archipelago quickly dissolves when one considers the quotidian realities facing Boricuas (Puerto Ricans), including a $73 billion debt crisis and the imposition of a nondemocratically selected fiscal control board to "manage" this financial debacle.[3] In fall 2017, Hurricanes Irma and Maria ravaged the archipelago's already weakened infrastructure, leaving millions without power and access to potable water for months, among numerous other life-threatening problems.[4] After more than five hundred years of colonial rule, Puerto Rico's inhabitants and their environments continue to experience the repercussions of racist, heteropatriarchal logics of domination. Often in collaboration, the US government and corporations and local political elites have promulgated detrimental discourses, programs, and policies.[5] It is unsurprising, then, that many environmental activists consider confrontations with both the US hegemon and their local government as *una lucha doble* (a double struggle).[6] Additional dualities are visible in intersecting colonial and environmental injustices and the ways environmental organizing in Puerto Rico finds its roots in pro-independence histories and ideology.[7]

In this chapter, I draw from personal interviews and archival materials to examine links between Puerto Rican environmentalism and nationalism(s).[8] Jorge Duany writes that political nationalism is "based on the doctrine that every people should have its own sovereign government," while cultural nationalism is "based on the assertion of the moral and spiritual autonomy of each people."[9] Ana Ramos-Zayas and Darrel Wanzer-Serrano examine "the interstitial space and dialectical tension between political nationalism and cultural nationalism" in Puerto Rican communities in Chicago and New York City respectively.[10] In a different context, I document how these nationalisms and the "interstitial space" between them are mobilized by movement actors in Puerto Rico with an environmental emphasis.

Linking environmentalism and nationalisms must be approached cautiously, however. Struggles for political sovereignty in Puerto Rico have failed to galvanize widespread support for independence, even as anticolonialism is common and manifest in cultural symbols and performances. The reasons for this seeming contradiction are multiple and complex. They can be partly attributed to the limitations of the territory's dominant form of political nationalism.[11] According to Duany, "Puerto Rican nationalism throughout the twentieth century has been characterized by Hispanophilia, anti-Americanism, racism, androcentrism, homophobia, and more recently xenophobia—as well as a more positive attempt to define and uphold local values and customs."[12] In particular, Eurocentric discourses suggesting that racial mixing (*mestizaje*) in Puerto Rico has led to an absence or minimization of racism have functioned to advance white supremacy and antiblackness.[13] These oppressive tendencies point to the importance of engaging different articulations of nationalism in specific contexts to study the extent to which they enable and constrain self-determined, livable lives—and for whom.

I focus on the ways nationalisms are linked to environmental struggles and how these connections might bridge divisions arising from Puerto Rico's status. Environmental nationalism carries the potential to mobilize Puerto Ricans who have different political commitments and live in different locations (including the contiguous United States and the Caribbean) by appropriating and eclipsing political nationalism. Celebrating and defending Puerto Rican culture and heritage as a component of environmental struggles can foster the creation of more sustainable communities. Since, in the words of Manuel Valdés Pizzini, "assess[ing] the growth and development of the environmental movement in Puerto Rico [is difficult] due to a lack of sociological analysis," I detail the ways in which racism and discourses of putative colonial benevolence and docility have been used to oppress Puerto Ricans and advance proindustrial and development programs and projects.[14] Highlighting the concept of *strategic eclipse,* which draws on Phaedra C. Pezzullo's theorizing on how different articulatory elements interact, I show how various Puerto Rican activist discourses employ anticolonial ideology and national symbols to refuse environmental exploitation by linking environmentalism and cultural nationalism.[15] My focus on strategic eclipse offers a theoretical concept and tactical resource for environmental, climate, and energy justice struggles in Puerto Rico and elsewhere.

COLONIZING PUERTO RICO

Puerto Ricans exist in a legal limbo as the "United States' first and only citizen-immigrants." In 1917, following two decades of judicial ambivalence, the Jones Act was signed into law, "granting broader governing powers to a new Puerto Rican legislature and conferring US citizenship on all Puerto Ricans." Part of the reason for the long delay in this decision was overt judicial racism that considered locals an inferior "mongrel" race. Some Puerto Ricans opposed citizenship because they believed it would place the region under tighter US control and infringe on Puerto Rico's capacity for self-government. This "Puerto Rican problem" revealed a tension in supposedly US democratic values: how could the so-called "land of the free" deny its colonial possession sovereignty and liberation?[16] Despite this contradiction, since 1898 to the present, the United States has maintained a stranglehold on Puerto Rico's people and the environments in which they live.

Puerto Rico has experienced substantial environmental exploitation, including environmental degradation and environmental racism, because of its colonial status.[17] For four centuries, Spain practiced resource colonialism. After the US takeover following the Spanish-American War and the

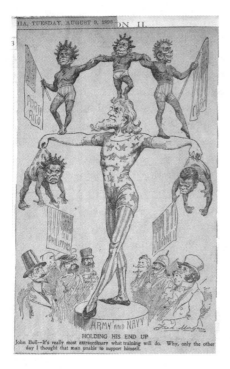

HOLDING HIS END UP

John Bull—It's really most extraordinary what training will do. Why, only the other day I thought that man unable to support himself.

Cartoon from *Philadelphia Inquirer*, 1898, depicting the putative inferiority of Puerto Rico and other US colonies maintained by the benevolent, generous, and powerful Uncle Sam and imposing the Anglicized spelling "Porto Rico."

Treaty of Paris in 1898, the US government and corporations drained Puerto Rico's wetlands to make areas "productive" for growth and construction and deforested much of the Big Island.[18] From 1898 to the early 1930s, Puerto Rico experienced the rise and demise of its sugarcane industry. On the heels of these ecological and economic disruptions came Operation Bootstrap, an industrialization program that dramatically and rapidly transformed the landscape.[19]

Following World War II, the US and Puerto Rican governments directed the Bootstrap initiative by encouraging migration to coastal areas, initiating a shift from rural, agrarian lifestyles to urban factory work. This effort paved the way for heavy industrialization and fossil-fuel consumption. While these rapid changes created some employment opportunities, few long-term jobs resulted.[20] The program was fueled by economic incentives for US companies, including tax exemptions, cheap labor, and "free" access to natural resources.[21] As Carmen Concepción notes, "The growth of capital intensive industries led to an even greater US control over the island's economy."[22] This physical and fiscal corporate invasion positioned Puerto Rico as a sacrifice zone for US expansionist projects and capitalism.

Colonial discourses of racial inferiority have legitimized and normalized the frequent siting of toxic chemical sites and fossil-fuel industries throughout Puerto Rico. During an interview, the lawyer and community activist Ruth Santiago noted that various US discourses have characterized Puerto Ricans as "any negative pejorative you can think of."[23] When discussing the relationship between the United States and Puerto Rico, Santiago remarked that the racist myth of Boricua docility and inferiority has resulted in resignation among some community members who, after nearly 120 years of US control, sometimes accept and reinscribe ideologies of colonial dependency. Nonetheless, Santiago and many of her neighbors have tenaciously resisted colonial oppression, often by organizing at the intersection of environmental and anticolonial concerns.

ARTICULATING ENVIRONMENTAL NATIONALISM

Colonialism is inextricably entwined with environmental degradation and global climate disruption. Perhaps not surprisingly, in Latin America and the Caribbean, green activism finds its "deepest roots . . . [in] resistance to conquest."[24] Many environmental and community organizations have worked to cultivate a sense of environmental nationalism that has led to coalitions among progressive and pro-independence organizations.[25] For example, the Vanguardia Popular and the Movimiento Pro Independencia (MPI) played a pivotal role in the 1960s antimining struggles in Adjuntas, Lares, and Utuado.[26] These groups are credited with imbuing nationalist movements with an environmental consciousness, as evidenced by MPI members' insistence that mining was "la colonización del subsuelo" (the colonization of the subsurface).[27] This recognition persisted in future decades: during the 1980s, as Barbara Lynch observes, "leading environmentalists in Puerto Rico linked environmental destruction and North American colonization and aligned themselves with the movement to declare independence from the United States."[28] Thus Puerto Rico's environmental and independence movements are, in many respects, co-constitutive.

These decades-long struggles exhibit several legal and political complexities that distinguish Puerto Rico from many other Western Hemisphere contexts. It is one thing to encounter interconnected environmental and colonial concerns in sovereign nations, as "culture, labor, intersubjective relations, and knowledge production [operate and control] well beyond the strict limits of colonial administrations."[29] It is an entirely different matter to consider the realities confronted by a territory under colonial rule. Engaging ecological challenges in Puerto Rico is especially complicated because

US legal codes (e.g., President Bill Clinton's 1994 environmental justice executive order and the 1920 Merchant Marine Act), federal agencies (such as the Department of Natural Resources and the Environmental Quality Board), and other factors and entities both help and hinder environmental, climate, and energy justice. Puerto Rico's political entanglement with the United States calls for tenacity and creativity on the part of movement actors.[30]

THEORIZING STRATEGIC ECLIPSE

The linkage of environmentalism and nationalisms and the movements associated with them offer insights for understanding and deploying different elements that can result in an eclipse effect—an interaction that partially or completely dims one element while illuminating the other. Pezzullo observes, for example, that in two Hollywood films (*A Civil Action* and *Erin Brockovich*) starring "sexy" actors who resist toxic corporate practices, sexiness eclipses environmental activism. "The linking of environmentalism with sexy stars brings increased attention," she notes, "but does it help or harm environmental efforts to be associated with what or who is sexy?" This articulatory effect of "outshining" moves Pezzullo to encourage scholars to critically examine the pitfalls and possibilities of such connections by being more specific "about the nature of the linkages we are studying."[31]

When linked together, environmentalism and nationalism(s) undergo transformations, suggesting that the eclipsing of one of the two elements need not always prove debilitating to progressive politics, given the importance of context. Environmentalism can link with cultural nationalism to dim political nationalism. Such a strategic move can enable interventions that resist exploitative logics, practices, and policies, regardless of whether individual actors support political independence, environmental advocacy, or both.

PRACTICING STRATEGIC ECLIPSE

In interviews, community activists frequently expressed their concerns for Puerto Rico's present and future by associating environmentalism with anticolonial advocacy. For example, Juan Rosario, a community leader and, at the time, a public energy utility board member, described his pro-independence convictions and his membership in Puerto Rico's oldest environmental organization, Misión Industrial.[32] Rosario insisted that

Puerto Ricans must struggle for independence. He also lamented that as the US mainstream environmental movement grew in the 1970s, Puerto Rican environmentalists became steadily less interested in connecting struggles to political sovereignty. He claimed that environmentalism on the Big Island now focuses more on depoliticized conservation issues than on resisting US corporate and government influence and their negative environmental effects. Thus, as environmental concerns eclipse political nationalism, less importance is placed on recognizing and uprooting logics of domination that undergird both anticolonial and environmental struggles. According to Rosario, groups like the Sierra Club have deprived Boricuas of control over their own problems. Expressing his pro-independence stance, he asserted: "I'm an environmentalist, but I'm a Puerto Rican first."

Unlike Rosario, the local Sierra Club chapter representative, Adriana González, supports the US organization's presence on the Big Island. She acknowledged, however, that the involvement of the US organization sometimes can create problems because of a lack of place-specific understanding. She explained: "I think the political status affects everything overall, and on the environmental side I would say it affects . . . how we value things here. People [from the United States] would think . . . less of Puerto Rico sometimes . . . just because either we aren't independent, or we're not represented on another thing. . . . We are ruled by a lot of the laws in the US. That is a big country with another type of resources, another type of wildlife, and a lot of the approaches that we have come from the US. . . . When we look at how we manage our landscape, it's totally different."[33]

González's statement points to the complexities posed by the US–Puerto Rico relationship and its detrimental effects on environmental advocacy, given the inability of some organizations, institutions, and individuals to adjust US mainland approaches and epistemologies to island geographies, Caribbean species, transnational environmental struggles, and Latin American culture and history.

While both Rosario and González draw on anticolonialism and environmentalism in articulating their positions, what distinguishes their remarks is how they believe these two elements function, or should function, in practice. Rosario foregrounds political nationalism, while González advocates for a differentiated approach to environmental organizing without arguing for the necessity of political independence.

Despite these intricacies and tensions, environmental nationalism has facilitated several grassroots victories in Puerto Rico, including the defeat of Vía Verde. The participation of diverse campaign actors, including US lawmakers and community members on and off the Big Island, exemplifies how the Puerto Rican nation transcends geopolitical borders.

Casting the greenwashed pipeline as a menace to healthy communities, activists resisted its associations with life, "green," and progress by calling it the "Vía de la Muerte" (Death Route). This rhetorical move is similar to the way Dakota Access Pipeline opponents shifted the colonial narrative by self-identifying as water protectors rather than protesters. In both cases, this reframing helped create broad-based coalitions for resisting these pipeline projects. As one study of the Vía Verde campaign observes, "The decision to organize the march against the pipeline in 2010 on May Day alongside labor unions powerfully reworked the common sense of the pipeline as an exclusively environmental issue, making it also about the perversity of capital accumulation strategies hidden as false solutions to the country's energy problems, and the implications for working class families."[34] By pointing out the project's multiple threats, including economic and environmental precariousness, Casa Pueblo members garnered greater support for their cause.

Alexis Massol-González, the founder of Casa Pueblo and winner of the 2002 Goldman Environmental Prize, insisted that Vía Verde's defeat was essential to protecting Puerto Rican culture and survival. Despite his decades of activist work, it was not until the proposed *gasoducto* protests that Massol-González engaged in civil disobedience, which led to his arrest at the White House with several other activists. He explained: " Nuestra lucha fue contra el gasoducto ... por el derecho a la vida, por la justicia a los pobres, en contra de la corrupción, y allí van todos los argumentos, incluyendo el ambiental. El ambiental está allí" (Our struggle was against the pipeline ... for the right to life, for justice for the poor, against corruption, and there go all the arguments, including the environmental argument, the environmental argument is there).[35] By describing Vía Verde as a threat to life and justice for the poor, instead of presenting a narrower environmental agenda separated from social considerations, he resists importing US mainstream environmentalism and instead advances an environmental justice perspective with a commitment to "liberty, solidarity, love, and dignity," as he expressed in an interview. Furthermore, Massol-González explained, he does not self-identify as an environmentalist, given his dislike for *etiquetas* (labels) that reduce complex, interlocking struggles to one dimension.

Massol-González's perspective resonates with his pro-independence ideology. Visitors at Casa Pueblo's headquarters, a spacious, bright pink home

Alexis Massol-González leads an anti-*gasoducto* march in Adjuntas, Puerto Rico, May 1, 2011. The banner reads: "The people already decided. No to the pipeline. Yes to forests, waters, and our people." Although the scene boasts several Puerto Rican flags, the US flag is absent. Source: Julissa Zoé Corporán.

in the mountainous region of Adjuntas, are greeted by paintings of three Puerto Rican independence movement leaders. Despite these visual representations of the group's political allegiances, Casa Pueblo members have learned to tone down their enthusiasm for political nationalism by emphasizing the importance of celebrating and preserving Puerto Rican culture. Decades ago, very poor attendance at the nonprofit's first event "led them to rethink their strategy. . . . They mobilized cultural ties to the territory through traditional music, dance, food, kite flying, reforestation activities and display of large banners showing the damage mining would cause to the landscape."[36]

The group's strategic shift to environmental nationalism persists today. On Casa Pueblo's gift-shop bags, decorated by community youth, statements such as "Amor para la patria" (Love for the country), "Historia para Puerto Rico" (History for Puerto Rico), and the presence of the Puerto Rican flag point to the interstices between political and cultural nationalism. Rather than place the Puerto Rican flag alongside the US flag, which is the typical pairing at many government buildings and monuments, the emblem of Puerto Rican nationhood appears alone (see the photo on the next page). The Puerto Rican flag carries connotations of both cultural pride and political resistance. US nation building in Puerto Rico has sought to control this symbol, perhaps most infamously in the 1948 Ley de la Mordaza (gag law). This legislation banned Puerto Rican cultural symbols to deter the leftist independence movement. Anyone caught waving a Puerto Rican flag, singing Puerto Rican songs, or performing other, similar acts risked up to ten years of imprisonment and high fines.[37] Although this draconian law was repealed in 1957, pro-independence and environmental activists are still often subject to heavy surveillance and punishment in Puerto Rico.[38]

In Casa Pueblo's grassroots guidebook, Massol-González and several coauthors, including his partner, Tinti Deyá Díaz, and son, Arturo Massol-Deyá, offer several organizing best practices:

- Know what you're fighting about.
- Develop solid arguments based on good research.
- Prepare the community to take the lead in the process.
- Stay away from partisan politics.
- Keep a steady hand at the wheel.[39]

The reference to eschewing partisan politics is explained in the section of the handbook describing the organization's successful defeat of open-pit mining by US extractive companies: "Given the highly partisan nature of Puerto Rican society, by staying away from politics Casa Pueblo not only avoided having the movement co-opted for other purposes, but was able to attract a widening circle of supporters from across the political spectrum, something that had proven difficult at the start."[40]

Decades later, Casa Pueblo continues to avoid party politics. These insights exemplify how different enactments of environmental nationalism might dim political nationalism to illuminate cultural nationalism in mobilizations for self-determination and environmental, climate, and energy justice.

Gift bags at Casa Pueblo's headquarters in Adjuntas, Puerto Rico. Photo by Catalina Maíre de Onís.

MOBILIZING FOR THE CHALLENGES AHEAD

Given Casa Pueblo's "pretty good batting average" with successful campaigns and the prominence of Massol-González's arguments in various media, the way Casa Pueblo strategically enacts environmental nationalism under his leadership can inform present and future struggles.[41] This discursive resource of strategic eclipse shapes different articulations of environmental nationalism among Puerto Ricans on the Big Island and beyond. Movement actors engage in environmentalism and cultural nationalism to strategically eclipse political nationalism. Though some interviewees expressed concerns about the dimming of independence efforts in favor of environmental concerns, organizing against the Vía Verde pipeline illustrates how strategic eclipse can cultivate community self-determination that refuses outside dictates and imposed energy futures. This tactic offers a means of bringing together pro-independence advocates who do not have environmental inclinations, environmentalists who do not favor Puerto Rico's political sovereignty, and those who might not align with either cause but who champion Puerto Rican culture and identity.

These findings carry implications for coalition building and the importance of recognizing shared concerns, especially amid the still-unfolding everyday disasters and community recovery efforts in Puerto Rico. This chapter seeks to inform advocacy that resists projects rooted in control and dependency that harm different environments and the peoples who care about and call these places home. As Katherine McCaffrey and Sheri Baver argue, there are "at least one hundred struggles since the 1970s in which Puerto Ricans have crossed party lines and banded together on issues."[42] Crossing party lines as well as geographic ones is increasingly significant for Puerto Rico in the aftermath of the hurricanes. As recent news stories attest, huge numbers of Puerto Ricans are migrating to the US mainland.[43] This ongoing and accelerated migration raises questions about how changing demographics may affect environmental and energy struggles and other intersecting issues by foregrounding a diasporic sensibility and the importance of long-distance environmental nationalism.[44] The haunting legacies of colonial practices might serve as cultural resources to establish diasporic networks that share hardship, hope, and healing across borders—even if efforts to heal colonial wounds are always already incomplete.[45]

While linking environmentalism and nationalisms allows for important recognitions about shared logics of domination that mark particular bodies (humans, water, and land) as disposable, and assists in broadening the concept of self-determination beyond political sovereignty, these relationships are complex. For instance, in Puerto Rico, disputes over how much influence the federal government should have in the Big Island's environmental decision-making process have driven a wedge between pro-independence and environmental activists. During the 1970s, some movement actors viewed US intervention as necessary for enacting and enforcing environmental laws; others saw this as a betrayal of Puerto Rico's potential for political sovereignty.[46] Thus, as I have argued elsewhere, coalitional politics must grapple with complex movement histories, legacies, and tensions.[47]

Furthermore, enactments of environmental nationalism with respect to strategic eclipse may not always "delink," or divest from, oppressive practices.[48] Thus, while environmental nationalism and strategic eclipse can bring people together to create more livable communities, this articulation also has the potential to alienate others and deny vital interconnections.[49]

One of the ways I have tried to record and complicate articulatory movement practices involves engaging those on the front lines with a commitment to praxis. A decolonial approach to reading these movement efforts requires critically documenting the lived realities of community members, including their reflections on mobilization campaigns and outcomes. This approach resonates with Karma Chávez's contention that we should "think about the courses of action that people have available to them, on the ground, as the starting points for theoretical analysis."[50] By accessing, assessing, and amplifying these discourses, activist scholars and other researchers can engage in praxis that values both academic and community expertise and the insights and imaginaries generated by these collaborations.

A study of the pipeline defeat would be incomplete without a discussion of a negative outcome of Vía Verde's demise—a proposed alternative "solution," known as the Aguirre Offshore Gasport. While the project is currently in limbo, the local public energy utility, the Federal Energy Regulatory Commission, and the US corporation Excelerate Energy are working to approve this gas port in southern Puerto Rico. According to Santiago, the project will detrimentally affect fishers' livelihoods and coral reefs and increase the territory's dependency on another fossil fuel (liquefied gas).[51] This energy proposal demonstrates that grappling with colliding economic, energy, and environmental crises also involves determining what counts as a "successful" campaign, and for whom.

In response to the disproportionate effects of energy colonialism experienced in the southern part of Puerto Rico, local community members were organizing for solar communities before the 2017 hurricane season and continue to do so. While Casa Pueblo has received attention for its commendable efforts to help distribute and implement solar devices and infrastructure, other, less well-known groups also are working hard in this area. For example, collaborators with the Iniciativa de la Bahía de Jobos have been planning Coquí Solar, a community solar project, for several years. Evincing the impure politics of colonial situations, the Sierra Club likely will fund this community project. Thus, despite the limitations of US-based organizations in Puerto Rico noted by Rosario and González, this solar project suggests that they can provide the financial resources necessary to give community members control over their own energy futures.

Given our collective, though uneven, contribution to anthropogenic climate disruption and environmental degradation, it is not hyperbolic to argue that what happens in one part of the world carries global effects. The relationship between environmental advocacy and nationalisms is crucial for imagining and enacting more just, sustainable communities within and beyond Puerto Rico. To quote Rosario, "We have the means to change. We need to change what's in our heads and in our hearts. [Life] is a creation. Let's re-create it. Let's start dreaming another one." Let us, indeed.

Acknowledgments: I thank the volume editors, Leilani Nishime and Kim Hester Williams, for their helpful suggestions and encouragement. I also thank Ruth Santiago, José Atiles-Osoria, Phaedra C. Pezzullo, John Arthos, and Darrel Wanzer-Serrano. The fieldwork for this chapter was funded in part by Indiana University's Office of Sustainability, the Organization for Research on Women and Communication, and the Waterhouse Family Institute.

1   J. Atiles-Osoria, "Environmental Colonialism, Criminalization and Resistance: Puerto Rican Mobilizations for Environmental Justice in the 21st Century," *RCCS Annual Review* 6 (2014): 3–21.

2   K. M. de Onís, "'Pa' que tú lo sepas': Translating Rhetorical Field Methods in Puerto Rico's Archipelago," in *Text and Field: Innovations in Rhetorical Method*, ed. R. Asen, K. Chávez, R. Howard, and S. McKinnon (Philadelphia: Penn State University Press, 2016). Puerto Rico is an archipelago consisting of the Big Island, Vieques, Culebra, Mona, and other, smaller islets. This chapter focuses on the Big Island, which has an environmental history related to but distinct from environmental struggles in Vieques and Culebra.

3   J. Duany, *Puerto Rican Nation on the Move: Identities on the Island and in the United States* (Chapel Hill: University of North Carolina Press, 2002). Locals often use the term *Boricua* to describe their heritage and nationality. The term is derived from Borikén, a name given to the Big Island by the Taíno people.

4   I have described the presence of energy colonialism before and after Hurricane Maria in popular press articles: C. de Onís, "For Many in Puerto Rico, 'Energy Dominance' Is Just a New Name for US Colonialism," *The Conversation*, August 21, 2017, https://theconversation.com/for-many -in-puerto-rico-energy-dominance-is-just-a-new-name-for-us-colonialism -80243; C. de Onís, "Puerto Rican Energy Researchers Excluded from Islands' Energy Transition Deliberations," *Latino Rebels*, October 16, 2017, www.latinorebels.com/2017/10/16/puerto-rican-energy-researchers -excluded-from-islands-energy-transition-deliberations/.

5   A. S. Dietrich, *The Drug Company Next Door* (New York: New York University Press, 2013); J. Duany, *Puerto Rican Nation*; D. Wanzer-Serrano, *The New York Young Lords and the Struggle for Liberation* (Philadelphia: Temple University Press, 2015).

6   Interview with A. Massol-González, Adjuntas, Puerto Rico, June 3, 2014.

7   J. Atiles-Osoria, "Environmental Colonialism, Criminalization and Resistance: Puerto Rican Mobilizations for Environmental Justice in the 21st Century," *RCCS Annual Review* 6 (2014): 3–21.

8   In 2014 and 2015, I completed seventy-five interviews with environmental activists, professors, and energy sector experts. I also engaged in participant observation and volunteer work.

9   Duany, *Puerto Rican Nation*, 5. This cultural nationalism includes celebrating cultural heritage sites, language, food, national heroes, and more.

10   A. Y. Ramos-Zayas, *National Performances: The Politics of Class, Race, and Space in Puerto Rican Chicago* (Chicago: University of Chicago Press, 2003); Wanzer-Serrano, *The New York Young Lords*, 73.

11   C. R. Venator-Santiago, "The Results of the 2012 Plebiscite on Puerto Rico's Political Status," *Latino Decisions*, December 28, 2012; C. R. Venator-Santiago, "Puerto Rico Votes on Statehood: Polls and Protest," *The Conversation*, June 12, 2017. The 2012 and 2017 plebiscites recorded 6 percent and 1.5 percent of voters supporting independence, respectively. However, these numbers disguise widespread discontent with restrictive status options on the ballot, which many voters leave fully or partially blank; the political maneuvering of certain parties that advocate for status votes when they think it benefits their agenda; and low voter turnout to signal protest.

12   Duany, *Puerto Rican Nation*, 24.

13   Ibid.; Y. M. Rivero, *Tuning Out Blackness: Race and Nation in the History of Puerto Rican Television* (Durham, NC: Duke University Press, 2005).

14   M. Valdés Pizzini, "Historical Contentions and Future Trends in the Coastal Zones: The Environmental Movement in Puerto Rico," in *Beyond Sun and Sand: Caribbean Environmentalism*, ed. S. L. Baver and B. Lynch, 44–64 (New Brunswick, NJ: Rutgers University Press, 2006), 54.

15   P. C. Pezzullo, "Articulating Anti-toxic Activism to "Sexy" Superstars: The Cultural Politics of *A Civil Action* and *Erin Brockovich*," *Environmental Communication Yearbook* 3 (2006): 21–48.

16   L. Thomas, *Puerto Rican Citizen: History and Political Identity in Twentieth-Century New York City* (Chicago: University of Chicago Press, 2010).

17   D. Berman Santana, *Kicking off the Bootstraps: Environment, Development, and Community Power in Puerto Rico* (Tucson: University of Arizona Press, 1996).

18   M. Meyn, "Puerto Rico's Energy Fix," in *Green Guerrillas: Environmental Conflicts and Initiatives in Latin America and the Caribbean*, ed. H. Collinson, 158–67 (London: Russell Press, 1996); Valdés Pizzini, "Historical Contentions and Future Trends."

19   The sugarcane industry suffered during the Great Depression, as demand for Puerto Rican sugar on the US mainland diminished (Berman Santana, *Kicking off the Bootstraps*). Mining, petrochemical and pharmaceutical industry pollution, US military activities (e.g., Agent Orange testing), and the privatization of public beaches are other environmental controversies that have been linked to Puerto Rico's exploitation as a US colony. See Atiles-Osoria, "Environmental Colonialism"; Dietrich, *The Drug Company Next Door*; McCaffrey, "Struggle for Environmental Justice."

20   Berman Santana, *Kicking off the Bootstraps*; C. M. Concepción, "The Origins of Modern Environmental Activism in Puerto Rico in the 1960s," *International Journal of Urban and Regional Research*, 19, no. 1 (1995): 112–28. As

rural community members moved to the cities in search of factory work, some Boricuas found themselves unemployed and living in coastal city slums.

21 Berman Santana, *Kicking off the Bootstraps*; Duany, *Puerto Rican Nation*; Meyn, "Puerto Rico's Energy Fix." It is difficult to determine a precise end date for Operation Bootstrap. Research suggests that this program lost its momentum in the 1990s, when the US government eliminated the tax loopholes that US corporations had exploited for years (Berman Santana, *Kicking off the Bootstraps*; Dietrich, *The Drug Company Next Door*). The effects of Bootstrap are, in many ways, irreversible and continue to shape everyday life in Puerto Rico.

22 Concepción, "Origins of Modern Environmental Activism," 113.

23 Interview with Ruth Santiago, Salinas, Puerto Rico, June 20, 2014. A Puerto Rican born in New York, Santiago moved to the Big Island with her parents when she was twelve and witnessed the economic and environmental aftereffects of Operation Bootstrap in "La Ruta del Hambre" (the Hunger Route), a name ascribed to the area because of its poverty. According to Santiago, Operation Bootstrap "has created an immense crisis."

24 B. Lynch, "The Garden and the Sea: U.S. Latino Environmental Discourses and Mainstream Environmentalism," *Social Problems* 40, no.1 (1993): 15. See also Atiles-Osoria, "Environmental Colonialism"; J. Colón Rivera, F. Córdova Iturregui, and J. Córdova Iturregui, *El proyecto de explotación minera en Puerto Rico (1962–1968): Nacimiento de la conciencia ambiental moderna* (San Juan: Ediciones Huracán, 2014); C. Concepción, "El conflicto ambiental y su potencial hacia un desarrollo alternativo: El caso de Puerto Rico," *Ambiente y desarrollo* 4, nos. 1–2 (1988): 125–35; Concepción, "Origins of Modern Environmental Activism"; C. M. Concepción, "Justicia, ambiente y movilización social en Puerto Rico," in *Puerto Rico y los derechos humanos: Una intersección plural*, ed. J. J. Colón Morera and Idsa E. Alegría Ortega (San Juan: Editorial Callejón, 2012), 193–220; McCaffrey, "Struggle for Environmental Justice."

25 Lynch, "The Garden and the Sea"; Valdés Pizzini, "Historical Contentions and Future Trends."

26 A group of university professors, scientists, and others joined the Vanguardia Popular during the mining struggles of the 1960s. Motivated by concerns about water contamination, deforestation, and natural resource extraction, they pushed for environmental reforms (Concepción, "Origins of Modern Environmental Activism"). Today those advocating for political independence tend to belong to the Partido Independentista Puertorriqueño (PIP) or the Frente Socialista de Puerto Rico/Socialist Front of Puerto Rico. Other pro-independence advocates avoid any affiliation, given the divisiveness of party politics.

27 Córdova Iturregui and Córdova Iturregui, *El proyecto de explotación minera*, 21.

28   Lynch, "The Garden and the Sea," 114.

29   N. Maldonado-Torres, "On the Coloniality of Being," *Cultural Studies* 21, no. 2 (2007): 243.

30   While Puerto Rico must abide by US federal laws, enforcement is often weak, especially regarding environmental policies and projects (Concepción, "Justicia, ambiente y movilización social").

31   Pezzullo, "Articulating Anti-toxic Activism to 'Sexy' superstars," 22, 29, 44. Like Pezzullo, I draw on articulation theory, which highlights the impermanence of different articulated elements on the basis of context and subordinate and dominant relationships. See L. Grossberg, "On Postmodernism and Articulation: An Interview with Stuart Hall," *Journal of Communication Inquiry* 10, no. 2 (1986): 45–60; S. Hall, "Race, Articulation and Societies Structured in Dominance," *Sociological Theories: Race and Colonialism* (Paris: Unesco, 1980), 305–45.

32   Interview with Juan Rosario, Cupey Bajo, Puerto Rico, June 13, 2014.

33   Interview with Adriana González, Rio Piedras, Puerto Rico, July 8, 2014.

34   G. A. García López, I. Velicu, and G. D'Alisa, "Performing Counter-hegemonic Common(s) Senses: Rearticulating Democracy, Community and Forests in Puerto Rico," *Capitalism Nature Socialism* 3(2017): 11.

35   A. Massol-González interview.

36   García López, Velicu, and D'Alisa, "Performing Counter-hegemonic Common(s) Senses," 6.

37   I. Acosta Lespier, *La mordaza: Puerto Rico 1948–1957* (Rio Piedras, PR: Editorial Edil, 2008).

38   Atiles-Osoria, "Environmental Colonialism."

39   A. Massol-González, E. González, A. Massol-Deyá, T. Deyá Díaz, and T. Geoghegan, "Bosque del Pueblo, Puerto Rico: How a Fight to Stop a Mine Ended Up Changing Forest Policy from the Bottom Up," *Policy That Works for Forests and People* (London: International Institute for Environment and Development, 2006), 8–9.

40   Massol-González et al., "Bosque del Pueblo," 9.

41   This "batting average" comment was mentioned by the late Carmelo Ruiz Marrero, a journalist and anti-GMO activist, following a public hearing at Puerto Rico's Capitol. Massol-González was instrumental in fighting open-pit mining and established the Bosque del Pueblo/People's Forest, a community-managed area (García-Lopez, Velicu, and D'Alisa, "Performing Counter-hegemonic Common(s) Senses").

42   K. McCaffrey and S. L. Baver, "Ni una bomba más: Reframing the Vieques Struggle," in *Beyond Sun and Sand: Caribbean Environmentalisms*, ed. S. L. Baver and B. Deutsch Lynch, 109–28 (New Brunswick, NJ: Rutgers University Press, 2006), 127.

43   I. Godreau, Y. Bonilla, and D. E. Walicek. "How to Help the University of Puerto Rico—and How Not To," *Chronicle of Higher Education*, November 27, 2017.

44 Duany, *Puerto Rican Nation*, 5.

45 Wanzer-Serrano, *The New York Young Lords*.

46 Concepción, "Origins of Modern Environmental Activism."

47 K. M. de Onís, "'Looking Both Ways': Metaphor and the Rhetorical Alignment of Intersectional Climate Justice and Reproductive Justice Concerns," *Environmental Communication* 6, no. 3 (2012): 308–27; K. M. de Onís, "Lost in Translation: Challenging (White Monolingual Feminism's) <Choice> with *Justicia Reproductive*," *Women's Studies in Communication* 38, no. 1 (2015): 1–19.

48 Wanzer-Serrano, *The New York Young Lords*, 11; Pezzullo, "Articulating Anti-toxic Activism to 'Sexy' Superstars."

49 P. C. Pezzullo and C. M. de Onís, "Rethinking Rhetorical Field Methods on a Precarious Planet," *Communication Monographs* 85, no. 1 (2018): 103–22.

50 K. R. Chávez, *Queer Migration Politics: Activist Rhetoric and Coalitional Possibilities* (Urbana: University of Illinois Press, 2013), 150.

51 K. M. de Onís, "'Pa' que tú lo sepas.'"

PART FIVE

SPECULATIVE FUTURES

CHAPTER THIRTEEN

"WOUND INTRICATELY THROUGHOUT MY SPHERE"

Spatial Subjectivity in Through the Arc of the Rain Forest

ASHLEY CHEYEMI MCNEIL

So, reader, join us as we ramble through these worlds of wonder.

JAKOB VON UEXKÜLL, *A STROLL THROUGH THE WORLDS*
OF ANIMALS AND MEN (1934)

I N the grand narrative of the United States, nature has historically been used as an ideological device for building the nation, "from sea to shining sea," to be the home of the God-fearing free and brave. So when the Japanese American author Karen Tei Yamashita published her first novel, *Through the Arc of the Rain Forest*, in 1990, locating her story in the depths of Brazil and questioning the very nature of what is "natural," she radically questioned the focus on US nationalism in the genre of Asian American literature.[1] Often categorized as magical realism, Yamashita's work critiques transnational capital, corporation, culture, community, technology, and consumption. Yet her narrative can also be read as an intimate study of living beings and their environment. Bringing together all the characters of the novel is the mysterious appearance of the Matacão, a massive polymer land substance, which emerges from the earth's core in the Amazon rain forest. On its discovery, the Matacão material is found to be highly transformable. It quickly becomes the basis of a lucrative industry: "Matacão plastic would infiltrate every crevice of modern life—plants, facial and physical remakes and appendages, shoes, clothing, jewelry, toys, cars, every sort of machine from electro-domestic to high-tech, buildings, furniture—in short, the myriad of commercial products with which the civilized world adorns itself."[2]

Through the Arc presents the natural in uncertain, unstable terms. As a polymer material, the Matacão is manipulated as an object to promote capitalistic, intellectual, religious, and mythical global pursuits that undergird nationalisms; yet as a *space*, the Matacão is constituted as a series of intermingling relations between humans, organisms, sentient beings, things, and beliefs that engage a subject-formation process untethered to the Western yoke of nature and nation. While *space* commonly carries connotations of separation, disconnection, or blankness, I argue that this perceived void is actually full of emanant relational capacities that resist the mutative impulses of Western doctrines of subjectivity. Space is not empty: it is emergent. This particular sense of space is what I call *spatial subjectivity*.

If we perceive nature as a space that is itself a subject and also engenders subjectivities, rather than as a rhetorical nation-building object, then we can work through covert mechanisms of oppression in radically productive ways. My proposal engages what the Asian Americanist Kandice Chuh defines in *Imagine Otherwise* as "subjectless discourse," which works to destabilize the structures in which subjects are permitted their subjectivity only through "conforming to certain regulatory matrices," such as race or nation.[3] Writing some thirteen years before Chuh's publication, Yamashita attends to the quagmire of constituting identity through nationalism.[4] The novel provides ample nationalistic rhetoric and tropes that could easily be used as bases of identity; but rather than situating subjects through national alignments, Yamashita imagines interrelational subjectivities brought forth through the Matacão (which, notably, is itself outside national jurisdictions).

To clarify how the space of the Matacão engenders subjectivities, I incorporate the Estonian ecologist Jakob von Uexküll's notion of the Umwelt. This term translates from German simply as "environment" or "surroundings." But Uexküll deepens the common understanding of the local, natural world to a more nuanced perspective of the connective relations that are intrinsic to a particular local environment. This distinction is aptly defined by the theorist Giorgio Agamben as "an infinite variety of [individual] perceptual worlds that, though they are uncommunicating and reciprocally exclusive, are all equally perfect and linked together as if in a gigantic musical score."[5] *Through the Arc* exemplifies Uexküll's theory when read as a series of intermingling Umwelten. A subject is constituted by its relations to other entities, and it can be not only human or nonhuman but also space itself—represented in Yamashita's text by the Matacão. Spatial subjectivity incites an acknowledgment of agency composed by the webs of such relations. When space is understood as both a subject and a constituter of subjectivities, it disrupts Western ideologies that traditionally locate agency in humanity or human institutions. This alternative understanding of subject formation is the central objective of spatial subjectivity.

NATIONALISM AND THE NARRATIVE OF
THE (UN)VIABLE SUBJECT

The final pages of *Through the Arc* describe the funeral procession of a young Brazilian spiritual leader, Chico Paco, who was accidentally caught in an assassin's line of fire. Chico Paco's death is a shock to his followers. They move his body from the site of his death, deep in the rain forest, back to his hometown on the northern coast of Brazil, a trek of hundreds of miles through the country's varied ecologies:

> Retracing Chico Paco's steps, the mourners passed hydro-electric plants, where large dams had flooded and displaced entire towns. They passed mining projects tirelessly exhausting the treasures of iron, manganese and bauxite. They passed a gold rush, losing a third of the procession to the greedy furor. They crossed rivers and encountered fishing fleets, nets heavy with their exotic river catch of manatee, *pirarucú, piramatuba, mapara.* They crowded to the sides of the road to allow passage for trucks and semis bearing timber, Brazil nuts and rubber. . . . They passed the government's five-year plans and ten-year plans, while all the forest's splendid wealth seemed to be rushing away ahead of them. . . . And when the rains stopped, they knew they had passed into northeast Brazil's drought-ridden terrain, the sun-baked earth spreading out from smoldering asphalt, weaving erosion through the landscape.[6]

Yamashita lyrically highlights a brutal double entendre: while the procession mourns the loss of their spiritual guide, they are confronted with the equally devastating, slow killing of the earth, which is being stripped of its natural resources for the benefit of capitalism and government. Yamashita evidences how nations are often built at the expense of the land to which they lay claim. Yet the mourners in the procession are not shocked at nature's death in process, despite their presumed meditation of death while in transit. Indeed, although the demise of the natural is evident, the mourners are concerned only with their own grief and loss, and even that devotion is limited in many who cannot resist an opportunity to mine the land for material wealth.

The mourners' apparent blindness to the ravaging of nature in the name of nation building should not come as a surprise. After all, nation and nature have long been yoked, almost always at nature's expense.[7] As the environmental theorist Christopher Manes contends, "Nature *is* silent in our culture (and in literate societies generally) in the sense that the status of being a speaking subject is jealously guarded as an exclusively human prerogative."[8] This silencing and, as Yamashita demonstrates, erasure of nature can assume a plethora of guises. For instance, in US school history lessons, we are taught that (certain categories of) humans are at the top of the hierarchy of the animal kingdom, at the teleological summit of consciousness and reason. The Asian Americanist and cultural theorist Lisa Lowe gives this frame of the "natural order" a more politicized scope: terming the Western anthropocentric epistemological model as "modern humanism," she usefully clarifies the expression to mean "the secular European tradition of liberal philosophy that narrates political emancipation through citizenship in the state . . . that confers civilization to the human person educated in aesthetic and national culture."[9] The grand narratives of nation and human subject, then, rely on the common internal logic of opposition to nature.

Yamashita is keenly aware of the nation-based humanism that Lowe articulates. While nationalism certainly can be a basis of social solidarity, its cohesive practice is also inherently an exclusionary one, which Yamashita's narrative works to counter. Nationalism can be a tool of oppression: it constrains identities, regulates citizenship, and sanctions belonging. Nature has also been used as a tool of exclusion: national identity, citizenship, and belonging have historically been available only to a specific category of subjects. Nation and nature, then, are not only used separately as exclusionary logics but also work together to reinforce the hierarchy of power that dictates humans to be rulers of all things, animate and inanimate. It is here that debates about legal subjects and place-based belonging can dominate discourses about nature, society, and the environment. Therefore it is also here that we should heed Judith Butler's warning that "oppression works not merely through overt prohibition, but covertly, through the constitution of viable subjects and through the corollary constitution of a domain of unviable (un)subjects."[10] The inherent oppressiveness of nationalism is rooted not so much in humans' (mis)use of nature as in the opposition of humanity and nature in the construction of the domain of viable subjects.[11] Deconstructing and repositioning the human requires that the same must be done with

ASHLEY CHEYEMI MCNEIL

nature, as the two are often defined in opposition to one another. The need to expand and reframe the process of subject formation espoused in *Through the Arc* is also the epistemological spirit of recent critical race theory in Asian American studies.

ASIAN AMERICAN STUDIES AND
SUBJECTLESS DISCOURSE

When Kandice Chuh published *Imagine Otherwise* in 2003, at a time of critical self-reflection in the field of Asian American studies, she tackled an impasse in the field: how to defend and espouse Asian American subjectivity without adopting the methods of oppression and erasure that it works against. Chuh acknowledges that we are at a tipping point in social history, at which the Western epistemology of who (or what) qualifies as a subject must be divested. This means extending notions of subjectivity to go beyond and dismantle traditional Western forms such as the category of the nation. Chuh shows how asserting the Asian American subject, or an Asian American subjectivity, works to reify the power relations that have flattened Asian American agency only by conceiving subjects solely within the framework that limits, marginalizes, and constrains them.

Working toward social justice, Asian American criticism inadvertently constructed the Asian American subject as an "epistemological object." In other words, if the traditional Eurocentric ways of knowing (epistemology) are simply recycled, even in new contexts such as critical race or transnational studies, then the outcome of what is known (object) will always be the same: the architecture of hegemony remains intact. Chuh insists that "emphasizing the internal instability of 'Asian American,' identity of and as the other—the marginal, the marginalized—is encouraged to collapse" and allows for a construction of Asian American identity that is not based in the binary logic of the (often hegemonic) subject and the (often marginalized) object.[12]

In this distinction, Chuh's theory harmonizes with environmental theories that challenge anthropocentric worldviews, as the limiting subject/object framework parallels the human/nature episteme. Of course, allying nature and subject formation is understandably precarious ground for minority scholars, as nature, territory, and nation so easily form a triumvirate of hegemonic authority.[13] Katherine Lee Bates's 1893 poem "America the Beautiful," quoted in my introduction, identifies the land of America as "a freedom beat" through "the wilderness," ruled by pilgrims, heroes, and patriots. Not only are humans meant to rule over nature, but it is only natural that they do so. It is in this sense of naturalization as a form of identity that the nation becomes a method of exclusion and covert prohibition for peoples who do not resemble the type of human described, for example, by Bates. Yet despite these qualifiers, I maintain that there is a liberatory potential in relating nature and subjectlessness.

Aligning with Chuh's discernment that "the inadequacy of nation as conceptual parameter for understanding the complexities of subject-formation" is not only "a question of accuracy" but also "specifically ideological," this chapter participates in her project of subjectless discourse by reimagining how nature and subjectivity function in Yamashita's novel.[14] However, while Chuh organizes her critique of Asian American studies by providing literary analyses that are not organized by an identity-based analytical category, I suggest that it may still be useful to attend to the subject/object framework, if, and only if, we can radically revise the construction and qualification of "subjects" and "objects."[15]

Space again emerges here as a productive response to Chuh's call for subjectlessness. *Through the Arc* imagines manifold spaces articulated as various capacities for relations, upending traditional philosophical distinctions between subject and object. For instance, the phrase "wound intricately throughout my sphere," which I take as the title of this chapter, is spoken by the omniscient narrator of the novel, who is embodied as a small, animated orb that spins inches in front of the forehead of the main character, Kazumasa Ishimaru. Kazumasa and his ball are spatially connected (the ball cannot be severed from Kazumasa's cranial vicinity) yet are consciously and physically independent of one another. Kazumasa's ball turns out to be made of the same material as the Matacão, but it is also an intelligent, nonhuman being endowed with consciousness and memory, which guides the reader through Yamashita's tale with first-person perspective and authority.

It is telling, I think, that the narrator is a ball. While the word *sphere* often connotes a hollow form, the ball challenges this assumed state of vacancy with its otherworldly sentience: it positions itself as a self-aware miniature of the Earth, homogeneously connected to the Matacão and its infinite, emerging capacities; it defies any established framework of subjectivity. The ball's agency is manifested through omniscient intelligence and critical consciousness. It exists more intricately in nature than humans can comprehend, exceeding our biological, semiotic, or narrative ability to describe it. Kazumasa's ball is revealed as the most knowing and affective character of the novel, shepherding the reader through the complicated relational web of everything and everyone engaging the Matacão. Spatial subjectivity, then, emerges as a potential not only to indelibly reinscribe the agency of nature but also to challenge the Western figure of the all-powerful human, in whom epistemology is self-reflexive and an absolute. By tracing intelligence and design through sentient beings' subjectivities by their relations to nature, other species, modes of power, and material forms, we transpose the genesis of subjectivity to the biosphere, so that human ontology is but one form of sentience among a vast, ever-changing sea of other subjectivities.

THE UMWELT AND SPATIAL SUBJECTIVITY

I now return to Jakob von Uexküll, an ecologist turned biosemiotician, to investigate more deeply how the space of the Matacão engenders its own subjectivity and constitutes the subjectivities of other beings. Uexküll defines the Umwelt as the *individual* ecology of a living being, which is constituted only by interactions with its local environment that hold significance for that specific being.[16] Uexküll often refers to the Umwelt as a "subjective-self-world," or, more endearingly, a being's "soap bubble" of existence. Classical science promotes a conception of a single world in which all living organisms and species are contained, hierarchically ordered from the biologically simplest species up to the most complex. Uexküll, however, does not subscribe to this single-world theory. In *A Stroll through the Worlds of Animals and Men*—his eloquent "picture book of invisible worlds"— Uexküll explains the deficiencies of such a single-sighted register of life. "We are easily deluded into assuming that the relationship between a foreign subject and the objects in his world exists on the same spatial and temporal plane as our own relations with the objects in our human world," Uexküll observes, presupposing the grounds of current-day environmentalism. "This fallacy is fed by a belief in the existence of a single world, into which all living creatures are pigeonholed. This gives rise to the widespread conviction that there is only one space and one time for all living things."[17] Instead, Uexküll contends, there are infinite perceptual worlds, in which each living being (or subject) is the master of its own subjective-self-world.[18] In the Umwelt, there is no objectively fixed realm of existence: the natural world is neither a singular entity nor an empty receptacle for life forms. Although the Umwelt is still based on a binary construction of subjects and objects (actors and their stimuli), the category of viable subjects is expanded beyond humankind, and the understanding of world is multiplied infinitely.

Importantly, though, while these multiple perceptual worlds—these Umwelten—are discrete and uncommunicating, so that "all animals, from the simplest to the most complex, are fitted into their unique worlds with equal completeness," all are linked together, as if in some enormous, purposeful musical score.[19] Consider the presence of a fig on a tree. The fig has different relations depending on the beings with which it interacts. In addition to being the fig of the growing tree, it is also the fig of the harvesting human, the fig of the snacking bird, and the fig of the spawning wasp. Thus there are multiple, intermingling Umwelten all in one place (the tree), created by a single subject (the fig). The final example of the Umwelt of the fig and the wasp is of special note, in that it demonstrates the harmonic composition in nature—what Uexküll alludes to as nature's "unknowing intelligence"—in which all Umwelten are interwoven.[20] The fig contains its flowers and seeds within the skin, which must be penetrated in order for pollination to occur. By fantastic evolutionary design, certain species of wasps have chosen the inner florets of figs as their nesting sites. The female wasp squeezes through the apex of the fig to deposit her eggs. As she does so, she sheds the pollen collected on her body. The apex of the fig is just large enough to admit the wasp, and the wasp is capable of identifying not only the particular species of Ficus (fig tree) her species of wasp is designed for, but also to determine which figs are uninhabited and unripe.

With the fig now pollinated and the eggs laid, the wasp's job is done. She dies, and the fig's acids are activated to consume the wasp's body, a process that ripens the fig. In Uexküll's scheme, the fig and the wasp are unaware of one another—the fig uses the wasp as its object, and the wasp uses the fig as its object in their respective Umwelten—yet they are clearly designed to enable a grand plan for the survival of nature. This unknowing intelligence is what Uexküll refers to as the compositional harmony of nature, stating that "this all-embracing interweaving [of subjects] cannot be referred to any particular formative impetus" but is rather attuned to "higher rules, which unite things separated even by time . . . without any reference to whether they depend on human purposes or not."[21]

Spatial subjectivity employs Uexküll's Umwelt theory, but the two are not the same. Where the Umwelt incites agency through the aspects of an environment that carry significance to the subject (only the species of wasp that is designed for a particular species of fig tree can squeeze herself inside the fruit to pollinate and ripen it) and form its subjective self-world, spatial subjectivity names the subject-formation process that occurs within Umwelten and fosters the unknowing intelligence of harmonic relations.

In *Through the Arc*, the Matacão is not only a specific geographic place but also has agency, in that it engenders multiple relations with and among other object-beings. The narrative that develops around the presence, use, and eventual failing of the Matacão plastic shows intricate systems of connectivity. Spirituality, technology, media, capitalism, material production, and social consumption are all narratively overlaid through an international cast of characters who travel to the Matacão and end up forming a community, as they recognize that each person and being has a unique relation with the baffling, magical polymer substance. Each character's connection to the Matacão and the ways in which each character's storyline consistently works toward interconnection substantiate the concept of spatial subjectivity. In addition to Kazumasa and his attendant, sentient floating orb, there is a host of other, equally magical characters. J. B. Tweep, a three-armed American CEO who personifies the neoliberal corporation, holds Kazumasa hostage for his satellite's ability to locate other sites of Matacão surfacings. The "native" character Mané Pena, capitalizing on his perceived indigenous authenticity, becomes an expert in the healing science of "featherology" and a local father-figure to newly arrived Matacão opportunists. He mentors Batista Djapan, who begrudgingly supports his partner, Tania Aparecida, as she builds an empire based on international carrier-pigeon communications, for which the Matacão serves a global base. Lastly there is Chico Paco, a spiritual pilgrim to the Matacão, who constantly promotes being in transit, even through his death.

Critics have approached the Matacão in differing and dynamic ways. Aimee Bhang examines the terrain of the novel as a mutant and speculative space of historically disavowed empire and present-day capitalist hubris.[22] Ursula Heise conceptualizes the Matacão as "primarily a destination," in that "the reader follows all the other characters [except for the native-born Mané Pena] on their journeys from far-flung places of origin to the rainforest."[23] Both Bhang and Heise highlight the interdependencies of globalism and nationalism through the valence of the "natural" world. By fruition, fortitude, or force, all the novel's characters seek the Matacão in an effort to settle and conquer it (either materially or ideologically, through capitalism or empire)—recalling again that master narrative of nature's subjugation to nation.

In many ways, although it is never a nation-state, the Matacão assumes the tropes of a nation. It is quickly settled into a distinct territory, mapped out, and claimed by numerous peoples and groups for various purposes, from capital gain to religious sanctity. Once settled, the Matacão is economically developed; it becomes a site for pilgrimages and religion; it instigates a new system of jurisprudence and legality; it has its own higher education system; it is a place that becomes a home and a livelihood; and it instigates a common sense of belonging. Yet Yamashita refuses to allow this burgeoning sense of nation to become the basis of subjectivity. Instead, it is the overlaid relations between the various beings and the natural—indeed, the relations enabled by the existence of the Matacão—that foster subjectivities.

Rather than interrogating space as a vacuum or as a tool of binary logic, I suggest that it can be approached relationally, as a nonnational grid of subject formation that does not have to hinge on Western ideas of body and territory. Articulating spatial subjectivity through the ecological philosophy of the Umwelt is one way to reimagine space, unsieved by Western, identity-based systems of knowledge. Although Uexküll seems unable to do away with hierarchical logic completely, he maintains faith in his nonscientific understanding of something other, "which lies beyond and behind" Western knowledge.[24] In their signals toward something beyond the domain of Eurocentric epistemology, Uexküll and Chuh make room for the concept of spatial subjectivity. Yamashita ponders a similar system of connectivity in her epigraph to *Through the Arc*, in which she notes, "I have heard Brazilian children say that whatever passes through the arc of a rainbow becomes its opposite. But what is the opposite of a bird? Or for that matter, a human being? What then, in the great rain forest, where, in its season, the rainbows are myriad?" Just as Yamashita protests the oppositions of binary logic, Uexküll approaches ecology through the multiplicity of subjectivities. Both Yamashita and Uexküll align with Lowe's appeal (which clearly resounds with Chuh's) to "imagine a much more complicated set of stories about the emergence of the now, in which what is foreclosed as unknowable is forever saturating the 'what-can-be-known.' We are left with the project of visualizing, mourning, and thinking 'other humanities' within the received genealogy of 'the human.'"[25]

CONCLUSION: IMAGINING OTHERWISE

Furthering his notion of these subjective-self-worlds, Uexküll elaborates that "these different worlds present to all nature lovers new lands of such wealth and beauty that a walk through them is well worth while, even though they unfold not to the physical but only to the spiritual eye."[26] Uexküll's Umwelt theory ultimately rests on perception, in the primary sense that each being perceives its own subjective self-world, but also in the secondary sense that readers can learn to see these worlds that are not our own (individually or collectively) with a sensory faculty beyond the visual. This revision deviates from canonized conceptions of being and consequently largely lacks the language to articulate such recension. As Manes keenly observes, "We must contemplate not only learning a new ethics, but a new language free from the directionalities of humanism."[27]

At first glance, this may seem an impossible project, but the works of Yamashita, Chuh, and Uexküll show it to be an ongoing, open invitation. They have already proposed a matrix of alternative approaches to subject formation. In his best-known monograph, Uexküll reminds us that we must be willing to look beyond the systems of what is known, as these systems instigate a blindness to Otherly beauty: "Many a zoologist and physiologist, clinging to the doctrine that all living beings are mere machines, denies their existence and thus boards up the gates to other worlds so that no single ray of light shines forth from all the radiance that is shed over them. But let us who are not committed to the machine theory consider the nature of machines."[28] Yamashita, too, points to the brilliance of such other worlds when she proposes the possibility of infinite beings created by the transformation of passing "through the arc of the rainbow . . . in the great rain forest" where "rainbows are myriad." Likewise, Chuh grounds her theory of subjectless discourse in a critique of the Western machinery of justified belief and, as her book title suggests, in imagining other ways to perceive agency. Uexküll's thought reverberates through Yamashita's and Chuh's works with his simple invitation: "So, reader, join us as we ramble through these worlds of wonder."[29] When all three writers are considered together, their perspectives illuminate spatial subjectivity as the harbinger of subjects that come into being relationally.

When nature is reframed through specificity of subject, "a new world comes into being," leaving subjectivity open to alternative articulations of language and knowing.[30] This is what Kazumasa's ball does for the reader, what the Matacão does for the biosphere, and what Chuh does for critical race studies. In Yamashita's imagining, this rhizomatic web of relations permeates not only individual beings but also human systems of thought that are often considered to be self-sustaining and self-perpetuating worldviews. In *Through the Arc*, capitalism, environmentalism, and globalism are nonopposing, interconnected forces of which there is no singular master manipulator. In a playful inversion of many ethical environmentalists' reading of nature as a morally empty space, Yamashita ignores the moral declinations in which these social systems are usually couched, espousing a neutral space of subject formation that operates outside the Western ideas of judgment and knowing.[31] In Yamashita's narrative world—which, of course, is not too different from the world we find ourselves in—a series of relations, individual yet interconnected, wax, wane, and are reconstituted into new formations of society and environment.

Ultimately, spatial subjectivity creates the possibility of infinite new imaginations of agency for all beings. The figure of Kazumasa's ball suggests that spatial subjectivity is wound not only throughout all Earth's life forms but also through all life forces—earthly and otherwise by its very sentient presence. As the novel progresses and the reader is introduced to the Matacão, it is understood from the opening paragraphs that the ball's existence has already cycled through extinction. "By a strange quirk of fate," Kazumasa's ball explains, "I was brought back by a memory . . . [and] brought back by a memory, I have become a memory, and as such, am commissioned to become for you a memory."[32] Kazumasa's ball is the only omniscient subject of the novel, importantly connected to the biosphere as "the voice that emerges from the depths of geology."[33] That the ball transcends any absolute sense of life and death—it is "brought back" and "commissioned to become"—indicates that spatial subjectivity is not conditioned to any single being, world, or even sense of time. Rather, it is braided into all systems of life, and we perceive it as series of recursive returns. This idea is reinforced through the nature of the earth itself. The earth's mantle manipulates non-biodegradable waste to form the Matacão; copper-colored butterflies thrive in the seemingly unnatural environment of an old, rusted junkyard in the forest; even the forest itself has a symbiotic relational manipulation, as it reconsumes vestiges of human civilization.

It is precisely this sense of return that illuminates a deeper meaning of spatial subjectivity in the novel. The final section is titled "The Return," though each individual chapter title is a cognate of death: "Typhus," "Rain of Feathers," "Bacteria," and "The Tropical Tilt." The most perfect organism imagined by Yamashita is the ecosystem of the past, still intrinsic in the forest: "The old forest has returned once again, secreting its digestive juices, slowly breaking everything into edible absorbent components, pursuing the lost perfection of an organism in which digestion and excretion were once one and the same."[34] And even though that "lost perfection" "will never be the same again," this gesture toward the return to that state of transformative, ambiguous, web of relational agency resonates deeply in the text and, ultimately, underpins the meaning of spatial subjectivity.

NOTES

Acknowledgments: This chapter has been shaped by many brilliant thinkers. A special thanks to Leilani Nishime and Kim Hester Williams for their dedication to this publication and perceptive comments through each writing stage; to Erin Suzuki for guiding me through two major early revisions with stalwart support; to the incisive reviewer of this collection; and to the discerning editors at the University of Washington Press.

1   Yamashita's oeuvre has received much critical attention for disrupting US-centered discourses of American studies and transnationalism. See Kandice Chuh, "Of Hemispheres and Other Spheres: Navigating Karen Tei Yamashita's Literary World," *American Literary History* 18, no. 3 (2006): 618–37.

2   Karen Tei Yamashita, *Through the Arc of the Rain Forest* (Minneapolis, MN: Coffee House Press, 1990), 143.

3   Kandice Chuh, *Imagine Otherwise: On Asian Americanist Critique* (Durham, NC: Duke University Press, 2003), 9.

4   While I focus on Yamashita's critique of nationalism through her positioning of the natural, it should be noted that race-based identity formation is tightly wound into constructions of nation. For further discussion, see Michael Omi and Howard Winant, *Racial Formation in the United States* (New York: Routledge, 1994).

5   Giorgio Agamben, *The Open: Man and Animal*, trans. Kevin Attell (Redwood City, CA: Stanford University Press, 2004), 40.

6   Yamashita, *Through the Arc*, 210.

7   In this essay I refer specifically to Western, Eurocentric nationalisms. Indigenous nationalisms, such as those of the Pacific and the Americas, often centralize nature, sea, and land in their formation of identity and nation.

8   Christopher Manes, "Nature and Silence," *Environmental Ethics* 14, no. 4 (1992): 339.

9   Lisa Lowe, "Intimacies of the Four Continents," in *Haunted by Empire: Geographies of Intimacy in North American History*, ed. Ann Laura Stoler (Durham, NC: Duke University Press, 2006), 192.

10   Judith Butler, "Imitation and Gender Insubordination," in *Inside/Out: Lesbian Theories, Gay Theories*, ed. Diana Fuss (New York: Routledge, 1991), 20.

11   For more on how "Man" has occluded the natural world, see Manes, "Nature and Silence," 350.

12   Chuh, *Imagine Otherwise*, 9.

13   Territory and nation can be mutually inclusive. Chuh, in particular, stresses that "territoriality literalizes nation, lending to it a palpability that contributes to its sense of inevitability." *Imagine*, 86.

14   Ibid., 88.

15   Chuh focuses on the *critique* of the subject rather than the subject itself (or, oftentimes, the reinscribed object). For example, Chuh organizes her study of Asian American texts by analyzing fluctuating categories of citizenship (chapter 1) and assessing how transnationality underpins racialization, which is itself a technology of hegemonic power (chapter 2).

16   Uexküll's use of *Umwelt* predates Martin Heidegger's famous application of the term. Publishing most of his work between the early 1890s through the late 1930s, Uexküll also directly influenced philosophers such as Ernst Cassirer, Maurice Merleau-Ponty, and Gilles Deleuze as well as Heidegger;

see Kaleiv Kull, "Jakob von Uexküll: An Introduction," *Semiotica* 134, no. 1/4 (2001): 12. Uexküll himself dedicated many of his works to Immanuel Kant: see Brett Buchanan, "Jakob von Uexküll's Theories of Life," *Onto-ethologies: The Animal Environments of Uexküll, Heidegger, Merleau-Ponty, and Deleuze* (New York: SUNY Press, 2008), 19–21.

17 Jakob von Uexküll, *A Stroll through the Worlds of Animals and Men: A Picture Book of Invisible Worlds*, reprinted in *Semiotica* 89, no. 4 (1992): 327.

18 This chapter examines the structure of the Umwelt as a means of revising the process of subjectification. However, Umwelten still form potentially racialized hierarchies, as each perceptual life-world depends on the number and sophistication of its interactive relations. See Neel Ahuja, "Intimate Atmospheres: Queer Theory in a Time of Extinctions," *GLQ: A Journal of Lesbian and Gay Studies* 21, nos. 2–3 (2015): 365–85.

19 Uexküll, "A Stroll," 324. While Uexküll often uses the terms *musical score* and *composition* to express the intelligent interweaving of nature, he also uses the words *chime, rhythm, melody, harmony,* and *symphony* to describe the relations of organisms; see Jakob von Uexküll, "The Theory of Meaning," *Semiotica* 42, no. 1 (1982): 25–82. For a list and definitions of the musical terms Uexküll uses throughout his oeuvre, see Buchanan, "Jakob von Uexküll's Theories of Life," 26–27.

20 See Katie Kline, "The Story of the Fig and Its Wasp," *EcoTone*, Ecological Society of America, May 20, 2011, www.esa.org/esablog/research/the-story -of-the-fig-and-its-wasp/. The post includes links to documentary video clips of the fig-wasp relationship.

21 Jakob von Uexküll, *Theoretical Biology*, trans. D. L. Mackinnon (New York: Harcourt, 1926), 254, 176.

22 Aimee Bahng, "Extrapolating Transnational Arcs, Excavating Imperial Legacies: The Speculative Acts of Karen Tei Yamashita's *Through the Arc of the Rain Forest*," *MELUS: Multi-Ethnic Literature of the United States* 33, no. 4 (2008): 123–44.

23 Ursula Heise, "Local Rock and Global Plastic: World Ecology and the Experience of Place," *Comparative Literature Studies* 41, no. 1 (2004): 142.

24 Thure von Uexküll, "Introduction: The Sign Theory of Jakob von Uexküll," *Semiotica* 89, no. 4 (1992): 281.

25 Lowe, "Intimacies of the Four Continents," 208.

26 Uexküll, "A Stroll," 320.

27 Manes, "Nature and Silence," 342.

28 Uexküll, "A Stroll," 319.

29 Ibid., 320.

30 Ibid., 319.

31 For example, Daniel Berthold-Bond argues that the "boundaries of ethical life entirely coincide with the sphere of the human world." "The Ethics of

ASHLEY CHEYEMI MCNEIL

'Place': Reflections on Bioregionalism," *Environmental Ethics* 22, no. 1
(2000): 8.

32 Yamashita, *Through the Arc*, 3.
33 Heise, "Local Rock," 147.
34 Yamashita, *Through the Arc*, 212.

CHAPTER FOURTEEN

REMEMBERING GOJIRA/GODZILLA

Nuclearism and Racial Reproduction in America's Asia-Pacific

YU-FANG CHO

THROUGHOUT the Asia-Pacific and in the United States, Gojira/ Godzilla—the king of monsters, who came into being as a result of US nuclear bomb tests in the Pacific in the 1950s—has been a popular childhood obsession and is recognized by Guinness World Records as the longest continuously running movie franchise.[1] Since its birth in the original Japanese *Gojira*, directed by Honda Ishiro in 1954, the meanings of this icon have shifted drastically from a solemn critique of nuclearism, militarism, and man-made environmental catastrophes in its earlier versions to what many consider to be kitschy children's entertainment.[2]

Just as this figure seemed to have been completely replaced by Hello Kitty on the global stage, the making of the 2014 movie *Godzilla* brought it back to the spotlight. This film was an immediate box-office success, grossing $524.9 million worldwide by the end of its theatrical run. This most recent American rendition brings back the political perspectives on nuclear weaponry in the original 1954 Japanese *Gojira* but reformulates them in light of contemporary concerns about the geopolitics of nuclear energy in the US-led transpacific military-industrial complex.[3]

This chapter discusses this latest "mutation" of Gojira/Godzilla as a metaphor for US nuclearism in Asia and the Pacific. I use the term *nuclearism* to refer to the dominant ideology that has defined the global geopolitical landscape since the nuclear bombings of Hiroshima and Nagasaki. This ideology legitimizes the use of nuclear weapons for imperial domination and mass destruction in the name of assuring world peace and achieving other political objectives. Specifically, this chapter examines the implications of Godzilla's recent mutation in two broad contexts: the shifting

220

representations and implications of this figure in transpacific contexts, and the ongoing struggles with (neo)colonial nuclearism in Asia and the Pacific that have remained largely absent from Western public discourse. The most recent American figuration of this global icon serves as a critical lens enabling us to unpack, critique, and redeploy the simultaneous absence and presence of indigenous Pacific Islanders and Asians in the US-centric racial logic of planetary security. Refiguring Godzilla as a symbol of nuclear power, this remake of the film revises the opposition to the United States and its violent nuclear bombings and testing in the Japanese original to project ambivalence toward a benevolent US presence in the Pacific. Placing a white American family at its center (in effect, representing white reproductive life as universal life), against the backdrop of intensive militarization of national and planetary security, this renarration transforms the devastating consequences of nuclear weaponry into an ambivalent embrace of nuclear power as a highly uncontrollable and unpredictable "natural" power while figuring global militarism as an organic form of "natural" defense that is immensely powerful yet untrustworthy.[4] This renarration elides the many sufferings and deaths that make white universal life possible—specifically the ecological and human costs of radioactive contamination caused by both nuclear weaponry and nuclear power in the Pacific.[5]

Gojira appeared nine years after the bombings of Hiroshima and Nagasaki in 1945 and two years after the end of the US occupation of Japan in 1952.[6] It draws inspirations from both Japanese folklore and contemporary Hollywood monster films to address fears and anxieties about the destruction wrought by war and nuclear weaponry. The US nuclear bomb testing that continued after World War II, and in particular, the 1954 *Lucky Dragon* incident, exacerbated such fears and anxieties.[7] On March 1, 1954, a Japanese tuna-fishing trawler by the name of *Lucky Dragon No. 5* (*Daigo Fukuryū Maru*), operating in the Pacific, was showered with radioactive fallout—later known as "ashes of death"—from the Castle Bravo nuclear test. This hydrogen bomb test explosion, carried out by the United States on Bikini Atoll, was referred to as "the worst nuclear test in US history" by the National Security Archives at Georgetown University. It had a total yield over 7,200 times more powerful than the bombings of Hiroshima and Nagasaki.[8] Also called the Bikini incident, the test spread deadly fallout across the twenty-nine populated atolls of the Marshall Islands and the surrounding oceans. This is a largely overlooked chapter of post–World War II nuclearism, with effects that persist today. Forcefully displaced from their homeland because of the test, the indigenous people of the Marshall Islands were then subjected to radiation and medical experimentation in the hasty and still incomplete resettlement process.[9] In Japan, the eventual death of the *Lucky Dragon*'s radio operator and the scare over radioactive tuna elevated anti-American hostility and antinuclear sentiment across Japan and crucially informed the making of *Gojira*.

It was at this very moment that the United States, in collaboration with the Japanese government, introduced nuclear power to Japan. The rhetoric framing nuclear power as a "peaceful use" of nuclear energy waged a sort of psychological warfare, seeking to erase the image of nuclear bombs as weapons of mass destruction of both humans and the environment. Specifically, the worldwide "atoms for peace" program sponsored by the United States presented nuclear energy as the basis of future economic prosperity and technological modernity.[10] In the decades that followed, as many nations embraced nuclear power as a "clean" alternative to coal to sustain modern life and economic development, indigenous peoples worldwide were disproportionately exposed to radioactive waste from nuclear power plants.[11]

While some critics find the antinuclear subtext of the 1954 *Gojira* didactic or even reductive, the film in fact mediates rather complex historical, cultural, and psychological landscapes across the Pacific.[12] Beyond its solemn messages about the tolls of war and its aftermath, and the utility and effects of science on humans and the environment, for postwar Japan, the film's figuring of external threat as a monster ultimately destroyed by scientific invention positions Japan as the victim and enables the reconstruction of national identity.[13] The sentiment behind the assertion of Japan's control over science and technology as a defense against foreign attacks also informed its embrace of nuclear power—a technology championed by the United States, Japan's former enemy turned occupier—as the path toward modernity.[14]

In 1956, the first American incarnation of Gojira reached the US market. Dubbed and retitled *Godzilla, King of the Monsters!*, this version of the film is narrated from the perspective of an American foreign correspondent in edited scenes. This dubbed version cuts almost one-third of the original film (about thirty minutes), removing or neutralizing sections that highlight antinuclear messages and the antagonism between the United States and Japan.[15] Sequels were further altered to fit the Hollywood monster film genre of that period, and particularly to appeal to the US consumer market of young adults and children.[16] While in the early days the gigantic, scaly beast was a powerful representation of a terrifying racial other and a reminder of the atrocities committed by the United States for American audiences, later versions gradually turned the king of monsters into a campy, cute, and kitschy object of affection. As Japan's economy revived in the 1970s, Gojira and the sentiments that it symbolized were tamed, domesticated, managed, and contained through infantilization, turning the terrifying monster into a friendly hero.[17]

THE 2014 *GODZILLA* AND THE NUCLEAR PACIFIC

The 2014 *Godzilla*, produced in the United States and in English, renarrates the preoccupation with militarism, science, and technology in the Japanese original in the context of early twenty-first-century US military dominance, advanced nuclear technology, and environmental crises. In addition to referencing the 2011 disaster at the Fukushima nuclear plant in Japan after a devastating earthquake, this American version also encompasses a broader geopolitical range of natural and man-made disasters that reach the US home front, from the Philippines, Japan, and Hawaiʻi to San Francisco and Las Vegas. The film's American perspective is most explicitly expressed by its focus on the fate of a white American family as both a national allegory and a tale of global security.

The prologue of the 2014 *Godzilla* recalls the 1956 American version with a fast-paced montage of archival materials. This segment features images of fossils and other records of prehistoric creatures, instantly establishing a sense of historical authenticity and immediacy by alluding to the original 1954 *Gojira* as an amphibious prehistoric monster. This opening montage also introduces two enduring themes in the Gojira/Godzilla narrative: the monster's antagonistic relationship with humans since prehistoric times, and the use of science, specifically military science, to secure the safety of humanity. The montage soon shifts this ethnocentric, antagonistic narrative to the militarized Pacific in the 1950s, reaching its climax when Godzilla emerges from the water. This moment immediately follows quick flashes of media references to the military rivalry between the United States and the former USSR, where "human" perspectives referenced previously become subsumed and represented by US perspectives.

In the 1954 *Gojira*, although Pacific Islanders are largely absent, their existence is hinted at through Japanese-looking and Japanese-speaking residents in a small fishing village on the fictional Odo Island. The reference to the *Lucky Dragon* incident elides and overshadows the devastating consequences of the same H-bomb test for indigenous people on Bikini Atoll and those living downwind from ground zero. By contrast, the prologue of the 2014 *Godzilla* portrays the histories of indigenous people in the Pacific as romanticized tales of American paternal benevolence. It draws a sharp contrast between these innocent, passive, primitive islanders and rational, action-driven, scientifically knowledgeable American men.[18] The black-and-white image of islanders in canoes watching Godzilla emerge from the ocean are followed by several images that showcase the holy trinity of the military, science, and technology. These images include historical footage of US soldiers on a military vessel, a news photo of a search (presumably for Godzilla) conducted by a submarine, and an image of recording devices and news coverage of scientific research. Here, Western men are portrayed as representatives of imperial benevolence, military violence, and scientific rationality. The news clipping of scientists studying bombs on Bikini Atoll is juxtaposed with the image of US military personnel who are shaking hands with and smiling at happy-looking islander children.

The introduction of Pacific islanders is followed by a cartoonish rendition of the islands, dotted with palm trees, juxtaposed with historical footage of US military operations that, as a quick geographical sketch suggests, span different islands in the effort to destroy the monster. At this point, the film's attempt at thematizing historical narration as a problematic act of completely rewriting history becomes evident. The bomb tests on Bikini Atoll caused casualties, radiation sickness, cancers, and other devastating consequences, including the radioactive contamination of fisheries. If the 1956 American *Godzilla* downplays the link between the monster's appearance and the H-bomb tests, the 2014 *Godzilla* appears to completely erase the genealogical complexity of this creature by framing it as a prehistoric monster awakened by the bomb. Instead of using the monster as a rhetorical tool to oppose the use of nuclear weaponry, the 2014 *Godzilla* instead appears to justify the use of such force against the already awakened monster.

However, one crucial yet easily overlooked detail in the opening montage calls into question the overall premise of the film. On the surface, the opening historical renarration seems to suggest that US bomb tests in the 1950s were not immoral acts that subjected humans, animals, and the environment to deadly consequences but rather noble endeavors to kill the monster to protect humanity. Yet the opening credits, which are displayed while the montage unfolds, simulate real-time editing on the screen by showing names on the running credits written over with white lines. This explicit display of "forced editing" fundamentally problematizes the narrative premise of the montage. This visual effect places two layers of narrative in tension: the deliberate fabrication and manipulation of history that attempts to pass as the authoritative truth is placed in opposition to self-reflexive deconstruction of this fabricated truth.

YU-FANG CHO

This narrative tension is evident in the juxtaposition of the swimming Godzilla with archival footage from Operation Crossroads. This footage was made famous by *Radio Bikini* (1987), a documentary film that exposed the reality and consequences of US nuclear bomb tests on Bikini Atoll in the 1940s. In this most recent Godzilla tale, the same footage that was used to critique US nuclearism seems now to be appropriated to create a completely opposite narrative. Moreover, by replacing Pacific Islanders and Japanese with US soldiers, and *Lucky Dragon No. 5* with a US battleship, this new narrative seems to displace the critique of US nuclearism in the original *Gojira* with a justification of the use of nuclear power, both past and present, framing Americans as the ultimate victims. However, as the opening montage evokes all of these familiar narratives of American imperial benevolence, the whited-out opening credits seem to call into question the film's own act of representation and narrative authority.

In Gojira/Godzilla narratives, the representation of various Pacific islands as the birthplace or habitat of monsters clearly registers the Western and Japanese colonial mentality.[19] The 2014 *Godzilla*, whose geographic scope extends to include the mainland US cities of San Francisco and Las Vegas, provides an opportunity to reflect on US nuclearism as an expansive, transpacific technological phenomenon. The main narrative of the film begins at a uranium mining site in the Philippines in 1999, where the discovery of an empty radiated spore—which, as the audience learns later, is the spore of a male MUTO (short for "massive unidentified terrestrial organism," a multilegged monster resembling a tardigrade)—causes alarms and prompts two scientists to carry out an investigation on site.

The setting in the Philippines serves as a reminder of US imperial dominance in Asia and the Pacific. The Philippines was, like many islands in the Pacific, home to US military bases, and the United States still exerts significant cultural, political, and economic influence there.[20] Moreover, the export of nuclear technology to the Philippines and other Southeast Asian sites after World War II was said to have saved the struggling new industry. The setting in the Philippines thus evokes a broader transpacific mapping of the 2011 Fukushima disaster. This highlights the ties between US military dominance in Southeast Asia and the Pacific and the establishment of US-based nuclear energy industry in the Pacific Rim, which can be traced back to US introduction of nuclear energy to Japan in the 1950s and in turn evokes the Fukushima disaster. The uranium mine in the film thus connects the histories of colonialism, militarism, and neocolonialism, with the formal colony continuing to function as a site of extraction of resources—in this case, uranium for both nuclear weapons and nuclear energy. The various islands and sites featured in the 2014 American *Godzilla*'s remapping of Asia and the Pacific thus evoke the extensive reach of the transpacific nuclear-military-industrial complex.[21]

NUCLEAR WEAPONRY, NUCLEAR ENERGY, AND NUCLEAR FAMILY

The film's initial setting in a nuclear power plant in Janjira (a fictional city in Japan) further highlights the connection between nuclear weaponry and nuclear power in the twenty-first century. In the original *Gojira*, a Japanese scientist, Dr. Serizawa, serves as the ultimate symbol of moral conscience, striving heroically to avert disaster. In the 2014 American version, this figure is replaced by a white American nuclear family, especially the father and son. The father, Joe Brody, is an engineer at the plant (his wife, Sandy, works at the same plant and dies trying to prevent damage to the reactor), and the early scenes of the film offer a sentimental depiction of his noble character.[22] Early on the morning of Joe's birthday, he detects increasing patterns of tremors akin to seismic activity in the Philippines. Sensing impending disaster, he rushes to alert the Japanese authorities. These tremors, as the audience learns later in the film, result from the male MUTO's calls for a female MUTO in Nevada, and they lead to the cracking and meltdown of the Janjira nuclear plant. Directly alluding to the 2011 Fukushima disaster, the narration of this event implicitly criticizes the Japanese government for covering up threats to public safety.

By shifting the narrative setting from a small Pacific island to Japan, the 2014 film also shifts from a critique of the US use of nuclear weaponry in the original Japanese version to a focus on the threats posed by nuclear energy, symbolized most explicitly by MUTOs. In the film, this disaster is presented primarily as the Japanese government's responsibility (although US culpability is referenced later in the film). This shift works both to erase the brutal history of US bombings and bomb tests and to reassign the responsibility for nuclear disasters. With its focus on the plight of the Brody family, the primary narrative of the film occludes and overwrites the consequences of nuclear power suffered by indigenous communities in the Pacific.

The emphasis on the Brody family's self-sacrifice, strong moral principles, and traumatic loss adds a heavy dose of nationalist, white, heteroreproductive sentimentality to the previous Godzilla narratives, which tended to portray all of humanity as under threat. This time around, whether the monsters attack Japan, America, or somewhere in between, the spectacle of catastrophes centers the white American family as a metaphor of national racial reproduction: it is white lives that matter, an idea that is extended universally as the film draws the audience's attention to the emotional duress the family suffers. In directing the audience to identify and sympathize primarily with the white family, the film both underscores and subtly problematizes the common structure of feeling in both the American "atoms for peace" narrative and the contemporary antiterrorist narrative. These narratives overshadow the afflictions and trauma enacted on indigenous communities in the Pacific and non-American racialized communities overseas, rendering their life and death irrelevant in the face of the threat to US national security as a planetary crisis.

Serving as the moral center of the film, this trope of the defense of the (white) American family also underscores the entanglement of nuclear energy and nuclear weaponry. Whereas Joe Brody is devoted to the nuclear power industry and is cast as the classic heroic, antiestablishment male scientist, his son, Ford, emphasizes the nationalistic narrative of the white male hero. Ford grows up to become an explosives expert in the US military. Fatally injured during the male MUTO's attack in Janjira, Joe tells Ford to keep his family safe, pointing up Ford's amplified responsibility for carrying on his father's legacy by stopping the current disaster from escalating into total destruction. The depiction of the chaos and catastrophes in the second part of the film underscores his heroic efforts to save both his immediate family and the human population of Tokyo, Hawai'i, and the greater San Francisco area.

Unlike previous Godzilla films, set mainly in locations outside the United States, the 2014 *Godzilla* stages combat scenes in US territories, first in Hawai'i and finally in San Francisco, while the Philippines and Japan serve as the backdrop. The setting of San Francisco, where Ford's wife and son live and where the violent battle between the MUTOs and Godzilla takes place, is significant in several ways. First, the Golden Gate Bridge, the city's landmark, provides an optimal staging ground for the visual spectacles that are central to monster films. Second, the border zone between land and sea highlights the motif of crossings and encounters, particularly the meeting of "nature" (creature) and humans. Third, as the gateway to the United States for transpacific migrants, San Francisco is the site of rich and complex histories of Asian immigration that often conjure up orientalist perceptions, such as overpopulation by racial others: it is thus, as is discussed below, an evocative setting for "alien attacks" that reference deviant Asian sexuality and reproduction. And finally, the Lawrence Berkeley Laboratory has been a crucial site for the circulation of nuclear materials across the Pacific.[23] These various dimensions of this setting allow the film to effectively infuse reflections on militarism and nuclear technology with concerns about orientalism, race, and reproduction.

Before the final showdown between Godzilla and the MUTOs in San Francisco, the havoc wreaked by the male MUTO's landing in Honolulu advances the film's two major themes: the vulnerable white American family in need of defense, and humanity's failed manipulation of science and technology, specifically nuclear weaponry. Ford's rescue of a Japanese boy, who is then reunited with his mother, foreshadows Ford's effort to rescue his own family in San Francisco in the final segment of the film. Ford's extension of his fatherly love to a child of a different race elevates his moral status and heroism. He is not only a loyal son, a loving father, and a courageous and patriotic American soldier, but he is also a rescuer of all humanity in peril. Notably, this family narrative continues as the script of reproduction develops in a parallel context. While Ford tries to catch a flight back to San Francisco to rescue his wife and son, the male MUTO flies to San Francisco to meet the female MUTO from Las Vegas, as scientists explain, to seek radiation in order to mate and reproduce.

AMBIVALENCE TOWARD NUCLEAR POWER

Before the violent confrontations between the MUTOs and Godzilla unfold in San Francisco, Joe, having observed seismic patterns similar to those that occurred in the Philippines fifteen years earlier, heads back to Janjira with Ford. This father-son mission reveals the cause of the power-plant disaster: the male MUTO has an electromagnetic pulse and can absorb electricity. As a result, when the Japanese military attacks the cocoon of the male MUTO with high-voltage electricity in an attempt to kill it, they actually facilitate its hatching. This failed attack can be read as a critique of the humanity's failure to manage nuclear power or, more generally, the limitations of technology— the classic motif of science gone awry. In other words, the technology that scientists have developed to gain control over and exploit the natural world to advance humans' self-interests has a completely opposite effect, engendering a vicious cycle of destruction.

The problematic marriage between science and the military is best illustrated in the failed operation of the multinational Monarch project. In the effort to kill the MUTOs, the US military joins forces with Dr. Serizawa of Japan and Dr. Graham of the United Kingdom. Taking place on a US battleship, the encounter between the two scientists obscures Godzilla's origin as man-made and casts the monster as a prehistoric creature with an origin in nature. As Dr. Graham and Dr. Serizawa explain, both Godzilla and the MUTOs came into existence millions of years before mankind, and their food source is radiation.

Dr. Graham's seemingly objective narrative about science and nature reframes the nuclear bomb tests as projects of pure scientific discovery. She explains that the Monarch project was established in the wake of the discovery of these creatures, specifically to study Godzilla, the predator at the top of the primordial ecosystem. Moreover, according to her narrative, the nuclear bomb tests in the 1940s and 1950s were in fact secret multinational military operations to eliminate Godzilla.

Graham's narrative rationalizes military actions through the language of science. It posits Godzilla, once a symbol of antinuclearism, as a justification for government secrecy in the name of public safety and also as nature's balancing force of the expansion of the multinational nuclear military complex. Here, Godzilla is darkly characterized as "a god for all intents and purposes, a monster." By contrast, perhaps alluding to Japanese folklore, Serizawa maintains a cautiously optimistic belief in the creature's ability to ultimately restore the balance of nature. These accounts represent divergent views on whether Godzilla's power is a natural occurrence or a result of dangerous human manipulation of natural forces. Serizawa's comment could also be read as an ironic reframing of man-made catastrophes—bombs, radiation, and mutation—as part of the natural order.

As the battle between the MUTOs and Godzilla escalates, science adopts a passive approach based on a belief in the balancing mechanism of nature, while the US military asserts an increasingly aggressive role. Despite Dr. Serizawa's caution and earnest plea, the US military insists on deploying nuclear weaponry in the name of protecting US citizens. The magnitude of the threat caused by the MUTOs is dramatized by the depiction of their mating, which produces millions of eggs. Taking place in San Francisco's old Chinatown, distinguished by red lanterns in the foreground, this mating scene of the "alien species" evokes the historical discourse of sexual deviancy associated with Chinese immigrants and reinforces the menace of alien invasion.[24]

The orientalist framing of San Francisco in this narrative of alien invasion obscures the more recent history of the area. The US government has actively engaged in and supported nuclear and military research in the Bay Area. High-tech industries in Silicon Valley have been key players in the transpacific nuclear-military-industrial complex, which includes Japan and Taiwan. This history is intimately tied to the testing of nuclear bombs in the Pacific, to US export of nuclear energy to the Asia-Pacific region after World War II, and to the human and environmental costs of these undertakings. The orientalist narrative displaces the consequences of this history—the production of excessive nuclear waste—onto the alien race.[25] Moreover, the female MUTO—the egg-producing alien body that came from the uranium mine in the Philippines—was secretly transported to Nevada by US agents when it was still dormant. This detail, implied in a passing comment by Graham, reveals that what is perceived to be an outside threat is in fact a direct result of the self-serving behavior of the US government.

In the final scene, with the MUTOs eliminated by Godzilla and Ford reunited with his son and wife, the crowd cheers for Godzilla as he makes his signature roar before entering the water and swimming away. Here, Graham's astounded reverence and wondering awe of Godzilla underscores Serizawa's earlier comment about the arrogance of man and the respect for the natural order. The news coverage of Godzilla's victory, headlined "King of the Monsters: Savior of Our City?" contradicts Serizawa's comment about humanity's arrogance. As the audience, we must also ask whether the ultimate triumph of the 2014 *Godzilla* forever brackets and erases the suffering of indigenous communities in the Pacific.

The whited-out opening credits in the prologue prompt us to question the film's surface narrative: it seems to romanticize the forces of nature over man-made technology, to frame consequences of human actions as part of the natural order, to denounce government secrecy, and to satirize the futility of military technology. While renarrating Godzilla as a force of nature that secures the reproduction of the white American heterosexual family and planetary security, the film also implicitly questions how narratives of a nuclear future have been made possible by deliberate erasures—for example, of traditional kinship networks, families, and ways of life at sites of the transpacific nuclear-military-industrial complex.[26] As a revered and powerful force, Godzilla is also highly unpredictable: thus the creature must retreat from the human world once its mission is accomplished. Whether we approach this "natural" force with aggressive control, passive acceptance, or empathetic reverence, we can imagine a disaster-free future only by willfully forgetting the contested genealogies of transpacific nuclear modernity that gave birth to Gojira and continue to shape what we make of the King of Monsters.

NOTES

1   The name of the monster in the 1954 original Japanese version, Gojira, was changed to Godzilla in the first American version in 1956. On the name's origin and change, see William Tsutsui, *Godzilla on My Mind: Fifty Years of the King of Monsters* (New York: Palgrave Macmillan, 2004), 26. On this figure as a product of the atomic age that draws on Japanese folklore, see Joyce E. Boss, "Hybridity and Negotiated Identity in Japanese Popular Culture," in *In Godzilla's Footsteps: Japanese Pop Culture Icons on the Global Stage*, ed. William M. Tsutsui and Michiko Ito, 103–9 (New York: Palgrave Macmillan, 2006). On childhood memory, see Tsutsui, *Godzilla on My Mind*, 1–12.

2   Aaron Gerow, "Wrestling with Godzilla: Intertexuality, Childish Spectatorship, and National Body," in Tsutsui and Ito, *In Godzilla's Footsteps*, 64. On the rise of consumer culture in the United States and the transformation of Godzilla, see Sayuri Guthrie-Shimizu, "Lost in Translation and Morphed in Transit: Godzilla in Cold War America," in Tsutsui and Ito, *In Godzilla's Footsteps*, 51–62.

3   See Susan Napier, "When Gojira Speaks," in Tsutsui and Ito, *In Godzilla's Footsteps*, 9–19; Christine R. Yano, "Monstering the Japanese Cute: Pink Globalization and Its Critics Abroad," in Tsutsui and Ito, *In Godzilla's Footsteps*, 153–66.

4   On this film as an allegory for transpacific networks and alliances designed to secure and stabilize the Asia-Pacific region for free trade, see Erin Suzuki, "Beasts from the Deep," *Journal of Asian American Studies* 20, no. 1 (2017): 11–28.

5   For a general overview of how such racial logic operates in Euro-American ecological discourses, see Elizabeth DeLoughrey and George B. Handley, "Introduction: Toward an Aesthetics of the Earth," in *Postcolonial Ecologies: Literatures of the Environment*, ed. Elizabeth DeLoughrey and George B. Handley, 3–39 (Oxford: Oxford University Press, 2011).

6   Facts about the bomb tests were suppressed during the US occupation. The *Lucky Dragon* incident and the release of *Gojira* were two events by which the Japanese public began to discover these facts after the suspension of US censorship. See Mark Anderson, "Mobilizing *Gojira*: Mourning Modernity as Monstrosity," in Tsutsui and Ito, *In Godzilla's Footsteps*, 22, 36n.4; Joanne Bernadi, "Teaching Godzilla: Classroom Encounters with a Cultural Icon," in Tsutsui and Ito, *In Godzilla's Footsteps*, 121.

7   Tsutsui, *Godzilla on My Mind*, 16–17, 20; "Introduction," in Tsutsui and Ito, *In Godzilla's Footsteps*, 6.

8   For a historical account of the antinuclear movement and the introduction of nuclear energy in Japan, see Muto Ichiyo, "The Buildup of Nuclear Armament Capability and the Postwar Statehood of Japan: Fukushima and the Genealogy of Nuclear Bombs and Power Plants," *Inter-Asia Cultural Studies* 14,

no. 2 (2011): 173. See also Toshihiro Higuchi, "An Environmental Origin of Antinuclear Activism in Japan, 1954–1963: The Government, the Grassroots Movement, and the Politics of Risk," *Peace and Change* 33, no. 3 (2008): 333–67; Guthrie-Shimizu, "Lost in Translation," 53; Bernadi, "Teaching Godzilla," 122.

9   Teresia K. Teaiwa, "Bikinis and Other S/pacific N/oceans," in *Militarized Currents: Toward a Decolonized Future in Asia and the Pacific*, ed. Setsu Shigematsu and Keith L. Camacho, 15–31 (Minneapolis: University of Minnesota Press, 2010).

10 Muto, "The Buildup of Nuclear Armament Capability," 186; Ira Chernus, *Eisenhower's Atoms for Peace* (College Station: Texas A&M University Press, 2002). For accounts of the effect on the Marshallese, see Holly M. Barker, "Radiation Communities: Fighting for Justice for the Marshall Islands," in *Life and Death Matters: Human Rights, Environment, and Social Justice*, ed. Barbara Rose Johnston (Walnut Creek, CA: Left Coast Press, 2011), 358–59; Barbara Rose Johnston and Holly M. Barker, *Consequential Damages of Nuclear War: The Rongelap Report* (Walnut, Creek, CA: Left Coast Press, 2008). On the legacies of nuclearism, see Barbara Rose Johnston, ed., *Half-Lives and Half-Truths: Confronting the Radioactive Legacies of the Cold War* (Santa Fe, NM: School for Advanced Research Press, 2007).

11 It is important to remember past and present indigenous antinuclear resistance, such as the Kanaka Maoli (Native Hawaiian) grassroots organization, whose 1976–97 activist efforts brought an end to over fifty years of US military training and weapons testing on the sacred Hawaiian island of Kaho'olawe. See Dina El Dessouky, "Activating Voice, Body, and Place: Kanaka Maoli and Ma'ohi Writings from Kaho'olawe and Moruroa," in DeLoughrey and Handley, *Postcolonial Ecologies*, 254–72.

12 Tsutsui and Ito, "Introduction," *In Godzilla's Footsteps*, 6.

13 Tsutsui, *Godzilla on My Mind*, 35–38, 105; Napier, "When Godzilla Speaks," 11.

14 Tsutsui, *Godzilla on My Mind*, 97–99.

15 For further discussion of the alterations, see Tsutsui, *Godzilla on My Mind*, 38–42; Guthrie-Shimizu, "Lost in Translation," 54–55. The 1954 *Gojira* was not released in the United States until 2004.

16 Tsutsui, *Godzilla on My Mind*, 39–42; Guthrie-Shimizu, "Lost in Translation," 57–60. For a summary of developments from the 1960s to 2000, see Tsutsui, *Godzilla on My Mind*, 113–40.

17 Napier, "When Godzilla Speaks," 11; Tsutsui, *Godzilla on My Mind*, 84–88.

18 For discussions of American military benevolence, see Mimi Nguyen, *The Gift of Freedom: War, Debt, and Other Refugee Passages* (Durham, NC: Duke University Press, 2012); Grace Cho, *Haunting the Korean Diaspora: Shame, Secrecy, and the Forgotten War* (Minneapolis: University of Minnesota Press, 2008).

19   Anderson, "Mobilizing *Gojira*," 27; Yoshikuni Igarashi, "Martha's Gigantic Egg: Consuming the South Pacific in 1960s Japan," in Tsutsui and Ito, *In Godzilla's Footsteps*, 83–102.

20   See Catherine Ceniza Choy, *Empire of Care: Nursing and Migration in Filipino American History* (Durham, NC: Duke University Press, 2003).

21   On the relationship between US militarism and tourism in the Philippines, see Vernadette V. Gonzalez, *Securing Paradise: Tourism and Militarism in Hawai'i and the Philippines* (Durham, NC: Duke University Press, 2013).

22   In the original version, there is only a love triangle, not a family. To American eyes, the woman represents the "good" side of Japan: vulnerable, grateful, and self-sacrificial.

23   See Lindsey Dillon, "Pandemonium on the Bay: Naval Station Treasure Island and the Toxic Legacies of Atomic Defense," in *Urban Reinventions: San Francisco's Treasure Island*, ed. Lynne Horiuchi and Tanu Sankalia (Honolulu: University of Hawai'i Press, 2017),140–58 ; Lindsey Dillon, "Race, Waste, and Space: Brownfield Redevelopment and Environmental Justice at the Hunters Point Shipyard," *Antipode* 46 (2014): 1205–21.

24   See Yu-Fang Cho, *Uncoupling American Empire: Cultural Politics of Deviance and Unequal Difference, 1890–1910* (Albany: SUNY Press, 2013).

25   See Yu-Fang Cho, "Nuclear Diffusion: Notes toward Reimagining Reproductive Justice," *Amerasia Journal: Asian American/Pacific Islander/Transcultural Societies* 41, no. 3 (2015): 2–25.

26   Ibid.

CHAPTER FIFTEEN

EARTHSEEDS OF CHANGE

Postapocalyptic Mythmaking, Race, and Ecology in
The Book of Eli *and Octavia Butler's Womanist Parables*

KIM D. HESTER WILLIAMS

>   i say that at the
> masters table only one plate is set for supper   i say no seed
> can flourish on this ground once planted then forsaken   wild
> berries warm a field of bones
> bloom how you must i say
>
>   LUCILLE CLIFTON, "MULBERRY FIELDS"

TAKEN from her collection *Mercy*, Lucille Clifton's "mulberry fields" expresses images of a master's table where there is only "one plate" and forsaken ground where seeds cannot flourish. Clifton's poetics of domination, neglect, and death, posed against the determination of "wild" life to "bloom," gestures toward my central concern: the material and imaginative relation between race and ecology. I focus here on apocalyptic speculative narratives that reify yet also reenvision the relationship between race and "nature." The racial speculative narrative exposes the enduring, false claims of a post–civil rights and postracial society while imagining how humans in ecological decline can be "saved" by earth's most "wretched" racial inhabitants. Apocalyptic representations of ecological collapse offer imaginative critical responses to the problem of hierarchical difference and ecological crisis. The movie *The Book of Eli* (2010) and Octavia Butler's novels *Wild Seed* (1980), *Parable of the Sower* (1993), and *Parable of the Talents* (1998) contend with environmental deterioration and ecological demise by using race and gender, specifically Black male and female figuration, to imagine future possibilities for human survival and redemption.

The Book of Eli reifies race and gender mainly through the representation of the male protagonist, Eli, as the atypically violent "magical negro," a Christ-like savior expressive of traditional Christian ethics, whose death is necessary to save humankind from slavery and ecological apocalypse.[1] In contradistinction, Butler's Black female protagonists, Anyanwu and Lauren Olamina, reenvision human value and purpose through African-centered cultural practices, a reinscription of Christian ethics as "Earthseed" verses that foreground positive ecology, and a womanist ethics of care and communalism.[2]

The Book of Eli and Butler's stories portray the consequences of ecological disconnection from both the land and its inhabitants and the psychically damaging isolation that ensues. In *The Book of Eli*, African American melancholy becomes essential to redeeming the earth as Eli confronts apocalyptic scarcity, human corruption, and the hoarding of economic and natural resources. Conversely, Butler's speculative discourses reveal dialogic landscapes of race, gender, and ecology that represent, in concert with a womanist ethics of care and communalism, an ecofeminist intervention. Butler's fiction is intensely occupied with social change as a necessary remedy for "the mutually reinforcing oppression of humans and of the natural world."[3]

Octavia Butler's dystopian logic is, relatedly, a method for understanding human imbrication in compromised and often toxic environments where therapeutic restoration is necessarily facilitated, not hindered, by the natural world.[4] Her postapocalyptic narratives confront "the dialectical unity of the individual and the collective" while also advocating for mutually beneficial, nondestructive ecological relations.[5]

ELI'S PATH: RACIAL ECOLOGIES OF REVELATION AND REDEMPTION

Apocalyptic representations of ecological collapse often display lone survivors who are left to rebuild a society. In *The Book of Eli*, we are introduced to a survivor of nuclear apocalypse who is also a "magical negro" figure. The terms *magic negro* or *magical negro* are most often associated with contemporary Hollywood's infamous characterization of African Americans as imbued with mystical powers or spirituality deriving from folk wisdom. These characters typically possess an intuition that allows them special insight into the human condition, which in these narratives is deployed primarily to aid white protagonists in realizing their full human potential and gaining a deeper self-awareness, while also realizing that self-interest must yield to the common good.[6]

Although Eli, played by Denzel Washington, does not possess any mystical or supernatural power, he is nonetheless portrayed as being hyperintuitive, largely because of the loss of his eyesight as a result of nuclear exposure. This detail is inconspicuous until near the end of the film: for most of the film, we experience Eli's hyperintuition and hypersensitivity as an intrinsic part of his identity, a notion that is further promoted by the explicit Black figuration of Eli's body. In the opening scene, we see Eli wearing a hazmat suit and mask while hunting for food in a clearly devastated environment. Once Eli finds shelter and removes the suit and mask, his racial identity is revealed.

Eli's deep brown pigment is not the only signifier of his "race." As the scene progresses, he locates a salvaged iPod and scrolls to Al Green's song, "How Can You Mend a Broken Heart?" As he listens, he turns up the volume so that Green's melancholy lyrics and melodic blues progression permeate the scene and become the only sound we hear. The Al Green song infuses the beginning of the film narrative with a decided blues aesthetic. As Amiri Baraka observes, "Blues (Lyric), its song quality, is . . . the deepest expression of memory. Experience re/feeling. It is the racial memory."[7] This description epitomizes the film narrative's postapocalyptic illustration of dystopian alienation and chaos. The song's blues aesthetic invokes a "re/feeling" of Black Atlantic slavery, "a racial memory" of loss, subjugation, and dispossession. Eli's racial embodiment also signifies both the afterlife of slavery and the contiguous vulnerability of nature to the relentless threat of human domination and destruction, a symbolic function of Black subjectivity that is reinforced throughout the scene and the film.[8]

While the Al Green song plays, the scene shifts, cutting to Eli using a KFC (Kentucky Fried Chicken) wet wipe to wash his body. Subsequent jump cuts show Eli's back and shoulders covered by scars that evoke the brutal whippings routinely inflicted on enslaved African Americans. The scarring can also be read as parallel to the scarring of the land. Eli embodies not only the legacy of slavery but also the abuse and neglect of the environment; his suffering is visually and audibly rendered. It is not a debased nature that is displaced onto Eli's body, as Stacy Alaimo has rightly observed in her critique of the pairing of the racial other with nature as abject.[9] Nor is nature romanticized. Rather, the natural world and its inhabitants are in a state of captivity, and Eli's symbolic function, communicated at the outset of the film, prepares us for his crucial role in securing the survival and redemption of the land and its inhabitants.

The only other explicitly foregrounded and visible person of color in the film is a Black man who is killed moments after he first appears on screen for his failure to keep Eli captive. We can infer from this dearth of people of color in the film that the purpose of Eli's path is white redemption. This representation of Eli is analogous to what Toni Morrison famously identified as American Africanism.[10] The function of the Black body as simultaneously a commodity, a sign of social and cultural rupture, and the means of white redemption is part of a long history of dependent racialization in which the Black figure is fixed in struggle, pain, and suffering yet is called on to redeem the impossible dream of freedom. Such interminable Black pain and suffering, which exclusively serves the purposes of white redemption, confounds communalism.

No fictional Black figure evidences this more clearly than Harriet Beecher Stowe's title character, Uncle Tom.[11] Stowe associated her own frustration, as a woman marginalized and oppressed by an entrenched patriarchy, with the "plight of the slave." *Uncle Tom's Cabin* aptly sheds light on a labor system that reduced women, workers, and slaves to object status and which could be sustained only by the suppression or absence of systems of consideration and care. Such disregard necessarily extends to stewardship of the natural environment, which is also relegated to object status by the forces of capital accumulation and exploitation.

Yet some (Black) bodies continue to carry an incongruous weight of oppression and ethical, ecological responsibility. Uncle Tom is brutally killed, or rather sacrificed, to punctuate Stowe's Calvinist critique of American patriarchy and capitalism. Her portrayal of Uncle Tom's "stoical ethic" of Christian virtues and devotion to God's grace and promise of salvation proved to be the greatest catalyst for arousing the readers' sympathy for the enslaved and resistance to legalized human bondage.[12] Nevertheless, Uncle Tom's death leaves a dispirited and broken community, and Stowe's critique thus remains incomplete. Tom's separation from his community, resulting from the oppressive labor practices necessitated by slavery, and finally the cruelty of the slave driver Simon Legree result in Tom's death—a permanent separation.

Additionally, George and Eliza's self-imposed exile to Liberia at the end of the novel evidences the failure of American democracy and the idea that there is no viable space for Black people to live—and certainly not to thrive or, in Clifton's poetics, to bloom. At the beginning of Stowe's narrative,

George abandons religion and faith, as he feels 'God' has abandoned him: "I an't a Christian like you Eliza; my heart's full of bitterness; I can't trust in God. Why does he let things be so?"[13] At the end of the novel, he abandons America as well. *Uncle Tom's Cabin* promotes religious solidarity and sacrifice despite the fragmentation of self and community experienced by all of the characters, and most starkly by the Black members of society. How does the Christian ethic of seeking the "ultimate good" produce a productive, positive ecological kinship, that is, a more just and livable world? To put it in James Baldwin's terms, "What exactly is the 'good' of society?"[14]

Baldwin's crucial question points directly to *The Book of Eli*'s similar uses of a Christian ethos of salvation and self-sacrificing, suffering love. *The Book of Eli* centers on spiritual revelation and redemption through self-sacrifice. Eli has not only acute intuition but also unique spiritual insight because he possesses the last copy of the King James edition of the Bible. All other copies of the Bible were destroyed in a nuclear explosion that "tore a hole in the sky." Some survivors, including Eli, were sheltered from the nuclear flash and emerged one year later into the desolate landscape. As Eli contemplated his own survival, he heard "a voice" that led him to a book—the Bible. He explains that "the voice told me to carry the book out West. Told me the path would be laid out for me, that I'd be led to a place where the book would be safe, told me that I'd be protected against anyone, anything that stood in my path." At this postapocalyptic crossroads, Eli accepts his calling and spiritual path to redeem society. In the thirty years that have elapsed since his discovery, Eli has been reading the braille copy of the Bible each day and has memorized its words, moral lessons, and instructions. The biblical passages that he recites reinforce the precepts of obedience to God's law and punishment for disobedience or transgression. During a fight scene, he is confronted by numerous men who have been instructed by Carnegie, a tyrant who controls one of the surviving towns and seeks to gain control of more populated areas, not to allow Eli to leave with the book. Before killing most of them to escape and protect the book, Eli recites from Genesis: "Cursed be the ground for our sake. . . . Thorns and Thistles it shall bring forth . . . for out of the ground we were taken . . . for the dust we are and to the dust we shall return." Notably, Eli's interpretation of the passage substitutes the pronoun *we* for the original *thou*, emphasizing a Calvinist view of a collective original sin for which humans must perpetually suffer and make amends.

The Book of Eli is grounded in an apocalyptic Revelation narrative in which the Genesis reference signals what Douglas Robinson theorizes as "the two temporal boundaries" between Adam, as the "first man," and

Christ, as "the last Adam," wherein "Adam or mortal man is bounded and Christ is the boundary."[15] Eli simultaneously occupies the role of the bounded mortal man and that of Christ as the boundary, that is, the beginning and the end (of time). The biblical name Eli, in fact, can be read as indicative of a temporal end (or apocalypse) as punishment for the wickedness of humans.[16] It further indicates God's moral supremacy over humans who, because of original sin, can never completely escape wickedness and depravity but who can be "saved." Again we must ask, what is the "good" of society? What is Eli's relation not simply to God but to the land and its inhabitants?

Eli's focus remains on delivering the book, if not in its physical form, in the form of his word-for-word memorization and recitation of the scriptures, after reaching a sanctuary located in what appears to have been San Francisco, California. With the help of Solara, a character coded as a white female, he manages to complete the task, after which he simply dies. Solara pays respects to Eli at his burial site, leaving a white flower evocative of the white smock Eli wore while reciting the Bible. This symbol also recalls Eli's explanation to Solara that faith is a "flower of light in the field of darkness"— again referring to Genesis and God's desire for light as representative of the "good." Eli's body ultimately becomes associated with both faith in God and the ecological relations of light/sun and field/land. Eli's faith is further expressed in a voiceover of his final words, where he thanks God for keeping him "resolute" on his path, "knowing that I have done right with my time on earth. I fought the good fight. I finished the race. I kept the faith."

As the film concludes, we discover that Eli's faith and good fight seem to have been deployed in the service of preserving European-centered culture and patriarchal theological traditions. Lombardi, the leader of the sanctuary, tells Eli they have been restoring books and other cultural artifacts to "rebuild civilization," proudly boasting that they have obtained works by Shakespeare, an almost complete set of the *Encyclopedia Britannica*, and several Mozart and Wagner records. To the voiceover of Eli's final words, Lombardi places the transcribed edition of the King James Bible on the Alcatraz sanctuary library shelf, between the Torah on one side and the Quran on the other. A subsequent scene shows the "Alcatraz" edition of the King James Bible, dictated by Eli, being replicated en masse on the sanctuary's new printing press.

The last scene of the film depicts a lone Solara, mirroring the opening scene of Eli, carrying with her Eli's possessions and a copy of the reprinted Bible while she listens to Eli's iPod as she heads back home. We can assume that she will deliver the Bible and its moral lessons along with word that "civilization" is being rebuilt. The restored civilization that is represented in the Alcatraz scene, however, is one that does not reflect Eli's cultural origins, his blues aesthetic, or other multicultural and diverse traditions that are absent from the film. In this civilization, *where is Al Green*?

The prescribed "good of society" in the film is not only Eurocentric: it is a theological path that does not address the exploitation and deterioration of the earth or the perpetual "slow violence" of racism, sexism, economic dispossession, and imperialism.[17] Nor is it clear how the revival of European culture and traditional Judeo-Christian theology will produce positive and productive ecological relations that promote life, as opposed to the antagonistic relations that precipitated the apocalypse. In considering the film's omission of these concerns, it is useful to reflect on Ivonne Gebara's insistence that "theology is a cultural product. And official theologies are cultural products of our hierarchical and masculine philosophies and ideologies." Gebara furthermore insists that traditional religions and Christian traditions "are not able to open new possibilities for our struggle for justice and happiness."[18]

Like Stowe's theological figuration and uses of Uncle Tom's symbolic death, Eli's death translates to an incomplete critique of American patriarchy and capitalism and the consequent demise of the environment. The traditional theological redemption privileged in the film, articulated by the recital of the patriarchal scriptures, does not extend to redemption of the land or any ecological relation beyond anthropocentrism and the supremacy of God. Furthermore, the film's final indication that society will be rebuilt by reinstating Eurocentric history, art, and culture offers no "new possibilities" for justice, sustainability, and life—not for Eli and not for Black people.

PARABLES OF MUTUALITY: OCTAVIA BUTLER'S
POSTAPOCALYPTIC ECOFEMINIST THEOLOGY AND
WOMANIST ETHICS OF CARE AND COLLECTIVISM

go. go. go into
the forest.

walk among
the deer.

GIOVANNI SINGLETON, "DAY 49," IN *ASCENSION*

An ecofeminist approach to environmental apocalypse necessitates a new ecological relation, what Gebara identifies as "a new believing in connectedness."[19] Relatedly, in the Hemispheric Institute of Performance and Politics publication *E-misférica: Caribbean Rasanblaj* article, "Groundings on *Rasanblaj* with M. Jacqui Alexander," Alexander elaborates on the concept of *rasanblaj* as a necessary project of reassembly and reimagination, "a constant element of supreme self—and collective reflexivity" and a pathway of "possibility and potential."[20] It is from this point of entry of *rasanblaj* that Octavia Butler's womanist ethics and ecofeminism take the reader on a journey of reassembly through reimagining. Butler fuses the past and present while also looking toward a future in which society will be redeemed not by death but by a renewal of life that extends to "the stars."

Specifically, Butler's 1980 novel *Wild Seed* and her two Parable novels, *Parable of the Sower* and *Parable of the Talents*, express a dynamic intersubjectivity that is crucial to *rasanblaj*—that is, reassembly and collectivism. Butler's work demonstrates how a deepened connection to others and to the land can mitigate the historical tension between other(ed) bodies and the disintegration or destruction of the natural environment. Butler's stories of slavery and apocalypse express a rigorous attention to care and connection. While intensely introspective, Butler's female protagonists function as heroes within the narrative who extend themselves, necessarily, while also preserving the supreme self to form what Alexander expresses as a "collective reflexivity." Butler engages an ecofeminist theology foregrounded by a concept of God that reassembles the supreme self with the collective environment and Spirit. As Alexander explains: "The way of Spirit [is] bringing together the far-flung, dismembered parts of ourselves into one place that is anchored in the Land. She, like Ocean, has the capaciousness to hold us. . . . It's in that capaciousness that we plant food, learn to make medicine, and come home to our wholeness."[21]

Butler's "way of Spirit" is made explicit at the beginning of chapter 1 in *Wild Seed*. The novel chronicles the relationship between two immortals: Anyanwu (Sun Woman), an African female shapeshifter, and Doro, a masculinist entity who violently possesses bodies and controls groups of telepaths and others with special abilities. When we are introduced to the protagonist, Anyanwu, she is expressly described as "an oracle. A woman through whom God spoke."[22] God speaks through Anyanwu by way of her stewardship over the land, the animals, and her people. She has borne generations of Africans for whom she has cared deeply and who have cared for her. This ecological relation of stewardship is also symbolized in the beginning chapter, by Anyanwu's tending her garden full of coco yams and various herbs that she "grew as medicines for healing" (4). Even when her magic frightens the people, she uses her abilities to convince them of its usefulness. As she tells Doro, she once transformed into "a sacred python" that "brought me luck. We were needing rain then to save the yam crop, and while I was a python, the rains came. The people decided my magic was good" (15). Butler's positive depiction of Anyanwu as a python is decidedly different from the Old Testament representation of the serpent as temptation and Eve as the embodiment of original sin. Butler instead focuses on a positive ecological interrelation, a "unity of spirit," that mitigates the unequal relations of power that Anyanwu could easily exploit but instead chooses to use for protection and healing.

Anyanwu is a not only an oracle and healer: she exemplifies "the way of Spirit" through her ability to adopt various human and animal forms, from her original Igbo female body to that of an elderly Igbo priestess, a Black man, a white male plantation owner, a leopard, a large bird, a dolphin, and a dog. She physically connects with others by inhabiting their experience. The antagonist of the novel, Doro, is likewise endowed with supernatural powers, but his power to "take over" the bodies of other humans and animals results in the immediate death of the original owner of the body. Doro uses this ability to perpetuate his existence, as well as to frighten and enslave masses of people. These include generations that he has fathered and especially what he calls the "wild seed," people possessing special abilities, like Anyanwu. In contrast to Anyanwu, Doro's ability and need to consume bodies has made him insensitive to the feelings and experiences of others and has intensified his disconnection. Doro's longing for Spirit and connection can be interpreted through Butler's drawings, which represent him as a horse whose gentle gaze and stance are neither dominating or indicative of being dominated (see the drawing below). Conversely, in the story, Doro is a violent tyrant and lonesome Soul who ultimately seeks connection and the way of Spirit that Anyanwu, through her connection and embodiment of various animals, invokes throughout the novel.

The story begins in 1690, when Doro discovers Anyanwu living in her West African village. She agrees to travel with Doro to live on several American plantations in the mid-nineteenth century. The novel ends with Anyanwu settling in California a few years before the Civil War. Doro wishes to possess Anyanwu and to use her to breed more "wild seed" progeny. Although he is able to keep her captive for a time, he is never able to fully possess her. Instead, Anyanwu's "presence seemed to be slowly awakening several long dormant emotions in him" (144). Anyanwu's constant attention to intersubjectivity—within and against the master-slave relation—repels Doro's power and dominance. In spite of his psychological torment and abuse, "he would not have her life" (197).

Octavia Butler, "Drawings of Horses," 1960, Box 32, Butler (Octavia E.)
Papers, courtesy of the Huntington Library, San Marino, California.

Butler expresses in *Wild Seed* what Elizabeth Spelman identifies as the
concern with a "specificity of slavery" precipitated by the demands of a
"labour of suffering" that is directly linked to racial(ized) ecologies—that is, to
a very particular experiential slavery: an entangled kinship not just of racial
bodies but of water, fire, and earth.[23] Through Anyanwu, Butler illustrates
an African cosmology that negotiates dislocation and slavery with "manifestations of locatedness, rootedness, and belonging that map individual and
collective relationships to the Divine."[24] She attempts to disrupt racial and
gender hierarchies by representing the complex relations between Anyanwu
and Doro, who must come to realize Anyanwu's true worth as a "medium
of spirit": "Anyanwu never told Doro that she could jump all but the widest
of the rivers they had to cross. . . . But Doro was not used to thinking as she
did about her abilities, not used to taking her strength or metamorphosing
ability for granted. He never guessed, never asked what she could do" (30).
What Anyanwu can do is to heal the physical and psychological wounds—
the "labours of suffering"—of racialized bodies and to insist on instilling
in Doro and every "body" a respect for all land, sea, and life.

This is most apparent in the scenes where Anyanwu transforms into the dolphin body, the form that she most identifies with outside her human form, "the best body she had ever shaped for herself." Butler writes how, as a dolphin, Anyanwu was "seeing differently . . . breathing differently" (82) and was "alone, but surrounded by creatures like herself—creatures she was finding harder to think of as animals. Swimming with them was like being with another people. A friendly people. No slavers with brands and chains here. No Doro with gentle, terrible threats to her children, to her" (84).

Amie Breeze Harper characterizes this ecofeminist approach in Butler's speculative fiction as "a holistic understanding of humanity's role in maintaining or destroying Earth's ecosystem."[25] In the end, Doro begs Anyanwu not to leave him and to promise to go on living. While he does not agree to stop killing or to completely release Anyanwu, he does agree that "he would not interfere with her children at all" (278). Anyanwu is left to continue protecting and healing generations, to continue nurturing and promoting life and herself, to *live*.

Read alongside *Wild Seed*, Octavia Butler's Parable stories are consonant ruminations on the spirit and empathy as a response to America's hegemonic history of slavery. These speculative narratives serve as a transformative antidote to empire and domination by inculcating—through ecowomanist protagonists—an individual and collective "love ethic."[26] As Madhu Dubey observes, "Slavery in *Parable* appears more centrally a descriptor of the present than as a historical reference point. . . . Butler pursues the extrapolative logic of futuristic science fiction to heighten dystopian present-day practices that are fostering new forms of servitude."[27] *Parable of the Sower* begins in the year 2024. The protagonist, Lauren Olamina, is the fifteen-year-old daughter of a Black Baptist preacher who is also a college professor. Lauren, her father, stepmother, and brothers live in a walled community located in Robledo, a suburb of Los Angeles. Lauren's journal entries depict a dystopian society riddled with drugs, violence, debt slavery, and an acute shortage of food, water, and shelter, as well as the encroachment of a Christian fundamentalism that becomes embedded within the government.

While Lauren's father adheres to and preaches a traditional Judeo-Christian theology similar to the Christian ethics espoused and embodied by Eli, he also inculcates and encourages Lauren to maintain a strong environmental consciousness. She is encouraged by studying the books in her father's library, which include volumes on "survival in the wilderness" and

"California native and naturalized plants and their uses, and basic living: log cabin-building, livestock raising, plant cultivation, soap making" (57–58). She explains to her friend Joanne that one particular plant book "about California Indians" offers insightful information about "the plants they used, and how they used them" (59). This indigenous agricultural knowledge helps form the basis of Lauren's Earthseed spirituality and new ecological relations—her reassembly and reimagining of community. Lauren's initial inscription of her Earthseed "belief system" uses "seed" as a metaphor for her newfound spiritualism:

> Godseed is all there is—all that
> Changes. Earthseed is all that spreads
> Earthlife to new earths.
> The universe is Godseed.
> Only we are Earthseed.
> And the destiny of Earthseed is to take root among the stars. (77)

She reveals the ecological source for her inspiration:

> The particular God-is-Change belief system that seems right to me will be called Earthseed . . . today, I found the name, found it while I was weeding the back garden and thinking about the way plants seed themselves, windborne, animalborne, waterborne, far from their parent plants. They have no ability at all to travel great distances under their own power, and yet they do travel. . . . There are islands thousands of miles from anywhere . . . where plants seeded themselves and grew long before any humans arrived. Earthseed. I am Earthseed. (77–78)

Lauren's belief reinscribes Christ's parable of sowing seed in "good earth" by extending the possibilities for positive human growth and its potential through community. Her spirituality is based on discovery and embracing change but also on recognizing that human survival will be achieved by the persistence of community: "*We persist*" (Butler's emphasis, 135).

Like Anyanwu in *Wild Seed*, Lauren Olamina possesses special abilities that help her rebuild community. Lauren has hyperempathy syndrome, a condition that postapocalyptic children suffer as a result of their mothers' having taken the drug Parateco, or "Einstein powder," while pregnant. The drug enhances intelligence but has deleterious side effects, especially for the unborn child. While many critics describe Lauren's condition as one that enables her to actually feel the physical pain of others, Butler has explicitly rejected this reading. In a *Science Fiction Studies* interview she insists that Lauren "is not empathic. She feels herself to be."[28] This declaration relates to Anyanwu as well as to Lauren Olamina. Lauren's hyperempathy syndrome can be read as a device that enables Butler to offer new ways of "feeling" in addition to new ways of envisioning community and ecological relations. Butler's larger ecofeminist purpose is to engender collectivism through connection. Lauren "feels herself" to be empathic because, like other characters who suffer from hyperempathy syndrome, she suffers desperately from a lack of connection—to other characters, to other living beings, and to the land. The need for connection is never resolved for Eli in *The Book of Eli*. It is also the need that Doro, in *Wild Seed*, longs to resolve through Anyanwu.

CONCLUSION

Nathaniel Mackey's ecopoetics in his "Song of the Andoumboulou: 33" locates meaning in leaves and wood. His poetic expression invites us to reorient ourselves and our ecological relations:

> A sudden rain, so we ducked
> under leaves. Wood became shed,
> > meaning
> Tree. Trunk, unembraceable,
> > beckoned,
> wide girth we'd have given the
> world to've been one with, run
> > with, roots
> above ground.[29]

The desire to be, as he writes, "one with, run with, roots above ground" resonates with Butler's explorations of the crucial need to form new ecological relations. How do we return to the embrace of nature, to hapticality—that is, a sensibility and feeling for connection—or love, as a renewed interconnectedness and embodiment of spirit in which we can be rooted "above ground"?[30] Octavia Butler's speculative response to this question is her offering of a Black womanist sowing of "wild seed" possibilities for transgressive convergences of race and ecology in the present "future."

"Octavia E. Butler and Large Tree," Amazon River region, 1985, Butler (Octavia E.) Papers, OEB 7185, courtesy of the Huntington Library, San Marino, California

NOTES

Epigraph: Lucille Clifton, excerpt from "mulberry fields," in *The Collected Poems of Lucille Clifton*, ed. Kevin Young and Michael S. Glaser (Rochester, NY: BOA Editions, 2010).

1   *The Book of Eli*, directed by Albert Hughes and Allen Hughes (2010; Burbank, CA: Warner Brothers).

2   Emilie Townes, *Womanist Ethics and the Cultural Production of Evil* (New York: Palgrave Press, 2006). Townes's womanist ethics is an elaboration of Alice Walker's concept of womanism, expressed in her book *In Search of Our Mothers' Gardens*. Womanism emphasizes Black women's wisdom, community, beauty, and critical thought. Townes's womanist ethics extends womanism to the "lived theological issues" and ethics of Walker's womanist discourse.

3   Greta Gaard and Lori Gruen, "Ecofeminism: Toward Global Justice and Planetary Health," *Society and Nature* 2 (1993): 1–35.

4   Greg Garrard, *Ecocritcism* (London: Routledge), 108.

5   Jonathan Scott, "Octavia Butler and the Base for American Socialism," *Socialism and Democracy*, 20, no. 3 (2006): 106–7.

6   See Kim D. Hester Williams, "NeoSlaves: Slavery, Freedom, and African American Apotheosis in *Candyman*, *The Matrix*, and *The Green Mile*," *Genders* 40 (November 2004), www.colorado.edu/gendersarchive1998–2013

/2004/11/01/neoslaves-slavery-freedom-and-african-american-apotheosis
-candyman-matrix-and-green-mile; Krin Gabbard, *Black Magic: White
Hollywood and African American Culture* (New Brunswick, NJ: Rutgers
University Press, 2004); Heather Hicks, "Hoodoo Economics: White Men's
Work and Black Men's Magic in Contemporary American Film," *Camera
Obscura* 18, no. 2 (2003): 27–55; Matthew W. Hughey, "Cinethetic Racism:
White Redemption and Black Stereotypes in 'Magical Negro' Films," *Social
Problems* 56, no. 3 (August 2009): 543–77; Cerise L. Glenn and Landra J.
Cunningham, "The Power of Black Magic: The Magical Negro and White
Salvation in Film," *Journal of Black Studies*, 40, no. 2 (November 2009):
135–52.

7   Amiri Baraka, "The Changing Same (R&B and New Black Music)," in *The
LeRoi Jones/Amiri Baraka Reader*, ed. William J. Harris (New York: Thunder
Mountain Press, 1991), 189.

8   Saidiya Hartman, *Lose Your Mother: A Journey along the Atlantic Slave Route*
(New York: Straus and Giroux Press, 2007), 6–7. Hartman defines the
afterlife of slavery as the residual consequence of the establishment "of a
measure of man and ranking of life and worth that has yet to be undone . . .
black lives [that] are still imperiled and devalued by a racial calculus and a
political arithmetic that were entrenched centuries ago . . . skewed life
chances, limited access to health and education, premature death, incarceration, and impoverishment" (5).

9   Stacy Alaimo, "'Skin Dreaming': The Bodily Transgressions of Fielding
Burke, Octavia Butler, and Linda Hogan," in *Ecofeminist Literary Criti-
cism: Theory, Interpretation, Pedagogy*, ed. Greta Gaard and Patrick D.
Murphy (Urbana: University of Illinois Press, 1998).

10 Toni Morrison, *Playing in the Dark: Whiteness and the Literary Imagination*
(Cambridge, MA: Harvard University Press, 1992). Morrison's influential
critical examination employs the term *American Africanism* to describe
"the denotative and connotative blackness that African peoples have
come to signify, as well as the entire range of views, assumptions, readings, and misreadings that accompany Eurocentric learning about these
people" (6–7).

11 Harriet Beecher Stowe, *Uncle Tom's Cabin* (New York: Penguin Books, 1981).

12 Nathan Huggins Genovese and Ann Douglas, "Introduction," *Uncle Tom's
Cabin* (New York: Penguin Classics, 1981), 27.

13 Ibid, 62.

14 James Baldwin, "Everybody's Protest Novel," in *Notes of a Native Son* (New
York: Beacon Press, 1955).

15 Douglas Robinson, *Western Translation Theory: From Herodotus to Nietzsche*
(New York: Routledge, 1997), 70–71.

16 In Samuel 1:2 it is prophesied that Eli's sons' continued sinfulness will cause
Eli and his family to be punished, with all male descendants dying before

reaching old age and being placed in positions subservient to prophets from other lineages.

17   Rob Nixon, *Slow Violence and the Environmentalism of the Poor* (Cambridge, MA: Harvard University Press, 2013). Nixon defines *slow violence* as "violence that occurs gradually and out of sight, a violence of delayed destruction that is dispersed across time and space, an attritional violence that is typically not viewed as violence at all" (2).

18   Ivonne Gebara, "Ecofeminism: A Latin American Perspective," *Cross Currents* 53, nos. 1–2 (2003): 98.

19   Ibid. The section epigraph is from giovanni singleton, "Day 49," in *Ascension* (Denver: Counterpath, 2012), 58.

20   M. Jacqui Alexander, "An Ideological Reassembly of Another Kind," *Caribbean Rasanblaj* 12, no. 1 (2015).

21   Ibid.

22   Octavia Butler, *Wild Seed* (New York: Warner Books, 1988), 4. Subsequent citations of this work appear in parentheses in the text.

23   Elizabeth Spelman, *Fruits of Sorrow: Framing Our Attention to Suffering* (Boston: Beacon Press, 1997).

24   M. Jacqui Alexander, *Pedagogies of Crossing: Mediations on Feminism, Sexual Politics, Memory, and the Sacred* (Durham, NC: Duke University Press, 2005), 290–91.

25   Sandra Jackson and Julie E. Moody-Freeman, eds., *The Black Imagination: Science Fiction, Futurism and the Speculative* (New York: Peter Lang Press, 2011), 110.

26   bell hooks, "Love as a Practice of Freedom," in *Outlaw Culture: Resisting Representations* (New York: Routledge, 2006).

27   Madhu Dubey, "Octavia Butler's Novels of Enslavement," *A Forum on Fiction*, 46, no. 3 (November 2012): 358.

28   Stephen W. Potts, "'We Keep Playing the Same Record': A Conversation with Octavia Butler," *Science Fiction Studies* 23 (1996): 335.

29   Nathaniel Mackey, "Song of the Andoumboulou: 33," in *Whatsaid Serif* (San Francisco: City Lights Books, 1998), 94.

30   Stefano Harney and Fred Moten, *The Undercommons: Fugitive Planning and Black Study* (Wivenhoe, England: Minor Compositions, 2013).

AFTERWORD

Collective Struggle, Collective Ecologies

LEILANI NISHIME AND KIM D. HESTER WILLIAMS

E COLOGICAL degradation is pervasive, but so is resistance, and so is our insistence on life in the undercommons. Stefano Harney and Fred Moten represent the undercommons as the subversion of neoliberal economic logic. It is a space and time of refusal and reimagination, as Jack Halberstam explains, that is "always here" and expressed as fugitive planning against "a call to order" and submission.[1] *Racial Ecologies* calls attention to our fugitive, dissenting relation to the neoliberal, carceral nation-state. It demands improvised forms of resistance and survival against subjugation. Yet we first must recognize the "slow death" perpetuated by the gears of the capitalist machinery rather than be numbed into apathy through the steady creep of environmental disaster or our dissociation from ecological crisis that occurs "elsewhere" or "out there."[2]

The ecological justice we are proposing involves attention to the historically pernicious relations of humans to the planet and the corollary, intersecting exploitation of ethnic and racial difference. As Jessi Quizar and Dian Million remind us, the deleterious consequences of climate change disrupt the human food and water supply. In the United States, the effects are particularly acute for low-income workers, poor and working-class Latinos, Asian Americans, American Indians, and African Americans, many of whom labor in food service and agricultural industries and, at the same time, disproportionately suffer from food deserts—impoverished areas where healthy food is difficult to find—and food insecurity. Racialized and Indigenous communities around the world are also more vulnerable to the effects of major environmental disasters, such as earthquakes, tsunamis, floods, fires, and drought, intensified by climate change and the toxic effects of industrialization detailed in the chapters here by Catalina de Onís, Sunny Chan, Zoltán Grossman, and Million. We are currently witnesses to "climate apartheid," as in the examples of Hurricane Katrina; the water contamination scandal in Flint, Michigan; the Dakota Access Pipeline; and a multitude of environmental disasters that interrupt the promise of prolific differences.[3] The fault lines of political, social, economic, and environmental conflict continue to threaten the ethnic and cultural diversity that have positively shaped the global populace.

This inequality of suffering is not only the historical result of colonialism, slavery, and economic dispossession; it is also bound up in the profoundly dialectical relationship of racialized and gendered bodies to the land itself, and in the "sorrow and suffering" of labor that was, and continues to be, extracted from these bodies for the purposes of mass profit and the propagation of empire.[4] Dominique Bourg Hacker, Yu-Fang Cho, Stephen Nathan Haymes, Tiffany Jeannette King, and Ana Elizabeth Rosas trace the histories of the suffering of communities of color as a result of environmental degradation and the capitalist exploitation of natural resources that began long before Hurricane Katrina. The 1739 Stono Rebellion in South Carolina, precipitated by the harsh and repressive labor conditions requisite for the mass production of rice crops, was one of countless examples of destructive mass agriculture and exploitation of land that deepened the suffering of enslaved Africans while plantation slaveholders profited mightily.[5] We see again and again the troubling intercourse between capitalist economy, race, and ecology. Labor markets founded on the persistence of privatization and property "rights" repeatedly result in the exploitation of the land, producing simultaneous wealth and dispossession over and against communal structures of care and subsistence.

In the face of these seemingly intractable problems, the authors in this book show us how communities of color respond to disasters using their own knowledge systems. The limits imposed by dominant structures of power shape but do not stop their resistance. The chapters in this volume can serve as relational sites for navigating both embodied racialized identities and ecological space and place. By focusing our attention on diverse lived experiences and speculative futures, Ashley Cheyemi McNeil, Min Hyoung Song, Julie Sze, Erica Tom, and Kim D. Hester Williams teach us how marginalized communities contest their compromised environments while envisaging the formation of more generative and just environmental relations. They contemplate historical, racial, and spatial contexts that represent a broader view of the cultural dimensions of environmental ethics. The perspectives of subjugated communities, their particularized experiences of the natural world, and their responses to ecological disaster reveal multiple ways of understanding our environmental relations. The explorations of affect, alternate and "spatial" subjectivities, trans-corporeality, mutual avowal between human and animal, communalism, and collectivity presented here suggest alternative pathways toward ecological and social justice.

As discourses in and about Flint and Standing Rock have shown, we can reframe the public conversation about environmental threats. This reframing entwines environmental issues with racial justice rather than resorting to a universalizing discourse that flattens out the differences between groups. Action in Flint and at Standing Rock addresses the intersection of race and ecology most effectively when it responds in ways specific to the historical and social context. At Standing Rock and in the courts, water protectors continue their work opposing the Dakota Access Pipeline. As we write this afterword, the federal courts have just ruled against the permits issued immediately after Donald Trump's inauguration that allowed the pipeline to cross the Missouri River.[6] While the case centered on violations of environmental law, the decision was undergirded by the failure of the Army Corps of Engineers to account for the environmental effects on the hunting and fishing rights accorded to the Standing Rock Sioux Tribe as a sovereign nation.

In Flint, residents continue to fight for clean water even as their supply remains contaminated, and the intense public interest in the crisis has faded. In a report issued in February 2017, the Michigan Civil Rights Commission concluded that racism was a factor in the Flint water crisis.[7] Despite national reporting that delinks race from Flint's polluted water supply, local activists refuse to ignore the long-standing history of state divestment from African American communities described by Quizar. Their fight addresses deficiencies in infrastructure and the unequal allocation of resources to repair that infrastructure. Their path toward environmental justice looks very different from that of the Standing Rock Sioux. As Haymes argues, we need to multiply our notion of a singular ecological ideal to the everyday practices of small ecologies. Through the lens of small ecologies, we can locate the fight for clean water in historical and cultural contexts that require contextually specific responses.

This volume concludes in solidarity with local and global resistance to the destruction wreaked on the planet by colonialism, neoliberal capitalism, and modern empire. We additionally call for a fugitive ecological relation to the neoliberal state. Elaborating on the ideas of Lisa Lowe, we must be attentive to the "freedoms yet to come" that are further revealed by the intimacies of our distinct yet shared transnational (under)commons and "the possibilities that lay within." Lowe urges us "to think beyond [the] received liberal humanist tradition" and develop new questions and alternatives to what Ana Rosas describes in this volume as stifling "ecological boundaries."[8] We continue to insist on the life and health of our communities, and we commit ourselves to the struggle that the philosopher Sylvia Wynter has so eloquently and forcefully proposed: "We must now collectively undertake a rewriting of knowledge as we know it."[9] We must at once preserve and rewrite the knowledge of our past, present, and future relations. We hope that this *Racial Ecologies* collection moves us toward that crucial transformative task.

NOTES

1   Jack Halberstam, "Preface," in Stefano Harney and Fred Moten, *The Under-commons: Fugitive Planning and Black Study* (New York: Minor Compositions, 2013), 15.

2   See Rob Nixon, *Slow Violence and the Environmentalism of the Poor* (Cambridge, MA: Harvard University Press, 2013); Dorceta Taylor, T*he Environment and the People in American Cities, 1600s–1900s: Disorder, Inequality, and Social Change* (Durham, NC: Duke University Press, 2009); Julie Sze, *Noxious New York: The Racial Politics of Urban Health and Environmental Justice* (Cambridge, MA: MIT Press, 2007).

3   See Naomi Klein, T*he Shock Doctrine: The Rise of Disaster Capitalism* (New York: Metropolitan Books, 2008) and *This Changes Everything: Capitalism vs. The Climate* (New York: Simon and Schuster, 2015).

4   Elizabeth Spelman, *Fruits of Sorrow: Framing Our Attention to Suffering* (Boston: Beacon Press, 1997).

5   See Peter H. Wood, *Black Majority: Negroes in Colonial South Carolina from 1670 through the Stono Rebellion* (New York: W. W. Norton, 1996); Daniel C. Littlefield, *Rice and Slaves: Ethnicity and the Slave Trade in Colonial South Carolina* (New York: W. W. Norton, 1991); Eugene Genovese, *From Rebellion to Revolution: Afro-American Slave Revolts in the Making of the Modern World* (Baton Rouge: Louisiana State University Press, 1992); Edda Fields-Black, *Deep Roots: Rice Farmers in West Africa and the African Diaspora* (Bloomington: University of Indiana Press, 2008); Judith Ann Carney, *Black Rice: The African Origins of Rice Cultivation in the Americas* (Cambridge, MA: Harvard University Press, 2009); Peter Charles Hoffer, *Cry Liberty: The Great Stono River Slave Rebellion of 1739* (New York: Oxford University Press, 2010).

6   "In Victory for Standing Rock Sioux Tribe, Court Finds That Approval of Dakota Access Pipeline Violated the Law," *Daily Native American*, August 4, 2017.

7   "The Flint Water Crisis: How We Got Here and What's Next," *Michigan Live*, June 27, 2017, www.mlive.com/news/flint/index.ssf/2017/06/the_flint_water _crisis_where_i.html.

8   Lisa Lowe, *The Intimacies of Four Continents* (Durham, NC: Duke University Press. 2015), 175.

9   Katherine McKittrick, ed., *Sylvia Wynter: On Being Human as Praxis* (Durham, NC: Duke University Press. 2014), 18.

CONTRIBUTORS

DOMINIQUE BOURG HACKER is a PhD candidate in English literature at the University of Wisconsin, Madison, focusing on contemporary African and Caribbean literature and ecocriticism. Her publication in a special issue of the *Journal of the African Literature Association* analyzes expressions of South African environmentalism in Nadine Gordimer's *Get a Life.*

SUNNY CHAN is a PhD candidate in English literature at the University of Wisconsin, Madison, specializing in experimental poetry of the Asian diaspora. She has also studied English and creative writing at the University of Alberta and the University of British Columbia, on unceded Musqueam territory. In her creative nonfiction work, which has been published in *The Puritan, Ricepaper, Interfictions,* and other journals, she explores raced and gendered relationships between human and nonhuman life. Her academic work has been published in *WestCoastLine, Journal of the Midwest MLA,* and *Contemporary Literature.*

YU-FANG CHO is associate professor of English and global and intercultural studies at Miami University. She is the author of *Uncoupling American Empire: Cultural Politics of Deviance and Unequal Difference, 1890–1910* (SUNY, 2013) and articles in *American Quarterly, Transnational American Studies, Amerasia,* the *Journal of Asian American Studies, Cultural Studies* and *Meridians: Feminism, Race, Transnationalism,* among others. She is also the coeditor of the 2017 special issue of *American Quarterly,* "The Chinese Factor: Reorienting Global Imaginaries in American Studies." She has received fellowships from the Bancroft Library, the Huntington Library, the Pacific Rim Research Program at the University of California, the Institute of Global Conflict and Cooperation at the University of California, and the National Research Institute of the Humanities and Social Sciences in

255

Taiwan. Her current book project investigates the relationship between race, reproductive justice, and nuclearism in America's Asia Pacific.

CATALINA MAÍRE DE ONÍS is an assistant professor in Willamette University's Department of Civic Communication and Media. She studies rhetoric, social movements, (de)coloniality, race, and the environment, especially in relation to global climate disruption and electric energy controversies. Her dissertation examined discourses of decarbonization and climate and energy (in) justice in Puerto Rico. She is committed to coalitional politics, field methods, and disrupting English monolingualism and US monoculturalism in her scholarship and teaching. Her essays have been published in *Communication Monographs, Communication Theory, Environmental Communication, Women's Studies in Communication,* and *Women & Language.* She has also contributed a chapter to *Text + Field: Innovations in Rhetorical Method* (Penn State University Press, 2016) and a chapter about ethnographic research practices to the *Routledge Handbook of Environmental Justice* (Routledge, 2017).

ZOLTÁN GROSSMAN is professor of geography and Native American and world Indigenous peoples studies at the Evergreen State College, in Olympia, Washington. He is the author of *Unlikely Alliances: Native Nations and White Communities Join to Defend Rural Lands* (University of Washington Press, 2017) and coeditor of the anthology *Asserting Native Resilience: Pacific Rim Indigenous Nations Face the Climate Crisis* (Oregon State University Press, 2012). He was cochair of the Indigenous Peoples Specialty Group of the American Association of Geographers (AAG) in 2008–10, a recipient of the 2014 AAG Enhancing Diversity Award, and an International Geographical Union observer at the 2008 climate change session of the United Nations Permanent Forum on Indigenous Issues. He earned a PhD in geography with a graduate minor in American Indian Studies in 2002 as a Udall Fellow at the University of Wisconsin, Madison, and taught at the University of Wisconsin, Eau Claire, from 2002 through 2005. He was a cofounder of the Midwest Treaty Network during the Wisconsin Ojibwe spear-fishing conflict and later helped bring together Native nations with their former adversaries in sport-fishing groups to protect the inland fishery from mining projects.

STEPHEN NATHAN HAYMES is Vincent de Paul Associate Professor of Philosophy of Education and Critical Educational Theory at DePaul University, Chicago. He teaches courses in Africana education, international studies, and peace, justice, and conflict studies. His current research focuses on the political ecology of education and Afro-descendent communities in the Americas. He serves on the International Ethics Commission of Truth and the pedagogical team of the Comisión Intereclesial de Justicia y Paz, a Colombian nongovernmental organization concerned with human rights. He is the author of *Race, Culture, and the City: Pedagogy for Black Urban Struggle*, which won the Gustavus Myer Outstanding Book Award on the Subject of Human Rights in North America. He has written numerous articles on social memory, Africana philosophy of education and thought, and race and ecology. He serves as a coeditor of the *Journal of Poverty*.

KIM D. HESTER WILLIAMS is professor of English and American multicultural studies at Sonoma State University. Her current scholarship considers race, ecology, and Black ecopoetics, with particular attention to the work of the science fiction writer Octavia Butler. She is working on a manuscript that examines the hyperconsumption and romanticizing of Black expressive culture and its dialectical correspondence to discourses and practices of anti-Blackness that, ultimately, reveal whiteness as racial crisis. Hester Williams has published essays on the representation of race, gender, and economy in new media, popular culture, and film. She has also served as chair of the Media and Cinema Division of the Cultural Studies Association and currently serves on the editorial board for the journal *Genders* and as a consultant for *Legacy*.

TIFFANY LETHABO KING is an assistant professor in the Department of Women's, Gender, and Sexuality Studies at Georgia State University. King's research exists at the intersections of Black studies, Native studies, Black geographies, and Black gender and sexuality studies. King is currently working on a book manuscript that explores the ways that Black studies' theorizations of conquest and the human put pressure on the hegemonic pull of contemporary discourses and the institutionalization of white settler colonialism as an explanatory frame for social relations in the Western Hemisphere.

CURTIS MAREZ is professor of ethnic studies at the University of California, San Diego. He is the author of *Drug Wars: The Political Economy of Narcotics* and *Farm Worker Futurism: Speculative Technologies of Resistance*. Marez is completing a third book, titled *University Babylon: Hollywood and the Making of Modern Student Bodies*. He is the creator of *Cesar Chavez's Video Collection*, an interactive digital book. He is the former editor of

American Quarterly, past president of the American Studies Association, and former chair of ethnic studies at the University of California, San Diego.

DIAN MILLION (Tanana Athabascan) is an associate professor in American Indian studies and an affiliate faculty member in Canadian studies and the Comparative History of Ideas Program at the University of Washington. She is the author of *Therapeutic Nations: Healing in an Age of Indigenous Human Rights* (University of Arizona Press, 2013); "There Is a River in Me: Theory from Life," in *Theorizing Native Studies*, edited by Andrea Smith and Audra Simpson (Duke University Press, 2014); and "Felt Theory: An Indigenous Feminist Approach to Affect and History" (*Wicazo Sa Review*, Fall 2009), among other publications and poems. Dian Million takes meaning from a lifelong commitment to learning, teaching, and acting on issues of Indigenous sovereignty and racial and social justice.

ASHLEY CHEYEMI MCNEIL is a PhD candidate in literary studies at Georgia State University and in American Studies at Johannes Gutenberg University in Germany. Her research employs new humanist theoretical frames to focus on narratives of interraciality, illuminating Asian American subjectivities that subvert constrictive Westernized notions of identity. She is a Student Innovation Fellow at the Center of Excellence for Teaching and Learning in Atlanta.

LEILANI NISHIME is associate professor of communication at the University of Washington. She received her PhD in English at the University of Michigan and was an associate professor of American multicultural studies at Sonoma State University. She is the author of *Undercover Asian: Multiracial Asian Americans in Visual Culture* and the coeditor of *East Main Street: Asian American Popular Culture* and *Global Asian American Popular Cultures.* She has published widely in anthologies and journals such as *Cinema Journal*, the *Journal of Asian American Studies, Critical Studies in Media Communication, Communication Theory,* and the *Quarterly Journal of Speech.* She has served on the boards of the Association of Asian American Studies, the Critical Mixed Race Studies Association, and the *Seattle Globalist,* and she is an organizing member of the Seattle Asian American Film Festival.

JESSI QUIZAR is an activist-scholar, a teacher, and a parent of four. Her work centers on the operation of and resistance to racial capitalism, with particular attention to racial political ecology, critical food studies, urban land and resource struggles, and social movements of people of color. She is inspired by the work of longtime activists of color in Detroit and elsewhere who creatively cultivate alternative and traditional economies and ways of being. Jessi is a member of the Critical Ethnic Studies Association's national steering committee and an assistant professor of ethnic studies at Northern Arizona University.

ANA ELIZABETH ROSAS is associate professor of history and Chicano/Latino studies at the University of California, Irvine. She is the author of *Abrazando El Espiritu: Bracero Families Confront the US-Mexico Border*, which was awarded the Immigration and Ethnic History Society's Theodore Soloutos Memorial Book Award for the best book on immigration history. She is currently researching the gendered configuration and impact of relentless displacement on Mexican immigrant family life in Mexico and the United States.

MIN HYOUNG SONG is professor of English at Boston College. He is the author of *The Children of 1965: On Writing, and Not Writing, as an Asian American*, which won several book prizes, and *Strange Future: Pessimism and the 1992 Los Angeles Riots*, as well as the editor of the *Cambridge History of Asian American Literature* and *Asian American Studies: A Reader*. He has served as the editor of the *Journal of Asian American Studies* and is at work on a book manuscript tentatively titled *Climate Lyricism*.

JULIE SZE is professor of American Studies at the University of California, Davis, and was the founding director of the Environmental Justice Project of the John Muir Institute for the Environment. Sze's research investigates environmental justice and inequality; culture and environment; race, gender, and power; and urban and community health and activism. Sze's book Noxious New York: The Racial Politics of Urban Health and Environmental Justice won the John Hope Franklin Publication Prize, awarded to the best book in American studies. Her second book is called *Fantasy Islands: Chinese Dreams and Ecological Fears in an Age of Climate Crisis* (University of California Press, 2015). She is editor of *Sustainability: Approaches to Environmental Justice and Social Power* (New York University Press, 2018).

ERICA TOM is an American studies scholar, poet, and multispecies ethnographer. She teaches in the English and American multicultural studies departments at Sonoma State and is a development associate at the Center for Law, Inequality, and Metropolitan Equity at the Rutgers Law School. She is also the director of arts and education at Belos Cavalos, an equine experiential organization located in Kenwood, California, where she develops trauma-informed equine experiential programs. Her scholarly and poetic work has been published in *Humanimalia, Volt, Pomona Valley Review,* and *Women's Studies Quarterly.* She earned her BA in English, with a minor in classical studies, from the University of Washington in 2007; her MA in English from Sonoma State University in 2012; and her PhD in American studies from Rutgers University, Newark, in 2017.

INDEX

Conservationist, The (Gordimer), 99
contaminated water. See water
    pollution
Coulthard, Glen Sean, 23–24, 26
Counihan, Clare, 96–97
courts. See judiciary
Cowen, Deborah, 24
Coyle, Marcia, 171, 172
"creative class" (Florida), 22, 24
critical race studies, 209, 215
cultural nationalism, 186, 187, 190, 194,
    195
Curtis, Kezia, 78–79, 80, 84, 86
Curtis, Wayne, 76, 80, 81

Dakota Access Pipeline (DAPL), 5, 6, 19,
    20, 21, 25, 192, 251
Dangerous Crossings: Race, Species,
    and Nature in a Multicultural Age
    (Kim), 12, 125
Darwin, Charles, 31–32
Davis, Angela, 138n24
Day, Ikyo, 8
DDT, 111
De Brahm, William: Map of South
    Carolina and Georgia, 66–75
deep-sea oil exploration, resistance to,
    153–69
Deepwater Horizon oil spill, Gulf of
    Mexico, April 2010, 157, 160
deforestation, 188
Deloria, Vine, Jr., 30
demonstrations. See protests and
    demonstrations
De Onís, Catalina Máire: "Es Una
    Lucha Doble," 185–202
Detroit, 76–89
Deyá Diaz, Tinti, 194
diesel emissions, 110
disasters, xi, 58, 173, 185–86, 196, 251.
    See also environmental disasters
documentary films, 173, 225
dolphins, 244

"dominionistic" values, 40
Douglass, Billy, 131
Duany, Jorge, 186
dumps, solid-waste. See landfills
dry cleaners, 176–77

Earlimart, California, 108, 109
"earth ethic" (Leopold), 45, 46
ecocentrism, 42, 45
ecofeminist literature, 235, 240–46
ecological disasters. See environmental
    disasters
ecologies of liberation (Haymes). See
    "slave ecologies" (Haymes)
ecotourism, 160
electricity. See energy and energy
    policy
electronics industry. See high-tech
    industry
Eli (biblical figure), 248n16
El Pueblo Para el Aire y Agua Limpio,
    110
emergency managers: Michigan, 77–78,
    87n2
Empalme, Sonora, 139–50
empathy, 126, 130, 133, 137n12, 244,
    245–46
"empty" land, 21, 25, 31
energy and energy policy, 197, 222.
    See also oil industry; natural gas;
    nuclear energy
enslaved Africans, 36, 42–43, 44,
    47, 71–74, 86; Kellert view, 41; in
    map cartouches, 66–74; rebellions,
    251
environmental disasters, xi, 23, 153, 157,
    160, 163, 250–51. See also nuclear
    disasters
environmental ethics, 34–49
environmentalism, 3, 7, 37, 109,
    114–15; "African relational,"
    37, 46; Asian Americans and,
    170–73, 181–82; nationalism and,

189–90, 196; Puerto Rico, 186, 187,
190–91, 192, 195, 196; racist, 91, 93;
Uexküll, 211
"environmentalism" (word), 34
environmental justice, 3, 7, 11, 25–26,
117; Asian Americans and, 170,
171, 175, 180, 182; Flint, Mich., 252;
Greenpeace and, 158; Kettleman
City, 108, 109, 112, 114, 118–19;
Puerto Rico, 192; women and, 108,
112, 113, 114
environmental justice movement, x,
110, 112, 170, 171, 173, 175, 182
environmental nationalism, 186, 187,
189–90, 193–94, 195, 196
Environmental Protection Agency.
See California Environmental
Protection Agency; US
Environmental Protection Agency
(EPA)
environmental racism, 6, 25–26, 171–73;
Asian Americans, 170, 171–72, 173,
175, 176, 179, 180, 181; Flint, Mich.,
4, 252; Puerto Rico, 186, 187; Silicon
Valley, x, xi
epistemology, 26, 30, 34–35, 37–39,
42, 211, 214; critical race theory,
209; E. O. Wilson, 42; humanism,
208; indigenous and non-Western,
xii, 25, 26, 35, 47; in maps, 67;
St. Lawrence Island, 30
equine assisted learning (EAL) and
therapy, 123–38
erasure, 100, 208, 209, 222; in films,
224, 226, 230; in literature, 92
Espiritu, Yen, 175
ethics. See morality and ethics
"ethics of avowal" (Kim), 125–26, 134
eugenics, 114
Eurocentrism, 34–39, 186
Evergreen State College, 153
evolution, 38–39, 212
Excelerate Energy, 197

*Faith, Food and Family in a Yupik
Whaling Community* (Jolles and
Oozeva), 29–30
Fala, Tony, 166
Fanon, Frantz, 43
farming. See agriculture
farmworkers, xi, xii, 109, 111, 178.
See also Latino farmworker
communities
Feedom Freedom Growers, 76–77,
80–89
feminism, 8–9, 114; Indigenous, 26.
See also ecofeminist literature;
womanism
fetal health, 111
Fielding, Maureen, 97
figs, 212
Filipino immigrants, 178
films, 190, 220–33, 234–40. *See also*
documentary films
Finlayson, John, 162
Finney, Carolyn, 7
fishing: African Americans, 41, 86;
Japan, 221, 222, 224; New Zealand,
153, 154, 155, 162, 163; Puerto Rico,
197; Standing Rock, 252
Flint, Michigan, 4, 5–6, 11, 251, 252
Florida, Richard, 22, 24
food, 19, 39; deserts, 250; insecurity,
28–29, 30. *See also* urban
agriculture
Foreshore and Seabed Act (New
Zealand), 156–57, 158, 159, 163
formaldehyde, 177
fossil fuels. *See* oil industry; natural gas
Foucault, Michel, 6
fracking, 19, 160
France, 155
Fukushima nuclear disaster, 2011, 223,
225, 226

Gage, Rikirangi, 159
Gaia principle, 45–46

gardening, 41, 76–77, 80–89; in fiction, 91, 94–100, 102n28

garment industry, 113, 176, 177

Garner, Tony, 137n12

gas pipelines. *See* Vía Verde gas pipeline

Gebara, Ivonne, 240

genocide, 6, 42, 43

gentrification, 22, 39

Gibbs, Lois, 111, 112

Gilmore, Ruth Wilson, 3, 83, 109

Gioielli, Robert, 7

global warming. *See* climate change

Godzilla (2014 film), 220, 223–30

Godzilla: King of the Monsters (1956 film), 222–23

Gojira (1954 film), 220, 221, 222–23, 225, 226

Gologergen, Sandra, 28, 29

Gong Lum v. Rice, 174

Gonzales, David, ix–x

González, Adriana, 191

Gordimer, Nadine: *Conservationist*, 99

Gordon, Lewis R., 34, 43

Great Britain. *See* Britain

Green, Al, 236

Greenaction, 110

"green capitalism," 39

"green gentrification," 39

greenhouse gas emissions, 179–80

Green Party (New Zealand), 160, 165

Greenpeace, 155, 157, 158–59, 160–61, 162, 164

Greensill, Angeline, 156, 161

Grossman, Zoltán: "Maori Opposition to Fossil Fuel Extraction in Aotearoa New Zealand," 153–69

Guenther, Lisa, 126

Gwich'in, 20, 21, 32

Halberstam, Jack, 250

Hansen, James, 54

Haraway, Donna, 10, 12, 138n26

Harawira, Hone, 159

Harper, Amie Breeze, 244

Harrison, Jill, 108, 110

Hartman, Saidiya, 248n8; *Scenes of Subjection*, 65–66

Harvey, David, xi

Harvey, Stefano, 250

Hawai'i, 178, 227, 228, 232n11

Hawaiian Sugar Planters' Association (HSPA), 178

Haymes, Stephen Nathan: "An Africana Studies Critique of Environmental Ethics," 34–49; *Race, Culture, and the City*, 41

hazardous waste: in Hollywood films, 190; Kettleman City, California, 107, 110, 111, 117, 118–19; New Orleans, 173; Puerto Rico, 189; Richmond, California, 177; Silicon Valley, 176; St. Lawrence Island, 30; UCC report, 171–72

Head, Bessie, 90; *Between the Lines*, 90; *Question of Power*, 91, 93, 94–101, 102n28; *When Rain Clouds Gather*, 93–94, 97

health, 6, 83, 107–22; St. Lawrence Island, 30. *See also* fetal health

Hearne, Vicki, 127–28

Hegel, Georg, 44

Heise, Ursula, 213

Henderson, James Sakej, 29

Hernandez, Victoria, 147–48, 149

Hernandez Lorenzo, Daria, 115

Hester Williams, Kim D.: "Earthseeds of Change," 234–49

Highfield, Jonathan, 90, 94, 97

high-tech industry, ix–xi, 176, 179, 230

historical erasure. *See* erasure

homeownership, 78

Homies, ix–x

Hong, Grace, 9, 10

hooks, bell, 41–42, 47

horse racing, 132, 134

horses, 123–38, 242, *243*
housing, 22, 78, 118
Howard, Tim, 155, 162–63
Huggan, Graham: *Postcolonial Ecocriticism*, 92
Hughes brothers: *The Book of Eli*, 234–40, 246
humanism, 68, 102n28, 208, 214
hunger, 28–29, 30
hunting, 29–30
Hurricane Katrina, xi, 173, 251
Hurricane Sandy, 58
Hurricanes Irma and Maria, 185–86, 196

Idle No More, 21, 153
Iizhik Gwats'an Gwandaii Goodlit. *See* Alaska National Wildlife Refuge (ANWR)
Imagine Otherwise: On Asian Americanist Critique (Chuh), 206, 209–10, 214, 215
immigrants and immigration, 81, 108, 112, 113; Asian, 177–78, 227; occupational hazards, 113; women, x, 113, 120–21n22. *See also* Bracero Program
Immigration and Naturalization Service (INS). *See* US Immigration and Naturalization Service (INS)
Indians, American. *See* Asian Indian Americans; Native Americans
indigenous peoples, 19–33, 42; Arctic regions, 20, 23, 27, 28–30, 32, 120n21; New Zealand, 153–69; Pacific islands, 176, 177, 221–22, 223, 224, 227, 230; radioactive waste and, 222. *See also* Native Americans
indigenous studies, 7
indigenous women, 27, 113, 119
indigo, 67–73
individuality, 37
industrialization: Puerto Rico, 188

Inhofe, James, 55
intersectionality, xii, 9, 10–11, 114, 117, 125, 133
iron sands, 156

James, Sarah, 32
Japan: *Lucky Dragon* incident, 1954. See *Lucky Dragon* incident, 1954
Japanese immigrants and Japanese Americans, 174, 177–78
Japan–US relations, 220–33
Jimenez, Noël, 128–30, *129*, 134–35
Jolles, Carol, 29–30
joy, 47, 133
judiciary, 81, 180, 181, 252; New Zealand, 155. *See also* US Supreme Court

Kellert, Stephen, 42; *Value of Life*, 40–41
Kenderdine, John, 162
Kettleman City, California, 107–12, 114–22
Key, John, 163
Keystone XL pipeline, 154
Kheel, Marti, 46
Kim, Claire Jean: *Dangerous Crossings*, 12, 125, 134
Kinder Morgan, 181
King, Tiffany Jeannette: "Racial Ecologies," 65–75
Kings County, California, 110, 119
Kiwis against Seabed Mining (KASM), 156–57, 164
Korean immigrants and Korean Americans, 176–77
Kuokkanen, Rauna, 26, 27

labor, 45, 83, 84–85; African American, 44; exploitation, xii; high-tech industry, x, 176, 179; South Africa, 91; toxics exposure and, 176–77, 179. *See also* Bracero Program

Misión Industrial, 191

Missouri River (Mni Sose), 20, 23, 24, 252

"model minority" stereotype, 174–75

monster films, 220–33

morality and ethics, 23, 25, 35–37, 40, 186; in *Book of Eli*, 238, 239, 240; ecocentric, 42; in Godzilla films, 224, 226, 227, 228; identity and, 34; womanist, 241; Yamashita, 215. *See also* environmental ethics; "ethics of avowal" (Kim)

Morgensen, Scott Lauria, 25

Morin, Peter, 26

Morrison, Toni, 3, 237, 248n10

Moten, Fred, 250

motherhood, 107, 108, 109, 111–12, 114, 117

Movimiento Pro Independencia (MPI), 189

Murkowski, Lisa, 32

Murkowski, Frank, 32

Murupaenga-Ikenn, Catherine, 164

music, 59, 236; Uexküll, 206, 211–12, 218n19

nail salons, 113, 177

nationalism, 186, 187, 191, 194, 195, 205–8, 217n7; in films, 226. *See also* cultural nationalism; environmental nationalism; political nationalism

National Party (New Zealand), 155, 157, 159, 165

Native Americans: enslavement, xii; hazardous waste sites and, 171–72; in fiction, 245; Pacific Northwest treaty rights, 153, 154; Standing Rock, 5, 6, 19, 21, 23, 25, 153

native peoples. *See* indigenous peoples

natural gas, 197. *See also* Vía Verde gas pipeline

"natural horsemanship," 127, 128, 130

"negativistic" values, 40

New Orleans, 173

New Zealand, 153–69

New Zealand Energy Company, 160

New Zealand First, 165

Ngai, Mae, 141

Ngata, Tina, 160

Nguyen, Viet Thanh, 174

nihilism, prevention of, 47

Nixon, Rob, 6, 50, 93, 171, 249n17

nonpartisan politics, 194

Norwegian state oil company. *See* Statoil

nuclear disasters, 223, 225, 226

nuclear energy, 220, 222, 223, 225, 226, 227

nuclearism, US. *See* US nuclearism

nuclear weapons testing, 155, 220–26, 229, 230, 231n6, 232n11

Nunavik, 120n21

nursing mothers. *See* lactating mothers

Oakland, California, 178–79

occupational hazards, 113

oil industry: Alaska, 32; health hazards, 6; New Zealand, 153–69; pipelines, 5, 6, 19, 20, 21, 25, 154, 155, 192; rail shipment, 181; refineries, 178; Richmond, California, 178; spills, 153, 157, 160, 163

Oil on Ice, 32

Okihiro, Gary, 174

Omnivore's Dilemma, The (Pollan), 58

Ong, Paul, 175

Onís, Catalina Maíre de. *See* De Onís, Catalina Máire

ontology, 26, 38, 44

Oozeva, Elinor Mikaghaq, 29–30

Open City (Cole), 51, 52–58, 60

Operation Bootstrap (Puerto Rico), 188, 200n21, 200n23

orientalism, 227, 229

Other, 4, 9, 43, 45, 299, 227, 236;
Godzilla/Gojira as, 222; nonhuman,
215
ownership of homes. *See*
homeownership
ownership of land. *See* landownership
Oxnard Strike of 1903, 174

Pacific Islanders, 176, 177, 221–22, 223,
224, 227, 230; hazardous waste
sites and, 171–72; New Zealand,
153, 166
Palestinians, xii
Parable of the Sower (Butler), 234–35,
241, 244–46
Parable of the Talents (Butler), 234–35,
241
Park, Lisa Sun-hee: *Silicon Valley of
Dreams*, x, xi
Patterson, Orlando, 44
patriarchy, 27, 237, 239, 240; Puerto
Rico, 186; South Africa, 90, 93, 99.
See also protectionism, patriarchal
PCBs. *See* polychlorinated biphenyls
(PCBs)
Pellow, David Naguib: *Silicon Valley of
Dreams*, x, xi
People of Color Environmental
Leadership Summit, 1991, 176
Perkins, Tracy, 112
permaculture, 39
Peru, 158
pesticides, 6, 93, 110, 111, 177; drift, 108,
110
Petrobras, 157–60
Pezzullo, Phaedra C., 187
Philippines, 225, 226, 227, 230
Pinderhughes, Raquel, 173
pipelines, 154, 155. *See also* Dakota
Access Pipeline (DAPL); Vía Verde
gas pipeline
Pizzini, Manuel Valdés, 187
plaasroman, 91–93, 95, 96, 100, 103n38

place-making, African American,
41–42, 44
plebiscites: California, 179–80; Puerto
Rico, 199n11
poetry, 19–20, 59, 234, 240, 246
police: New Zealand, 156, 159; Standing
Rock, 5, 20, 24
political nationalism, 186, 187, 190, 191,
193, 194, 195
political sovereignty. *See* sovereignty
Pollan, Michael: *Omnivore's Dilemma*,
58
pollution, 108, 110, 114, 115; health
impacts, 107, 113, 118. *See also* water
pollution
polychlorinated biphenyls (PCBs), 110
Porter, Ruben Taipari, 162, 164
Postcolonial Ecocriticism (Huggan and
Tiffin), 92
power, electrical. *See* energy and
energy policy
Power in Asians Organizing (PAO), 177,
178–79
pregnant women, 113, 245–46. *See also*
miscarriages
prehistoric humans, 39
prisoners: equine assisted learning and
therapy, 123–24, 126–35
prison industrial complex, 138n24
privatization, 77, 199n19, 251
progress, xi, 22, 25, 30, 35, 41, 71, 192
protectionism, patriarchal, 114
protests and demonstrations: New
Zealand, 156, 157, 159, 161, 163, 164,
165; Puerto Rico, 192, *193*
public health. *See* health
public health services, 140
Puerto Rico, 185–202

Question of Power, A (Head), 91, 93,
94–101, 102n28
Quizar, Jessi: "Working to Live,"
76–89

race, 3–4, 7, 11, 24, 127, 133, 251, 252;
Chuh, 206; climate change and, 51;
Detroit, 82; in film, 228, 230, 235,
236; identity formation and, 217n4;
Kettleman City, 107–10, 112, 114, 117;
Kim, 125; in literature, 11–12, 52, 53,
60, 234, 235, 236; Native Americans
and, 21, 22, 23, 25; nature and, 234;
Puerto Rico, 187; South Africa, 99.
See also critical race theory;
racialization; racism
Race, Culture, and the City (Haymes),
41
"racial ecologies" (term), 4, 119
racialization, 8, 9–10, 117, 243; in films,
237; of Indigenous peoples, 21, 22,
23, 25; of land use, 110
racialized transcorporality. *See*
"transcorporality" (Alaimo)
racial other, 222, 227, 236
racism, 3, 9, 43, 133, 171, 173, 174; anti-
black, 43, 81, 125–26, 133; fictional
treatment, 52, 57; Gilmore on, 3, 83,
109; South Africa, 91, 92–93, 100;
"slow violence" of, 240. *See also*
environmental racism
radioactive contamination in films,
220–33
rain forests in fiction, 205–16
Ramirez, Teresa, 139
Ramos-Zayas, Ana, 186
Ray, Sarah Jaquette, 114
*Red Skin, White Masks: Rejecting the
Colonial Politics of Recognition*
(Coulthard), 23–24
relationality, 36–37
religion, 239, 240; African, 36, 241;
African American, 47, 86. *See also*
Christianity
reproductive justice, 107, 108, 112–16, 119
resistance to deep-sea oil exploration.
See deep-sea oil exploration, resistance to

Richmond, California, 177, 178, 181
Rickard, Eva, 161
Rise of the Creative Class, The (Florida),
22
Robinson, Douglas, 238–39
Rodriguez, Cristina, 145
Romero, Magdalena, 115
Rosario, Juan, 191, 197
Royal, Lorene, 163–64
Ruiz Marrero, Carmelo, 201n41
rural African American culture, 41
"rural" and "urban." *See* "urban" and
"rural"

Sample, Maxine, 90, 93, 99
San Francisco, 180, 181; in films, 225,
227, 228, 229, 239
Santa Clara County, California, 172
Santiago, Ruth, 189, 200n23
savanna (biosystem), 39
Saxton, Ketana, 164
*Scenes of Subjection: Terror, Slavery,
and Self-Making in Nineteenth-
Century America* (Hartman),
65–66
Schleifer, Jay, 127, 134
Schwarzenegger, Arnold, 109, 117
science fiction (speculative fiction), 12,
59, 234–35, 240–46
Sea Shepherd, 159
Second Chances Horse Program
(SCHP), 123–24, 126–35
Senate, US. *See* US Senate
settler colonialism, xii, 5, 13n6, 21, 25
sewage sludge, 109
sexual harassment, 145, 146
sexuality, 96–97, 227, 229
Shaffer, Gwen, 176
Shah, Nayan, 180
shapeshifters in literature, 241–44, 245
Sierra Club, 191, 197
Silicon Valley, ix–xi, 120–21n22, 176,
230

Tom, Erica: "Humanizing Animals," 123–38

tourism, 153, 159, 160, 162. *See also* ecotourism

Townes, Emilie, 247n2

toxic exposure, x, xi, xii, 107, 108, 109–10, 113–18, 121n21; Asian Americans, 176–77, 179; New Zealand, 158

toxic waste. *See* hazardous waste

Toxic Wastes and Race in the United States, 171–72

"transcorporality" (Alaimo), 107–8, 109, 112, 113, 114, 117–18, 119

Trans-Pacific Partnership (TPP) Agreement, 164, 165

transportation, 79, 181

Trans-Tasman Resources, 156

Treaty of Waitangi, 153–55, 161, 162, 164

trees, 86, 212, 247; fig, 212; in map cartouches, 68, 69, 74n10; in poetry, 246; symbolic removal of, 158. *See also* deforestation

Tremper, Jim, 127, 129, 132

Uexküll, Jakob von, 205, 206, 211–12, 214, 215, 217n16, 218n19

Umwelt, 211–12, 214

Uncle Tom's Cabin (Stowe), 237–38, 240

"undercommons," 250

unemployment, 79, 140, 199n20

unions, x, 79, 111, 174, 192

United Church of Christ (UCC), 171, 172, 175

United Farm Workers, xi, 111

United Kingdom. *See* Britain

United Nations, 30; Declaration on the Rights of Indigenous Peoples, 158

Unlikely Alliances (Grossman), 154

uranium mining in films, 225–26

urban agriculture, 39, 76–77, 80–89

"urban" and "rural," 21–22, 24–25, 31

US Army Corps of Engineers, 252

US Census, 22–23

US Environmental Protection Agency (EPA), 108, 111, 172

US Immigration and Naturalization Service (INS), 140

US-Japan relations in films. *See* Japan–US relations in films

US military, 199n19, 225, 228–29, 252; Hawaii, 232n11

US nuclearism, 220–33

US Resource Conservation and Recovery Act, 172

US Senate, 32, 55, 109

USSR. *See* Soviet Union

US Supreme Court, 174, 180

utilitarianism, 40

Valley Fever (fungal infection), 116

The Value of Life: Biological Diversity and Human Society (Kellert), 40–41

Van den Heever, C. M., 92, 94, 95, 103n38

Vanguardia Popular (Puerto Rico), 189, 200n26

Vía Verde gas pipeline, 185, 192, *193*, 195, 197

Vick, Michael, 125

Vietnamese Americans, 173

Village Called Versailles, A (Chiang), 173

violence, slow. *See* "slow violence" (Nixon)

Vital, Anthony, 91

Wallkill Correctional Facility (WCF), 123–24, 126–35

Wanzer-Serrano, Daniel, 186

Warnes, Christopher, 92

wasps, 212

waste, hazardous. *See* hazardous waste

water pollution, 4, 5–6, 11, 251; post-hurricane, 186

weather: conflation with climate, 54

Weil, Kari: *Thinking Animals*, 127, 128, 137n16

West, Cornel, 47

whaling, 29–30, 158

When Rain Clouds Gather (Head), 93–94, 97

white flight, 79

whiteness, 43

white supremacy, 180, 186

White Writing: On the Cultures of Letters in South Africa (Coetzee), 92

Whyte, Kyle, 5, 13n6

Wild Seed (Butler), 234–35, 241–44, 245, 246

Wilkins, Michael, *135*

Williams, Raymond, xiii

Wilson, Edward O., 38–39

Wistrand, Asta, 163

Wo Lee, 180

womanism, 235, 241, 244, 246, 247n2

women, indigenous. *See* indigenous women

women, migrant. *See* migrant women

women, pregnant. *See* pregnant women

work. *See* labor

Wynter, Sylvia, 253

Yakini, Malik, 83

Yamashita, Karen Tei: *Through the Arc of the Rain Forest*, 205–16

Yick Wo v. Hopkins, 180

Yupik, 28–30

Zeitlin, Benh: *Beasts of the Southern Wild*, 59